PASTA & CO.

encore

PASTA & CO.

MORE FAMOUS FOODS FROM SEATTLE'S LEADING TAKE-OUT FOODSHOP

encore

marcella rosene

Printed in the United States of America.
01 00 99 98 97   5 4 3 2 1

Designed, produced, and distributed by Sasquatch Books,
615 Second Avenue, Seattle, Washington; (206) 467-4300

Cover design: Karen Schober
Interior design and composition: Kate Basart
Editing: Cynthia Nims and Rebecca Pepper
Indexing: Sigrid Asmus
Photograph on page vi: Jimi Lott

Library of Congress Cataloging in Publication Data
Rosene, Marcella, 1945-
Pasta & Co. encore : more famous foods from Seattle's
leading take-out foodshop / Marcella Rosene.
        p.   cm.
Includes index.
ISBN 1-57061-109-2
1. Cookery. 2. Cookery (Pasta) 3. Pasta & Co., Inc.
I. Pasta & Co., Inc. II. Title.
TX714.R672 1997
641.5—dc21   96-29751

Published by Pasta & Co., Inc.
1316 East Pine Street
Seattle, Washington 98105
(206) 322-1644
On the World Wide Web: http://www.pastaco.com
Provisions mail order: (800) 943-6362

Distributed by Sasquatch Books, (800)775-0817

PASTA & CO. LOCATIONS:	BELLEVUE STORE 10218 NE 8th Street Bellevue, Washington 98004 (206) 453-8760	QUEEN ANNE STORE 2109 Queen Anne Avenue N Seattle, Washington 98109 (206) 283-1182
UNIVERSITY VILLAGE STORE 2640 NE University Village Mall Seattle, Washington 98105 (206) 523-8594	DOWNTOWN STORE 1001 Fourth Avenue Plaza Seattle, Washington 98154 (206) 624-3008	BROADWAY STORE 815 East Pike Street Seattle, Washington 98122 (206) 322-4577

For mail order: Pasta & Co. Provisions: (800) 943-6362

◆

*This book is dedicated to those whose names are too many to list.
Wherever they are, they know who they are: They are Pasta & Co.
employees—past and present—who have in big and little ways worked
to keep the vision of highest quality and the magic of excellence.
Harvey and I are proud to count ourselves among them.*

◆

Pasta & Co. Managers celebrate Christmas, 1996

ACKNOWLEDGMENTS

Throughout this book, a number of our staff members—Lura Throssel, Lisa Szkodyn, David Shuler, Judy Birkland, Bonita Atkins—are named with the recipes they personally contributed to the Pasta & Co. repertoire. As with all good ideas freely given, thanks for them are never adequate to truly express their value. In addition to lending favorite recipes, Lura Throssel, our Prepared Foods Manager (in the photograph she's the one seated on the right, with the pretty long hair), must be singled out for her tireless, good-natured testing of recipes for this book; likewise, Richard Card, our Manager of Merchandising and Quality Assurance (he's seated on the left with our Bellevue Assistant Manager on his lap).

In addition, many thanks to all our store managers—Andy, Margaret, Marybeth, Lisa, and Kelly—and their staffs for showing pride in the project, whether by debating over cover art, sampling a recipe for dinner, or simply boasting to an interested customer that yes, indeed, we would have a third cookbook.

Credit goes to graphics designer Kristine Anderson of Twist, who years ago originated our "tomato label," now used on the cover of this book. At Sasquatch Books, designers Karen Schober and Kate Basart turned Kristine's original motif into the "look" of our book, all the while tolerating, with calm and understanding, my attempts to influence their efforts. Thanks also to Sasquatch Books for providing editorial direction through Joan Gregory (whose congeniality and insight made this project a true pleasure), Cynthia Nims, Rebecca Pepper, Justine Matthies, and Sigrid Asmus. A belated appreciation is due Seattle nutritionist Dr. Evette Hackman, who helped us in our very early efforts with lower-fat foods. Her steady, patient aid in analyzing our recipes and understanding government regulations was invaluable.

On a very personal level, I must, as always, thank my son Charlie, my parents Charlotte and Larry, my beagle Sam, and most of all, my always-encouraging husband, Harvey, for eating plate after plate of trial food. I am certain there have been at least fleeting moments when all of them (except Sam) wished I had never begun to cook.

And as with each of our books, gratitude is owed to Pasta & Co. customers. It is their continued enthusiasm for our successes and their understanding patience for our shortcomings that have afforded us the opportunity to come to print yet one more time. We are thankful for this chance for an encore.

Marcella Rosene

January, 1997

CONTENTS

INTRODUCTION

This is not a low-fat cookbook. Rather, it is—as each of our other two cookbooks have been—a veritable snapshot of how our customers eat. The first—*Pasta & Co.: The Cookbook*, published in 1987—reflected eating with great abandon and with curiosity for the new, the exotic, and the inventive. The second—*Pasta & Co. By Request*, published in 1991—demonstrated a definite preference for more homey and familiar fare. Now, in 1997, *Pasta & Co. Encore* shows a marked interest in healthy eating—not at the exclusion of taste and pleasure, but as a newly pivotal standard of measure. It is indisputable that our customers' growing concern about health, especially about fat in their diets, has irreversibly changed the way we at Pasta & Co. cook and think about food.

Not that this new standard applies to every meal or even to all parts of the meal. We still make, sell, and eat Fettuccine Alfredo, Beef Lasagne, Macaroni and Cheese—every fat-dense, delicious product we always have. But we also want the option of cooking and eating less fat at least some of the time. Accordingly, *Pasta & Co. Encore* contains a mix of recipes, from high-fat classics to new low-fat and reduced-fat innovations.

Demand for these options has meant a time of exploration and experimentation at Pasta & Co. It's brought a new reason to search out and try unusual ingredients—not for sport, as in the 1980s, but for healthier eating. It's meant exhaustive efforts to make low-fat products that will sell as successfully as those with higher fat. It's involved revising countless recipes to cut fat. And it's led to hard decisions about when foods need fat to ensure great taste.

There is another compelling issue at work in food today: Most of us are too busy to cook. That's why companies like Pasta & Co. have a business. That is also why we emphasize—in the foods we sell in our stores and in our recipes—the convenience of "prepare-ahead cooking"—a style of cooking designed for people who are too busy to cook but who are not willing to compromise on quality or taste. Every *Encore* recipe has "Prepare-Ahead Notes" that convey our extensive knowledge about the shelf life of the dish. Take advantage of this feature to plan your cooking ahead. You just may rediscover the time to enjoy the pleasures of cooking and serving food. There are also a number of recipes that include cooking with "Ready-Mades"— pre-made products that save time and produce astonishingly good food. You will find most of these recipes on pages 193 to 205, in the Hot Pastas and Sauces chapter.

So, here is *Pasta & Co. Encore*—a collection of more recipes that customers want and the tale of our efforts to create flavorful, lower-fat foods. After nearly two decades of business and two successful cookbooks, it is, of course, exceedingly gratifying and a bit humbling to hear that customers do indeed still want more. After all, encores—the giving of more in response to demand—are what good food and lasting businesses are all about.

ABOUT PASTA & CO. ENCORE CONTENTS AND ORGANIZATION

The idea of Pasta & Co. cookbooks is not merely to publish recipes, but also to pass along what we at the company have come to call "our inimitable kitchen wisdom"—the food finds we pride ourselves on, the stubborn opinions we've formed, and the tips and tricks one can learn only after making a recipe literally hundreds of times (as our cooks do). Much of this arguably valuable information is in the inside column of selected pages. It is here that you will find everything from notes on ingredients (as mundane as salt or as esoteric as specialty oils) to opinions about such topics as garnishing, wine-pairing, and poaching chicken. The material is referenced by page number both in relevant recipes and in the index.

Encore's chapters are quite self-explanatory, except perhaps the largest and most quintessentially Pasta & Co. one: Room-Temperature Foods. What is "room temperature"? It's any temperature between hot off the stove and cold out of the refrigerator that still maintains food in a wholesome state. It's a temperature that optimizes rather than masks flavors. And it's the absence of that awful onus for any cook that food must be served the minute it is made. What relaxed good eating this implies. In a few recipes, such as those containing fresh egg mayonnaise or shellfish, we specify serving dishes chilled, and certainly, many of our recipes are equally good hot or at room temperature. In these instances, you will find cross-references between the chapters on Room-Temperature Foods, Hot Entrées and Side Dishes, and Hot Pastas and Sauces.

As for hard-to-find ingredients, you should be able to obtain almost any ingredient called for (or at least a comparable one) from your local specialty grocer. If you cannot, you can order them from Pasta & Co.'s mail-order operation, Provisions, at 1-800-943-6362. You can also visit us on the Internet at http://www.pastaco.com.

New to this book, is, of course, our experience with lower-fat foods. Our discoveries are scattered profusely throughout the book. There are case studies that vividly illustrate the crafting of lower-fat foods, and recipe after recipe that gives a running chronicle of all that we have learned about making foods healthier. Watch for this Yellow Line Logo to indicate lower-fat recipes:

LOW FAT AT PASTA & CO.—
THE YELLOW LINE

In the early 1990s, when we were just a decade old, Pasta & Co. experienced a groundswell of customer interest in lower-fat eating. In response, a group of Pasta & Co. managers drafted a plan to significantly alter the way we cook at Pasta & Co. We committed ourselves to concentrating our new product efforts on lower-fat foods and to reviewing all our existing products for their fat content, revising where feasible. We were going for nothing short of a new taste standard in reduced-fat eating. After all, these new-fangled, lower-fat foods had to please our customers just as well, or better, than any other Pasta & Co. product. The new lower-fat foods were called Yellow Line, simply because the signs that identified them in the deli-case were yellow (the actual locomotive logo came several years later).

In 1991, when we launched the Yellow Line products, the popularly held understanding of "low fat" was any dish in which fat accounted for 30 percent or less of the calories. Then, in 1994, new government regulations changed the 30 percent rule, redefining "low fat" as dishes with less than 3.6 grams of fat per designated serving unit. Rather than reformulate and re-analyze all of our previously designated "low-fat" dishes, Pasta & Co. combined both systems under our Yellow Line logo.

Current criteria for Pasta & Co. Yellow Line recipes:

- ◆ No compromise in taste and quality compared with foods that have higher amounts of fat—if it doesn't taste really good, customers won't buy it.
- ◆ No more than 30 percent of calories from fat OR no more than 3.6 grams of fat per 1-cup serving.
- ◆ Vegetarian whenever possible.
- ◆ Relatively low in calories with the nutritional balance of vitamins, minerals, and fiber that naturally comes from using premium and varied ingredients.

PASTA & CO.'S
FAT-TRIMMING TIPS
THE TACTICS WE'VE USED FOR
MAKING OUR YELLOW LINE FOODS

Use these tips at will. No single one will make you a low-fat cook, but incorporating them into your own cooking repertoire (as we have into ours) is guaranteed to make you sufficiently fat-savvy, so that when you feel like eating and serving less fat, you can.

No. 1. Substitute good-quality, defatted stock or broth (page 40) for part or all of the fats called for in savory recipes. The advantages are obvious:

> 1 cup of oil = 1909 calories and 216 grams of fat
> 1 cup of stock = 39 calories and 1.39 grams of fat

No. 2. Revise the classic vinaigrette formula of 3 parts oil to 1 part acid (vinegar or lemon juice) to at least equal parts oil and acid. Such alternatives to the classic formula will pose challenges in terms of both taste and texture, but as you will see in these recipes, such challenges can be successfully met. (See Pasta Cooking Times for High-Acid Dishes, page 63, and Case Study: The Making of a Low-Fat Classic, page 68.)

No. 3. Rethink cooking methods, opting for those that require less, or no, fat. Steam, poach, grill, broil, and bake rather than sauté. Make good-quality nonstick cookware (page 129) an essential in your kitchen to help cut back on fat needed in cooking.

No. 4. Try sources of low-fat protein that come from combining legumes and grains—more particularly, beans and pasta or beans and rice. (See sections on Room-Temperature Beans, page 81, and Room-Temperature Grains, page 95.) Our culture has typically dismissed these centuries-old combinations as "starchy," but in fact, they are replete with lower-fat, higher-fiber eating possibilities.

No. 5. Identify the staples of low-fat cooking—ingredients you can count on for adding flavor and texture without fat. The list is quite endless. You can begin with such commonplace ingredients as onions, tomatoes, cucumbers, carrots, beans, tomato paste, lemon juice, vinegar, pasta, bread crumbs, mushrooms, and undressed salad greens. Then, as you'll see in the recipes in this book, you can explore such less familiar ingredients as barley, sumac, miso, dry-curd cottage cheese, quinoa, horseradish, water chestnuts, and dried figs.

No. 6. Identify big-flavor ingredients—low fat or not—that you can count on for stepping up flavor even when used in only small doses. The list will definitely include garlic, all kinds of herbs and spices, capers, anchovies, mustard—maybe even just a shot of heavy cream, cheese, butter, or olive oil as a final enrichment (page 77). On the subject of that much-maligned ingredient, salt, see page 90.

No. 7. Don't overlook the role of temperature in increasing and decreasing the flavor of food (page 67).

No. 8. Identify nonfat and low-fat ingredients that can act as thickeners and emulsifiers in the absence of fats. Some possibilities are tomato paste, mustard, nonfat yogurt cheese (page 6), arrowroot or cornstarch dissolved in water or stock, some puréed vegetables such as eggplant or roasted garlic, and puréed cooked legumes. (See especially the Soups chapter, page 35.)

No. 9. Identify flavor-enhancing techniques. For instance, oven roast vegetables (page 182), dry roast nuts, toast grains, reduce (boil down) stocks (page 82), heat spices, and conserve precious flavors by adding fresh herbs to dishes right before serving.

No. 10. Rethink the role of meats and fish in the menu. Consider them side dishes rather than entrées, garnishes rather than main ingredients.

No. 11. When serving higher-fat foods, exercise portion control. Serve smaller amounts of high-fat foods, filling out the plate with larger amounts of lower-fat foods.

No. 12. "Fool" the palate. Identify nonfat and low-fat ways to make foods taste "rich" and "creamy." Favorites for savory dishes include using nonfat yogurt cheese (page 6) and Quark (page 62). Others for either savory or sweet are:
- low-fat ricotta, plain or combined with nonfat yogurt, puréed to a creamy texture in the food processor
- nonfat cottage cheese, puréed to a creamy texture in the food processor
- 2 parts nonfat yogurt folded into 1 part stiffly beaten heavy cream

Most of these cannot be successfully heated, but can be spooned at room temperature over hot foods. Low-fat sour cream is a boon to many fat-watchers, and in most cases, it can be heated without separating.

No. 13. Become fat-conscious in your cooking. Look before you cook. Not every recipe can be converted to low fat, but almost every recipe can stand some fat-trimming. Think in terms of the "Fat Point" in a recipe: the point where there is just enough fat for your taste (page 188).

appetizers

IN OUR PREVIOUS BOOK, PASTA & CO. BY REQUEST, WE DESCRIBED APPETIZERS AS "'CONVERSATION FOODS'—FOODS WHICH, BECAUSE OF THEIR TASTE AND APPEARANCE, INTRIGUE GUESTS." SINCE THEN, WE HAVE RUN ACROSS AN EVEN MORE APT WAY OF DESCRIBING THEM. IN A DELIGHTFUL BOOK PUBLISHED IN 1994 CALLED LULU'S PROVENÇAL TABLE, AUTHOR RICHARD OLNEY TALKS ABOUT "AMUSE-GUEULES," WHICH HE SAYS MIGHT BE TRANSLATED AS "'MOUTH-AMUSERS' WHOSE ROLE IS TO EXCITE THE APPETITE AND THE IMAGINATION IN ANTICIPATION OF THE MEAL TO FOLLOW." THAT'S PRECISELY WHAT WE MEANT BY "CONVERSATION FOODS."

Slow-Roasted Romas and Pasta

You can use Slow-Roasted Romas in a variety of dishes. Here's one idea: Cut them into strips and combine them with roasted yellow peppers and blanched asparagus tips, and toss with perfectly cooked rigatoni or penne. All you'll need for sauce are the juices from the vegetables themselves, a little full-bodied stock, a dash of extra virgin olive oil, a generous sprinkling of freshly grated Parmesan, and some chopped parsley or cilantro.

Slow-Roasted Romas

Some of the best low-fat cooking involves very simple procedures that lead to myriad applications. Certainly that is the case with Slow-Roasted Romas. The only challenge in this recipe, in our kitchens at least, is scheduling oven time.

You can use these juicy morsels in infinite ways. We include them as an appetizer because each tomato half makes an edible, nonfat container for finger food. Think of them as a substitute for crackers or pastry shells. We like to fill them with Green Lentil Tapenade (page 4) or Roasted Eggplant and Pepper Purée (page 8). Another low-fat idea is to chop them up, fold them into seasoned Nonfat Yogurt Cheese (page 6), and serve them on dry-roasted breads. Don't care about grams of fat? Then fill them with the Green Olive Tapenade (page 25).

PREPARE-AHEAD NOTES:

♦ At first it may seem impossible to have your oven tied up for 5 to 6 hours, but keep in mind that you can interrupt the process for hours at a time and, within a 24-hour period, finish off the tomatoes at your convenience.

♦ The tomatoes can be refrigerated for up to 4 days. They also freeze well.

♦ Alternatively, if you're not concerned about fat, place the roasted tomatoes in a clean glass jar and cover with olive oil seasoned to taste with salt, pepper, herbs, and garlic. Make sure the tomatoes are submerged in the oil. Stored in the refrigerator, the tomatoes will keep for months.

INGREDIENTS:

4 pounds ripe Roma tomatoes (about 20)
¾ to 1 teaspoon fine sea salt

- Preheat oven to 200° F.
- Wash tomatoes and cut in half lengthwise. With a sharp paring knife, cut out seeds and core, leaving tomato shell intact. Reserve tomato pulp for use in Green Lentil Tapenade (see below).
- Place tomatoes, cut side up, on two foil- or parchment-lined baking sheets. Sprinkle with the salt.
- Roast tomatoes for 5 to 6 hours. Check the tomatoes after about 4 ½ hours. They are done when they are dry to the touch, but still plump and orangy red. Do not overdry. They should not be leathery. Some may be done before others. Remove those that are done and return remainder to oven for another 30 minutes. Repeat until all the tomatoes are done. Let tomatoes cool before serving.

Makes about 40 tomato halves

for more about
**PASTA & CO.
YELLOW LINE
DISHES**
turn to page xv.

Green Lentil Tapenade

*O*ur *Green Olive Tapenade (page 25) is arguably one of the best tapenades ever (the Mediterranean classic fat-dense with a combination of olives, anchovies, garlic, and olive oil). This lower-fat alternative takes advantage of the firm and meaty texture of green lentils (page 37) to eliminate more than half of the high-fat olives usually called for in a tapenade. The mixture can be spread on warm flour tortillas or naan (Indian flatbread), or used to fill Slow-Roasted Romas (page 3). Leftovers can be frozen. They also make a great seasoning for a vegetable soup.*

This is an idea borrowed from Julee Rosso's opus on lower-fat cooking, Great Good Food. *The book received some scorching reviews, but we credit it with being one of the first of its kind, full of more ingenious recipes than disappointing ones.*

Low-Fat Olives?

I t is difficult to mention the words "olives" and "low-fat" in the same breath. Ninety-four percent of the calories in olives come from fat. A single cup of brine-cured olives contains about 19 grams of fat. But fortunately, their intense, complex, and salty flavor makes a few go a long way. Accordingly, we have been able to use them in small quantities in a number of our lower-fat Yellow Line recipes.

For more about olives, see Choosing Olives, page 25.

Pitted Olives

I ncreasingly, you can find good-quality, imported olives *pitted*. Pasta & Co. stores, for instance, sell jars of pitted kalamatas. However, should you not find a ready source of pitted imported olives, do not settle for pitted California olives, which are comparatively bland in flavor. Rather, buy good-quality imported olives and pit them yourself.

How to Pit Olives:

P itting some olives is simply a matter of squeezing the olive very firmly between your thumb and middle finger until the pit slips out. For tougher-to-pit varieties, you need only a cutting board and a chef's knife. Place olive on cutting board and lay knife blade flat on top of the olive (as you do when you skin a garlic clove). With one hand, hold the handle of the knife, and with the other, make a fist and firmly whack the flat side of the knife. Remove the knife and you will find that the pit pops easily out of the olive, leaving the olive meat more or less intact.

PREPARE-AHEAD NOTES:

The tapenade will keep five days refrigerated or can be frozen. Return the mixture to room temperature or gently reheat before using. Re-season as needed.

INGREDIENTS:

> ½ cup green lentils, picked over and rinsed
> ¾ cup chicken or vegetable stock
> 1 tablespoon garlic, peeled and chopped
> ¾ cup tomato "cores" from Slow-Roasted Romas (page 3), or chopped canned tomatoes, drained of juice
> Additional stock, if needed
> ¼ cup imported olives, such as kalamata olives, pitted and coarsely chopped (see this page)
> 2 tablespoons capers, rinsed and drained
> Optional: 4 Slow-Roasted Romas (page 3—you will usually have two or three in a batch that turn out a bit misshapen; use these), coarsely chopped
> 1 tablespoon freshly squeezed lemon juice
> ½ teaspoon salt
> Freshly cracked pepper to taste
> ¼ cup finely chopped cilantro or parsley

TO TOP:

> Additional finely chopped cilantro or parsley
> Optional: 1 tablespoon extra virgin olive oil

♦ In a saucepan over medium heat, combine lentils, stock, garlic, and tomato cores. Bring to a low boil, cover, reduce heat to low, and simmer until the lentils are tender but still firm, about 20 minutes. Watch liquid level. Lentils should be almost dry, but do not allow them to scorch. Add a small amount of stock if necessary.

♦ Place the lentil mixture in a food processor equipped with a steel blade and process for 30 seconds, scraping down the sides of the bowl as necessary. Add the chopped olives, capers, Slow-Roasted Romas (if using), lemon juice, salt, and pepper. Process briefly. We like the mixture fairly coarse. If you prefer, process to a smoother purée. If the mixture seems dry, add a little additional stock; if it seems soupy, place it in a sieve and let excess liquid drain off before finishing recipe. Immediately before serving, fold in cilantro or parsley. Serve warm or at room temperature with a sprinkling of cilantro or parsley on top and, if you choose, olive oil drizzled over all (page 77).

Makes about 2 cups

for more about
**PASTA & CO.
YELLOW LINE
DISHES**
turn to page xv.

Nonfat Yogurt Cheese

This is, quite possibly, our favorite low-fat discovery. After all, a big part of successful lower-fat cooking involves deceiving the palate, and yogurt cheese does just that. It fools it into thinking it's experiencing something sinfully creamy and rich, like heavy cream or a high-fat cheese.

The nonfat yogurt cheese can be seasoned in numerous ways and served as an appetizer spread or dip. Recipes in this book that use yogurt cheese as an ingredient include Roasted Eggplant and Pepper Purée (page 8), White Beans with Low-Fat Greek-Style Dressing (page 88), Lentil Sauce (page 181), Second Skin Chicken (page 152), and Second Skin Fish (page 152).

PREPARE-AHEAD NOTES:

Allow 24 hours to make the yogurt cheese. Once made, it keeps for at least a week in the refrigerator.

INGREDIENTS:

> *1 cup plain nonfat yogurt (we like Mountain High or Altadena brand)*
> *Optional: ¼ teaspoon salt*

About Yogurt Cheese

Paula Wolfert, author of numerous acclaimed volumes on Mediterranean and Middle Eastern cooking, writes that within an hour from the time you begin to drain the yogurt, it will lose about 20 percent of its liquid and will be the consistency of light whipped cream—about right for use in salad dressings. By the end of 24 hours, it will lose about half its volume and will have acquired the consistency of sour cream. In this form, it is perfect for dips, sauces, and soups. If you want a very thick texture (almost similar to fresh goat cheese), allow it to drain even longer before using (adding the optional salt accelerates this process).

♦ Line a fine sieve with a paper towel, coffee filter, or double layer of cheesecloth. Spoon the yogurt into the sieve and set over a container to catch the liquid that the yogurt will give off. (The bottom of the strainer should sit at least 2 inches above the bottom of the container.) Stir in the salt, if using. Cover yogurt with plastic wrap, refrigerate, and allow to drain for 24 hours. The yogurt cheese is now ready to use. It will keep for up to two weeks refrigerated.

♦ Once made, season yogurt cheese according to your taste (or see the suggestions below), and serve as an appetizer spread or dip.

Makes 1 scant cup

SEASONING SUGGESTIONS FOR NONFAT YOGURT CHEESE:

♦ Add salt, fresh or dried herbs, and finely minced garlic to taste
♦ Add salt, cumin, oregano, and finely minced garlic to taste
♦ To the above mixture, add currants and/or raisins that have been plumped in hot water and well drained
♦ Fold in julienned Slow-Roasted Romas (page 3)
♦ Fold in a chiffonade (page 132) of fresh spinach leaves, cooked white beans, and salt and other seasonings to taste
♦ Fold in raw sesame seeds, dried oregano, fresh cilantro, cayenne, ground cumin, salt, and garlic to taste

Roasted Eggplant and Pepper Purée

*H*ere we use roasted eggplant (see this page) in combination with Nonfat Yogurt Cheese to create a creamy concoction, full of flavor but low in fat. The eggplant mixture alone, without the peppers, is also superb. You might add minced fresh tomato, some garden-fresh herbs, or capers; or substitute 3 poblano peppers, roasted and including juices, for all the bell peppers (poblano peppers are a touch hotter than bell peppers). The salient point here is that you have a great-tasting, low-fat base for any cook's flight of fancy. Serve the purée with good bread, crackers, warmed tortillas, or naan (Indian flatbread). The mixture can also be used to fill Slow-Roasted Romas (page 3), and it makes a superb room-temperature side dish with meat or rice.

PREPARE-AHEAD NOTES:

♦ Allow 24 hours for making the Nonfat Yogurt Cheese.
♦ Each step of the recipe can be done several days before serving, with final assembly at the last minute. Or the mixture can be assembled up to the addition of the cilantro and will keep for at least five days refrigerated. Return to room temperature and add the cilantro before serving.

INGREDIENTS:

2 pounds eggplant (approximately 2 average-sized
   eggplants), roasted or grilled (see this page)
1 ½ teaspoons finely minced garlic
1 to 2 teaspoons salt
1 ½ to 2 teaspoons ground cumin
⅛ teaspoon ground cinnamon
1 or 2 red bell peppers, roasted, including juices
   (page 9)

Low-Fat Tip: Roast Eggplants as You Would Potatoes

*N*utritionally, eggplant is great. The one problem is that it is usually cooked with lots of fat, especially olive oil. We have recently discovered that eggplant bakes in the oven as easily as a potato and yields up sweet-flavored eggplant meat without the addition of a drop of fat. What's more, baking in the oven eliminates the pesky need to salt the eggplant to remove bitterness. First, rinse eggplants and prick them at least an inch deep with a fork in a dozen places. (Don't omit this step. Eggplants can explode in your oven if not amply poked.) Place eggplants on a cookie sheet lined with foil. Bake in a preheated 375° F oven for approximately 40 minutes, turning the eggplants once during this time. When eggplants are very soft to the touch, remove from the heat and let cool. When cool enough to handle, skin the roasted eggplants and place them in a sieve for 15 minutes to let any bitter juices drain off.

We hesitate to jump to conclusions, but so far, we

have had excellent results substituting this method of cooking eggplant for the higher-fat preparations called for in most eggplant recipes. Try roasting the next time you prepare a favorite eggplant dish. We think you'll be pleased with the results.

Grilled eggplant is even tastier: Place the pricked eggplant on a grill about 8 inches above a charcoal fire that has burned down to embers. Roast, turning frequently for about 30 minutes, or until the flesh feels very soft and the outside is quite charred.

Rethinking Roasted Peppers

Early on, we learned that in lower-fat cooking, you need to make a special effort to conserve and enhance flavors. The Pasta & Co. technique for roasting peppers is a perfect illustration. After charring and steaming peppers, we used to hold them under cold running water as we rubbed off the charred skin. However, in reduced-fat recipes, where flavors need to be optimized, it is important to salvage the roasted pepper juices instead of rinsing them down the drain. So

1 green bell pepper, roasted, including juices
    (see this page)
½ to 1 cup Nonfat Yogurt Cheese (page 6)
1 to 3 teaspoons freshly squeezed lemon juice
Freshly chopped cilantro to taste

TO TOP:

Freshly chopped cilantro
Optional: 1 tablespoon extra virgin olive oil

♦ Roast or grill the eggplant as described in "Low-Fat Tip: Roast Eggplants as You Would Potatoes" on page 8. When eggplants are very soft to the touch, remove from the heat and let cool. When cool enough to handle, slice off stem end and strip off peel. Place the skinned eggplant meat in a strainer, weight with a small plate, and let drain for about 15 minutes.

♦ Place skinned and drained eggplant in work bowl of a food processor equipped with a steel blade. Add garlic, salt, cumin, and cinnamon. Pulse to a very coarse purée. (Texture can vary from very coarse to very smooth—your choice.) Remove eggplant mixture to a large bowl. Add peppers and their juices to food processor and pulse until finely diced. Reserve.

♦ Tasting as you proceed, fold yogurt cheese and lemon juice into the eggplant mixture (you may not need to use all of either ingredient—neither should overwhelm the taste of the eggplant). Fold in peppers, also to taste. Add cilantro. Adjust seasoning.

♦ To serve, bring to room temperature, place in serving dish, and top with additional cilantro and, if you wish, the optional olive oil (page 77).

Makes 3 to 4 cups

Sumac Spiced Cheese and Tomato Salad

his recipe is a lower-fat takeoff on a Lebanese dish recorded in Paula Wolfert's The Cooking of the Eastern Mediterranean. We replace half of the high-fat feta cheese with nonfat dry-curd cottage cheese (page 61), chop the feta to match the cottage cheese curds, and step up the seasonings for a delicious appetizer that's as appealing as the original dish with about half the fat. This dish is at its best with summer-ripe tomatoes and crisp parsley from the garden. But even off-season, the dish works well with grocery store produce. Serve with warm pita bread.

PREPARE-AHEAD NOTES:

The cheese mixture can be prepared, without adding the vegetables, at least three days before serving. Keep refrigerated. Return to room temperature before adding the tomatoes, onions, and parsley.

INGREDIENTS:

 ¼ pound feta cheese, drained of any brine
 2 cloves garlic, minced
 1 tablespoon fresh thyme leaves, or ½ teaspoon dried thyme
 1 teaspoon sumac (page 11)
 ¼ teaspoon freshly cracked black pepper (Pasta & Co. No. 4 Pepper Blend with Whole Allspice—page 53—works well here)
 ¼ pound dry-curd cottage cheese (page 61)
 ½ cup finely diced red onion
 3 medium tomatoes, cut into ½-inch dice (no need to seed, juice, or peel)
 ⅓ cup finely chopped fresh parsley
 Optional: 1 tablespoon extra virgin olive oil

we now use the following technique for roasting peppers:

Char the whole peppers evenly on all sides over a gas flame or under a hot broiler. Place them in a paper bag and close the bag, or wrap them in foil and allow the peppers to "steam" for about 15 minutes. Place a sieve over a measuring cup and, holding each pepper over the sieve so that you can catch the pepper juices, rub off the charred skin, and remove the stem and seeds. Use the meat and juices as you wish.

If Low-Fat Limits Your Options, Look for New Options

or the cook, the best part of lower-fat cooking is the opportunity—the sheer imperative—to look for and experiment with ingredients and techniques that we otherwise might never have bothered with. You'll find examples of these scattered profusely throughout this book. Already in this chapter, we've roasted tomatoes without oil, turned yogurt into a cheese, and baked eggplants like potatoes. In the recipe for Sumac

Spiced Cheese and Tomato Salad (page 10), we introduce two ingredients that, before our fat-cutting efforts, we had never used: dry-curd cottage cheese and sumac. This simply illustrates that cutting fat has made cooking a continual adventure, full of enchanting discoveries.

About Sumac

Ground sumac comes from a red berry and gives a distinctive, astringent flavor to dishes, as well as a rusty red color, not unlike paprika. It is used commonly in Middle Eastern cooking to flavor everything from yogurt to vegetables to meats. There is virtually no substitute for its unique flavor.

Sumac can be difficult to obtain (Pasta & Co. stores do stock it), but if you can't find it, don't despair. While the sumac adds a unique fillip to Sumac Spiced Cheese and Tomato Salad, the mixture is also extremely tasty without it.

♦ Lay the drained feta and the minced garlic on a cutting board. Sprinkle with the thyme, sumac, and pepper. Chop mixture coarsely until the pieces of feta are approximately the size of the cottage cheese curds. Place the mixture in a bowl.

♦ Fold in the dry-curd cottage cheese. Ideally, let the cheese mixture season for 2 to 3 hours. (If you're short of time, proceed with the remaining ingredients and serve immediately. You'll lose a little in the roundness of the flavors, but the mixture is still very enjoyable.)

♦ Add the onion and the tomatoes. Place in a serving bowl. Immediately before serving, re-toss the mixture and top with the parsley and the optional olive oil (page 77).

♦ Serve at room temperature.

Makes 4 to 5 cups

Asian Rice Rolls

Water chestnuts and shrimp are two ingredients that contribute texture and richness to dishes while adding very little fat. Here we combine these two ingredients with other low-fat ingredients: rice, green onions, and Thai spring roll rice papers.

The only other fat comes from the hot chili oil (which is a very small amount and could be replaced with Tabasco sauce) and the Bashan's Ginger Dressing. It is a Pasta & Co. favorite made with tamari, vinegar, canola oil, sugar, fresh ginger, and miso. Spread over 36 servings, the fat component is relatively low. If you wanted to make your own dressing, restricting the oil to about a tablespoon (be sure to use generous amounts of fresh ginger), you might make these Asian Rice Rolls even more irresistible.

The rice filling can be made up to a day before assembling the rolls; add the green onions right before assembly. The finished rolls will hold for at least a day, individually sealed in plastic wrap. Once cut and ready to serve, they can be held for several hours, covered with wet paper towels that have been wrung *very* dry.

INGREDIENTS:

> *1 cup raw jasmine rice*
>
> *½ cup Bashan's Ginger Dressing (or a ginger dressing of your own making)*
>
> *1 ½ cups (about 7 ounces) cooked shrimp, cut into ¼-inch pieces, or left whole if tiny*
>
> *1 can (8 ounces) water chestnuts, well drained and cut into ¼-inch dice*
>
> *⅓ cup thinly sliced green onions (most of a bunch, including the green part)*
>
> *1 to 3 teaspoons hot chili oil (depending on spiciness of your chili oil and personal preference)*
>
> *7 Thai spring roll rice wrappers*

TO TOP:

> *½ cup sliced green onions (slice very thinly on the diagonal)*
>
> *1 tablespoon lightly toasted sesame seeds*

♦ Cook rice according to package directions, being sure to salt the rice. Toss hot cooked rice with dressing and let cool. Stir in shrimp, water chestnuts, green onions, and chili oil.

♦ To moisten rice wrappers, dip quickly in a bowl of hot water, then lay each between 2 pieces of plastic wrap, stacking the wrappers. When done moistening all the wrappers, flip the stack over so that the wrapper that has been moistened the longest will be used first. When the wrappers are pliable, lift one, with its plastic wrap still underneath it, off the stack. Place ⅔ cup of rice mixture on the lowest quarter of the wrapper, forming a log that leaves a 1-inch border on three sides. Fold the side edges inward over both ends of the log. Then roll the log away from you until the wrapper has completely enclosed the filling. (Do not be concerned if wrappers tear. They'll stick when pulled back together. If a wrapper seems too dry, moisten with a sprinkle of water.) Wrap the rice roll very securely in the plastic wrap and roll a couple more times to round it. Repeat with remaining wrappers. You may need only 6 of the wrappers, depending on how carefully you apportion the filling.

♦ To serve, remove plastic wrap and, using a very sharp knife, slice each roll into 6 pieces.

♦ Place the slices on a serving dish (we think they are most attractive packed tightly together in mounds on a couple of small plates). You can cover them with damp paper towels wrung very dry and refrigerate for several hours before serving. To serve, remove paper towels and top with the green onions and sesame seeds.

Makes about 36 pieces

Shrimp Cakes

Sharon Kramis, a well-known Northwest food consultant, brought us the basics of this recipe. To keep the cakes low fat, bake them in the oven rather than pan-frying them. (Baking is also easier and we've found no compromise in taste.) The high-fat problem comes in serving the cakes with the rich remoulade, which is everyone's favorite way. Try them with squirts of freshly squeezed lemon juice instead; you may even prefer the low-fat mode.

Warning: Don't be tempted to cheat on the dicing; it's the tiny bits of perfectly cut ingredients that make the cakes remarkable.

PREPARE-AHEAD NOTES:

Next to their taste, the best thing about these shrimp cakes is that they freeze well. Wrapped securely in plastic wrap, they will keep for at least a month in the freezer—very handy to have ready for a party. They don't even need to be thawed before baking.

INGREDIENTS:

7 ounces white fish (cod or snapper is fine), cut into ½-inch cubes

1 teaspoon salt

Pinch cayenne

½ cup ice water (be sure it's ice cold)

12 ounces cooked shrimp—we use Chilean—cut into ⅛- to ¼-inch dice

¼ cup diced red bell pepper (1/16-inch dice)

¼ cup diced green onion (1/16-inch dice)

8 grinds black pepper

¼ teaspoon curry powder

1 package (6 ounces, about 3 cups) panko crumbs, available in the Asian food section of grocery stores (do not substitute regular bread crumbs)

for more about
**PASTA & CO.
YELLOW LINE
DISHES**
turn to page xv.

turn to page xv.

TO ACCOMPANY:

Remoulade (page 16)

♦ Combine fish, salt, and cayenne and refrigerate for 1 hour.

♦ Place fish mixture in work bowl of a food processor equipped with a steel blade. Process, while slowly drizzling in the ice water. Stop and scrape the bowl as needed. Fish should soon form a smooth mass. Remove fish to a bowl and stir in shrimp, red pepper, green onions, pepper, and curry powder.

♦ Place mixture on a large baking sheet and knead in all but about ⅓ cup of the panko crumbs. If the mixture binds nicely, do not use the reserved crumbs; if it is too moist, add them. Form into 1-inch patties. (Use about 1 tablespoon of the shrimp mixture per patty; you may choose to make larger patties for a first course or entrée serving. Cooking time will vary slightly, depending upon size.)

♦ The shrimp cakes can be wrapped well and frozen at this point.

♦ When ready to serve, preheat oven to 350° F. Place the fresh or frozen shrimp cakes on a clean baking sheet and bake for 10 minutes. Turn cakes over and bake an additional 3 to 5 minutes (depending on whether cakes were fresh or frozen). Do not overbake. Serve hot or at room temperature with the remoulade.

ALTERNATIVE COOKING METHOD:

♦ Heat a small amount of butter in a sauté pan over medium-high heat. Brown the fresh or frozen shrimp cakes on both sides. The 1-inch cakes should be completely cooked after about 4 minutes per side (break one open to make certain). Larger cakes should be browned first, then baked in a 350° F oven for 3 to 5 minutes (depending on whether they were fresh or frozen) to finish cooking. Do not overbake.

Makes 3 ½ dozen one-inch cakes

Remoulade

We originally introduced this remoulade to accompany the Shrimp Cakes (page 14). Since then, we've found that customers also love it as a tartar sauce substitute, a sandwich spread, and as a dip for blanched vegetables.

PREPARE-AHEAD NOTES:

The original inspiration for this recipe was the remoulade recipe in Bruce Aidells's book *Hot Links and Country Flavors*. We substituted commercially prepared mayonnaise for the fresh mayonnaise called for in Bruce's recipe. The result is a sauce that will keep in your refrigerator for at least a month; no need to leave this recipe until the last minute.

INGREDIENTS:

1 green onion, coarsely chopped
1 rib celery, coarsely chopped
1 clove garlic, peeled and coarsely chopped
¼ cup coarsely chopped parsley
1 ½ teaspoons sweet paprika
1 cup Best Foods mayonnaise
2 tablespoons prepared horseradish
1 ½ tablespoons tomato paste
1 tablespoon coarse-grained mustard
1 tablespoon freshly squeezed lemon juice
1 ½ teaspoons Worcestershire sauce
1 ½ teaspoons white wine vinegar
1 teaspoon Tabasco sauce

♦ Place the green onion, celery, garlic, and parsley in a food processor bowl equipped with a steel blade. Process until finely chopped. Shut off the machine. Add remaining ingredients. Process just until well blended (but maintain some texture from the vegetables).
♦ Taste for seasoning. Serve immediately or refrigerate.

Makes 1 ¾ cups

Endive Leaves Stuffed with Red Bread

For another fun finger-food appetizer, see the recipe for Pasta Brutta: Tortellini with Sun-Dried Tomatoes and Kabonossi, page 73. Coated in a thick, zesty dressing and served with toothpicks, the bite-sized tortellini make great party food.

This is a fun, very classy finger food to make for a large party. It's a great way to use up stale scraps of those expensive artisan breads we all buy these days. Let them pile up in the freezer until you have 10 ounces. Then make Red Bread.

Looking for something to stuff in whole boiled artichokes? Red Bread is a dazzling candidate: Remove the thistle from the cooked artichoke and pack in the Red Bread; right before serving, drizzle with your very best extra virgin olive oil.

PREPARE-AHEAD NOTES:

Red Bread can be made up to two days ahead of serving. The endive can be prepped up to five hours ahead and covered with damp paper towels. The leaves can be filled up to three hours ahead and also covered with damp paper towels. (Be sure to wring the wet paper towels very dry before using.)

INGREDIENTS:

10 ounces day-old bread, trimmed of all crusts and roughly broken into ½-inch pieces

¼ to ⅓ cup red wine vinegar—the best quality you have

⅔ cup Pasta & Co. Marinara Sauce (purchased or made according to recipe on page 180)

⅓ cup best-quality extra virgin olive oil

1 ½ tablespoons finely minced garlic

¼ teaspoon salt

8 grinds black pepper

¼ cup capers, rinsed and drained

¼ cup finely chopped parsley

6 or 7 heads Belgian endive

TO TOP:

Finely chopped fresh parsley or finely snipped chives
Optional: 1 tablespoon extra virgin olive oil for
drizzling over before serving

♦ Toss the bread with the vinegar and spread out in a shallow pan. Let sit for 10 to 15 minutes.

♦ Squeeze bread together into egg-sized balls; then, with a fork, break bread down into a coarse paste. Continue working with the fork, incorporating the marinara sauce, olive oil, garlic, salt, and pepper. (If the bread stubbornly resists binding into a coarse paste, place the mixture in a food processor equipped with a steel blade. Process, but do *not* purée. Keep the mixture coarse. Remove from processor and proceed with the recipe.) Fold in capers and parsley.

TIP:

If you have leftover marinara sauce, freeze it in ½- or 1-cup portions. The sauce will keep frozen for months.

TO ASSEMBLE:

♦ Cut endive heads about 1 inch above root end and separate each head into individual leaves. Fill each with about 2 teaspoons of Red Bread. Arrange the filled endive in an attractive pattern on a serving dish. Just before serving, sprinkle generously with parsley or chives and the optional olive oil (page 77).

Makes about 48 appetizers

Bonita Atkins's Pizza Crust

This is a much-requested recipe for the pizza dough we have made and sold for nearly a decade. Using semolina flour (the same high-gluten durum wheat flour we use to make pasta) makes for a durable, crisp crust. Use the dough for making either entrée- or appetizer-size pizzas. The dough freezes well. When you want to use it, allow two to three hours to thaw at room temperature and then proceed with forming the dough into a crust.

INGREDIENTS:

2 packages (¼ ounce each) dry yeast
1 ½ cups warm water (about 115° F)
1 teaspoon sugar
1 ½ cups all-purpose white flour
1 ½ cups semolina flour
1 teaspoon salt
2 tablespoons extra virgin olive oil
Additional all-purpose flour as needed
Olive oil, cornmeal or additional semolina flour, and toppings of your choice for baking pizza

♦ In a mixing bowl, dissolve the yeast in the warm water. Add the sugar and the all-purpose flour. Beat vigorously for 1 minute. Dough should be the consistency of a thick cake batter.

♦ Turn oven to 150° F. Open oven door, pull shelf partway out, and place dough on the shelf to rise for 30 minutes. Do not cover dough. (Although you can place the dough in any warm spot for this step, Bonita suggests that this is the most dependable way of getting just the right temperature.)

♦ At the end of 30 minutes, stir dough and add the semolina flour, salt, and olive oil. Mix well. Place dough on a floured surface and knead well for about 8 minutes, adding additional all-purpose flour as needed to keep dough from sticking. Form dough into two balls. At this point, you can freeze the dough for later use or make it into pizzas immediately.

♦ Each ball should make a thin-crust 13-inch pizza or a thick-crust 7-inch pizza. Knead each ball into a ½-inch-thick disk (if you are making smaller pizzas, cut each ball in half before kneading).

Makes crust for two 13-inch pizzas

WHEN READY TO MAKE PIZZA:

♦ Preheat oven to 500° F. Lightly brush a heavy-grade baking sheet with olive oil and dust with either cornmeal or semolina flour. (Lightweight pans will not yield a crispy crust.)

♦ Place dough on prepared baking sheet and press or roll to desired thickness (usually ⅛ to ¼ inch thick). If dough resists, let it rest for a few seconds, then continue pressing. (If you prefer using a pizza stone, place dough on a cornmeal-dusted wooden peel, proceed to form dough, then slide it onto the preheated stone to bake.)

♦ Add your choice of toppings, spreading them evenly and being careful not to overload the center of the pizza.

♦ Bake on lowest shelf of preheated oven 8 to 10 minutes, or until toppings and crust are golden (be sure to check bottom of crust). Remove to cooling rack.

Dots

For those times when you crave the elegance of canapés, you need Pasta & Co. Dots—2-inch disks of golden puff pastry. They can be served straight from the oven as simple little pastry puffs (you'll need no more than two per person). They can be split in half and filled with numerous concoctions, including Smoked Trout Mousse, Artichoke Gruyère Spread, Roasted Onion Gorgonzola Spread, and Sun-Dried Tomato Cream Cheese. All of these recipes are on the following pages.

And don't overlook Dots for dessert. Plan on three per person. Make pools of your favorite dessert sauce on each plate, and place the Dots in the puddles of sauce. You might fill them with whipped cream, chocolate mousse, or a dab of vanilla ice cream or just use them plain from the oven and top them with fresh fruit.

PREPARE-AHEAD NOTES:

We routinely make Dots and freeze them unbaked. This way they are ready to bake on the spur of the moment. Once baked, they can be set aside for hours and reheated in a 300° F oven for 5 minutes just before serving.

INGREDIENTS:

> 1 package (approximately 1 pound) frozen puff pastry (we use Dufour brand; other brands such as Pepperidge Farm work fine)
> 1 egg, beaten with 1 teaspoon water
> Optional: Toasted homemade bread crumbs (page 186)

♦ If you are going to bake immediately, preheat oven to 375° F.
♦ Lay the dough out flat according to package directions. Cut dough into 2-inch circles with a cookie cutter. To bake immediately, place circles on an ungreased cookie sheet. To freeze, place in a single layer in a pan suitable for freezer storage. Brush each circle with the egg wash and top with the optional bread crumbs, which add attractive

Product Spotlight: Neva-Betta Crackers

These best all-around little soda crackers are an appetizer lifesaver. Pasta & Co. stores have used and sold them for years. Although they can be eaten as a cracker, they have a slight indentation that makes them into an edible container for an endless number of dips and spreads. Try filling them with a spoonful of goat cheese, topping them with grated Parmesan, and running them under the broiler for a hot hors d'oeuvre.

texture. If you want to serve the Dots within a few hours, bake immediately in the preheated oven until golden brown and puffed (about 20 minutes).

◆ If you want to freeze the Dots for later baking (as we do), cover well with plastic wrap and place in freezer. When ready to bake, remove storage container from freezer. Dots may need to thaw slightly to remove from container. Place as many Dots on baking sheet as you need and proceed as above. The Dots do not need to thaw before baking.

Smoked Trout Mousse

This mousse is one of our favorite fillings for Dots (page 20); however, it is equally good spooned or piped onto Neva-Betta crackers (see this page), Belgian endive leaves, cucumber rounds, or any other edible bite-sized "container." It is also perfect for tea sandwiches with fresh watercress.

We make the mousse with a smoked trout produced for us by Hickey Foods in Sun Valley, Idaho. You can substitute any good-quality smoked fish.

PREPARE-AHEAD NOTES:

The mousse is best prepared two days before you plan to serve it, but whipping it up at the last minute is also perfectly acceptable. Leftovers freeze well.

INGREDIENTS:

8 ounces smoked trout (about 2 fillets), bones and skin removed
5 tablespoons Best Foods mayonnaise
2 tablespoons cream cheese, at room temperature
3 tablespoons freshly squeezed lemon juice
1 clove garlic, coarsely chopped
1 tablespoon capers, rinsed and well drained

*1 tablespoon very coarsely chopped parsley (it will
    be chopped again in the food processor)*
¼ teaspoon Tabasco sauce
Optional: ⅛ teaspoon cayenne

◆ Place trout, mayonnaise, cream cheese, lemon juice,
and garlic in work bowl of food processor equipped with
a steel blade. Process just until blended, keeping as much
texture as possible. Add capers, parsley, Tabasco, and
cayenne (if using). Process just until parsley is finely
chopped and well blended. Taste for seasoning.
◆ Refrigerate until ready to serve.

Makes 1 ½ cups, enough filling for at least 18 Dots

Pasta & Co. Spreads

A couple of years back, smack in the middle of our
efforts to develop lower-fat foods, we determined that
our customers wanted more quick appetizer options. The
answer was a line of four spreads—insufferably dense in fat
and enormously popular as party food.

PREPARE-AHEAD NOTES FOR SPREADS:

Since all four of these spreads will keep well in your refrigerator, you can have them on hand and integrate them
into your cooking in all manner of handy ways. All are
great spooned onto a baked potato, dolloped as an enrichment into a bowl of soup, or slathered on sandwiches.
They also freeze well.

Artichoke Gruyère Spread

*This is everyone's favorite for filling Dots (page 20). At room
temperature or gently warmed, it is perfect to spread on crostini or sturdy crackers, such as Neva-Bettas (page 21).*

Onion Crescents

Many of our
recipes call for
onions cut into "cres-
cents." To do this, cut an
onion in half from top to
bottom, lay the cut side
flat on a cutting board,
and slice into the onion
along its grain lines.
("Regular" onion slices are
usually cut *across* the
grain.) This produces little
wedges that, when cut
apart, look like crescents.
This particular cut of
onion is especially useful
in introducing texture to
dishes and for garnishing
them (page 91).

Roasted Garlic

Roasted garlic is a wonderful way to give a flavor boost to food. You may want to roast several heads at a time and have a supply ready for quick appetizers (just spread the mellow roasted garlic on thin slices of toast and serve). Roast the garlic with stock to add low-fat flavor, as well as creaminess to soups (see White Bean, Carrot, and Roasted Garlic Soup, page 38) and salad dressings.

- 1 or more whole heads garlic (if you can, get big, fat heads of Spanish Roja garlic— page 27—they're a specialty every fall in Pasta & Co. stores)
- 1 tablespoon stock or extra virgin olive oil per head of garlic
- ½ teaspoon Pasta & Co. House Herbs (or your choice of dried herb) per head of garlic
- Preheat oven to 325° F.
- Trim the garlic heads of any loose skin, keeping them firmly intact. Place in an ovenproof dish just large enough to hold the garlic. Drizzle the stock or oil over the heads and sprinkle with herbs.
- Place in oven and bake for about 45 minutes, or until skin is golden and

INGREDIENTS:

> 1 can (8.5 ounces) artichoke hearts
> ½ cup Best Foods mayonnaise
> ½ cup freshly grated Parmesan cheese
> ½ cup freshly grated Gruyère cheese
> ¼ cup thinly sliced green onions
> 5 grinds black pepper
> ⅛ teaspoon dried tarragon, crumbled between your fingers
> ⅛ teaspoon salt
> Pinch cayenne pepper

- Drain artichoke hearts and squeeze well with your hands, pressing out as much moisture as possible (this is important).
- Place the drained artichokes in bowl of a food processor equipped with a steel blade. Process until very finely chopped. Remove artichokes to a mixing bowl. Stir in mayonnaise, Parmesan, Gruyère, green onions, pepper, tarragon, salt, and cayenne. Mix thoroughly.

Makes 2 cups

Roasted Onion Gorgonzola Spread

This is wonderfully rich. For a change from Dots (page 20) or crackers, spread the mixture onto sliced pears or apples, moistened with a little freshly squeezed lemon juice. The recipe makes a fairly large batch. You can easily halve it.

INGREDIENTS:

> 8 ounces cream cheese
> 1 ½ tablespoons extra virgin olive oil
> ½ pound yellow onions, peeled and cut into ¼-inch-thick crescents (page 22)
> 3 ounces Gorgonzola cheese
> 1 small head of roasted garlic (see this page)
> 4 grinds black pepper

- Bring cream cheese to room temperature. Meanwhile, heat oil in a medium sauté pan over medium-high heat.

Add the onions and cook, stirring periodically to prevent burning. Reduce heat as onions begin to cook and brown. Continue cooking about 30 minutes, until onions are very brown and soft in texture. Reserve.

♦ Crumble Gorgonzola cheese into food processor bowl equipped with steel blade. Squeeze the roasted garlic from its skin and add to the processor bowl. Pulse several times to break up the Gorgonzola and the garlic. Add cream cheese and process in short pulses until thoroughly combined. Transfer mixture to a mixing bowl and fold in the reserved onion and black pepper.

Makes 1 ¾ cups

Sun-Dried Tomato Cream Cheese

So simple, and so popular. In addition to using it for canapés, spread it on sandwiches.

INGREDIENTS:

> *4 cloves garlic, peeled*
> *½ cup sun-dried tomatoes packed in olive oil, drained (reserve oil for another use)*
> *¼ teaspoon salt*
> *1 pound cream cheese, softened*

♦ Place garlic in food processor bowl equipped with steel blade. Process until garlic is minced, stopping a couple of times to scrape down sides of bowl. Add the drained sun-dried tomatoes and salt. Process until mostly smooth; some pieces should still be visible. Transfer mixture to a mixing bowl. In same work bowl, process the cream cheese until very smooth. Add tomato mixture and pulse just enough to thoroughly combine ingredients.

Makes 2 ½ cups

garlic meat is soft and buttery. Baste with the stock or oil every 10 minutes. Use additional liquid if necessary. When garlic is done roasting, remove from oven and let cool to room temperature.

♦ To use, squeeze the meat out of each clove. Be sure to use all the pan juices left from roasting either by drizzling them over the roasted cloves or adding them to soups or sauces.

Garlic Bread Spread

This is the best ever garlic butter. It is great for garlic bread or simply tossed with pasta.

INGREDIENTS:

> 8 ounces butter, softened (if using unsalted butter, you
>   may want to add salt to this recipe)
> 8 or 9 cloves roasted garlic (page 23)
> 2 cloves fresh garlic, peeled and put through a press
> ½ teaspoon dried basil
> ⅛ teaspoon sweet paprika

◆ Place softened butter, roasted garlic, and fresh garlic in food processor work bowl equipped with steel blade. Pulse to chop garlic and cream butter. When butter is smooth, mix in basil and paprika.

Makes 1 cup

Choosing Olives

Think of olives as an agricultural product whose quality is determined by wide variation in geography, weather, cultivation, processing, handling, and probably a host of other variables. The only quality about olives that is consistent is that they are inconsistent. Buy by taste, not by name. Varietal names, such as picholine, niçoise,

Green Olive Tapenade

In this very popular tapenade, we lighten the traditional mixture of olives, anchovies, garlic, and capers with the addition of grainy mustard, fresh parsley, and a generous dose of fresh lemon juice. We also use a mix of olives to give a more mellow flavor and spike them with an ample dose of oregano and just a touch of ground allspice. The result is a very lively taste and texture that has dozens of delicious uses. Use the sprightly mixture on crackers or bread, to season vegetables, to toss with pasta—there is almost no end to its uses. We especially like to serve it with Polenta Patties (page 28) or to use it for filling Slow-Roasted Romas (page 3).

Without the parsley, the mixture will keep, refrigerated, for months, so you may want to add parsley only to the amount of tapenade you plan to use immediately. The ratio is about 4 parts olive mixture to 1 part parsley. Even once the parsley is added, the tapenade keeps for up to a month.

INGREDIENTS:

> *7 to 9 garlic cloves, peeled*
> *1 anchovy fillet, well rinsed and drained*
> *Generous pinch ground allspice*
> *1 teaspoon dried oregano*
> *1 teaspoon Tabasco sauce*
> *1 ½ teaspoons coarse-grained mustard*
> *¼ cup pitted kalamata olives, well drained (page 5)*
> *⅓ cup pitted California black olives, well drained*
> *½ cup pitted green olives (the most flavorful you*
>   *can obtain)*
> *1 teaspoon capers, rinsed and drained*
> *1 ½ tablespoons freshly squeezed lemon juice*
> *½ cup extra virgin olive oil*
> *¼ cup finely chopped parsley*

◆ Place garlic and anchovy in work bowl of food processor equipped with steel blade, and process until minced. Add allspice, oregano, Tabasco, and mustard. Pulse to combine. Add kalamata olives, California olives, and green olives. Pulse several times, scraping sides of bowl with a rubber spatula as needed. Do *not* purée. The texture of the olives should be coarse—neither chunky nor pasty. Spoon mixture into a bowl and stir in capers, lemon juice, olive oil, and parsley.

Makes 1 ⅓ cups

gaeta, or kalamata, are only a tip to the qualities of the olive. For instance, picholines, most often associated with France, frequently hail from Morocco. Niçoises (thought to be a French classic) often come from Italy and Spain. While there are some moves toward a regulated designation of origin, generally the country where the olive is packed is indicated as the country of origin.

Even cost does not necessarily indicate quality in olives, although it can be a sign of the carefully controlled processing that produces optimum texture and flavor. Taste "bargains" before buying.

In general, olives should be firm textured yet tender, and without bruises. Next to their complex and varied flavors, the great thing about olives is their near-imperishability, especially if stored in their own brine or juices or in olive oil. Although they will keep well at room temperature, refrigeration definitely extends their shelf life. Be certain to return them to room temperature before serving.

Green Olive Gremolata

Here is another favorite olive concoction that's full of possibilities. Serve the high-flavor mixture on Neva-Betta crackers (page 21) as an easy appetizer. But don't stop there. The combination of raw garlic, lemon, and olives can be a marvelous flavor lift to a host of dishes.

This recipe is based on the traditional Italian garnish for ossobuco, called gremolata. Parsley, lemon zest, and raw garlic are minced together and sprinkled over veal shanks that have been braised in a garlicky tomato sauce. The very fine mince and the acid of the lemon zest tames the raw garlic. Adding olives and olive oil to the formula makes the mixture very versatile: spoon it over potatoes, stir it into hot beans, dollop it into soup. Try substituting orange zest for the lemon and fresh rosemary or sage for part or all of the parsley. For some dishes, you may also want to add a bit of anchovy to the minced mixture.

INGREDIENTS:

> 1 cup pitted green olives (page 5)
> Zest of 1 to 2 lemons, to taste (be sure there is no white pith on your zest to make it bitter)
> ¼ cup finely minced parsley
> 2 cloves garlic, finely minced
> About ¼ cup best-quality extra virgin olive oil (page 75)

◆ Finely mince the olives and the lemon zest. Mix both together with the parsley and garlic. Moisten with olive oil to taste; there should be enough oil to make the mixture shiny but not liquid.

Makes about ¾ cup

Don't Miss the Short-Lived Roja Season

Every fall, Pasta & Co. stores sell the year's best garlic: freshly harvested Spanish Roja garlic with big, easy-to-peel, juicy cloves. The variety is grown in very limited amounts by Northwest farmers, primarily because of its short shelf life. By December of most years, the garlic is past its prime, and we are forced to settle for more run-of-the-mill varieties.

Polenta Patties

Adding egg, chicken stock, semolina flour, and cream *changes the texture and flavor of classic polenta into a meatier substance with more complex flavors. This recipe originated in Cindy Pawlcyn's book* Fog City Diner Cookbook. *In it, Chef Pawlcyn uses a similar mixture to make polenta cakes the size of hamburger patties—a great vegetarian entrée possibility. Here, we take a slightly altered mixture and form it into bite-sized patties for appetizers. Of course, you can turn these patties into an entrée simply by serving several of them. The advantage of the smaller cakes is that you get more of what is perhaps the tastiest part of polenta: the crispy exterior.*

PREPARE-AHEAD NOTES:

The cakes can be prepared several days ahead before sautéing and serving.

INGREDIENTS:

- 1 cup heavy cream
- 1 cup chicken stock
- 1 ½ tablespoons butter
- ¼ teaspoon ground nutmeg
- ½ teaspoon salt
- ¼ teaspoon freshly ground black pepper
- ½ cup semolina flour
- 1 cup coarse-ground cornmeal
- ¾ cup grated cheese—cheddar, Parmesan, Gruyère, or fontina (or any combination)
- 1 egg, lightly beaten
- 1 tablespoon chopped parsley or minced chives
- Butter for sautéing
- Optional (but highly recommended): Pasta & Co. Green Olive Tapenade, purchased or made according to recipe on page 25, or dollops of sour cream

For other polenta recipes, see Baked Cheese Polenta (page 159) and Cheese-Seasoned Polenta (page 161).

encore

◆ In a large, heavy-bottomed saucepan over medium heat, combine the cream, stock, butter, nutmeg, salt, and pepper, and bring to a rolling boil. Stir in the semolina flour and cornmeal and continue to cook until the mixture thickens and is smooth, 5 to 8 minutes. (Watch closely, stirring as necessary to prevent sticking.)

◆ Remove from heat and add the cheese and egg, mixing thoroughly. Allow the mixture to cool. Add the parsley or chives and form into cakes, using ¼ cup for each appetizer patty.

◆ Immediately before serving, sauté the patties over medium-high heat in a little hot butter until golden brown on both sides and heated through. Serve hot or at room temperature, but do not hold longer than an hour after browning. (Leftover patties reheat quite well in the microwave: heat them for 2 minutes on high.)

◆ Serve with dollops of Pasta & Co. Green Olive Tapenade or sour cream, if desired.

Makes 12 to 14 appetizer patties

Marinated Chèvre

Even when *Pasta & Co.* first published this recipe in 1987, we called goat cheese a "foodie cliché," along with sun-dried tomatoes, balsamic vinegar, and yes, even pasta." But we also predicted that all of these truly good ingredients would survive their fad stages. And they have. Our stores still marinate chèvre daily according to this recipe.

Part of the appeal of this slightly pungent and very creamy cheese is that it complements so many other foods. It's a satisfying appetizer, served with good warm bread to sop up the herb-and-garlic-scented olive oil. It also goes splendidly with blanched asparagus and Couscous and Black Beans (page 92) to make a vegetarian, room-temperature entrée—stunning and easy.

PREPARE-AHEAD NOTES:

♦ You can make the marinade days before pouring it over the cheese. Just refrigerate to store.

♦ The cheese is best left in the marinade for at least 8 hours. However, since the cheese slices are fragile, it is best to let them marinate in their serving dish so that you won't have to move them before serving.

♦ The marinade will congeal under refrigeration. Bring the dish to room temperature to serve and the marinade will form a sheer, shiny coating for the cheese.

INGREDIENTS:

1 log (12 ounces) goat cheese (French Montrachet is a good choice)

1 cup best-quality extra virgin olive oil

1 ½ teaspoons dried chervil

1 ½ teaspoons dried thyme

1 teaspoon dried rosemary, finely crumbled

3 medium cloves garlic, put through a press

◆ Make sure the cheese is well chilled. Dip a sharp knife into a cup of hot water before slicing the cheese into 8 slices, each about ¾ inch thick (dip the knife before each slice to avoid crumbling). Use any "crumbles" in your next green salad, along with any extra marinade. Lay each slice in a serving dish in a single layer.

◆ Whisk together the olive oil, herbs, and garlic. Spoon marinade over cheese slices. Let marinate for several hours in the refrigerator. Return to room temperature and baste with the marinade before serving.

Makes 8 slices

Frittata Made Easiest

W*hen we need a stunning brunch dish, when we need a good-looking appetizer, or when we are looking for contrasting texture for a buffet of room-temperature salads, we go back to this bake-in-the-oven egg dish.*

Commonly, the frittata is considered the Italian version of the French omelet. Accordingly, it has some precise techniques that distinguish it, such as slow cooking over low heat in a heavy-bottomed skillet. And, unlike the French omelet, it is served flat rather than rolled.

Our version is more like a crustless quiche. The beauty of it is that it cooks unattended in the oven and comes out ready to serve with no last-minute hassle. It is exceedingly tasty at room temperature even a day after baking.

Frittatas, like omelets, invite infinite combinations of ingredients. The recipe that follows suggests only two— one with bacon and spinach and a vegetarian version with roasted bell pepper.

The recipe calls for a standard 9- or 10-inch pie plate. However, it's easy to double the recipe and bake it in an ovenproof porcelain fish platter (a shallow, long platter that holds 5 cups of liquid), or triple it and bake it in a 13-inch porcelain paella pan (a shallow, round dish that holds 8 to 10 cups of liquid). Cut oversized frittatas into strips or wedges and serve in expectation of raves.

Note: Do not overbake. The eggs should be firm and set but not stiff and dry.

PREPARE-AHEAD NOTES:

The frittata can be prepared up to eight hours before baking; ideal timing is to bring it out of the oven 30 minutes before serving.

FOR BACON FRITTATA:

> ¾ cup coarsely diced good-quality bacon (about 6 ounces)
>
> 1 large yellow onion, peeled and cut into ¼-inch crescents (page 22)
>
> 2 cups fresh spinach leaves, cut into a chiffonade (page 132)

FOR VEGETARIAN FRITTATA:

> 2 tablespoons extra virgin olive oil
>
> 1 large yellow onion, peeled and cut into ¼-inch crescents
>
> 2 cups fresh spinach leaves, cut into a chiffonade
>
> 1 bell pepper, preferably red, roasted, peeled, seeded, and cut into ¼-inch dice (for how to roast the pepper, see page 9)

FOR EITHER FRITTATA:

> 6 large eggs
>
> Optional: ½ teaspoon salt
>
> 8 grinds cracked pepper
>
> ¾ cup freshly grated Parmesan cheese

♦ For either version, generously butter a 9- or 10-inch pie plate and set aside.

♦ *For the bacon version,* sauté bacon until golden. Remove with a slotted spoon and place in the buttered pie plate. Drain off all but 2 tablespoons of the fat left in the sauté pan and add the onions to the pan. Cook over medium heat until browned and almost caramelized, about 30 minutes. When onions are done, add the spinach and cook just until wilted. Remove from heat and spoon onions and spinach evenly over the bacon in the buttered pie plate, making sure that they are evenly distributed. Let cool.

♦ *For the vegetarian version,* heat the olive oil in the sauté pan. Add the onions and sauté until browned. Add the spinach and cook just until wilted. Stir in the roasted pepper and remove from heat. Spoon the vegetables into the buttered pie plate, distributing evenly. Let cool.

♦ Meanwhile, beat eggs in a large bowl just until yolks and whites are blended. Add optional salt (the bacon version may not need it), pepper, and Parmesan cheese. Mix thoroughly.

♦ When onion/bacon/spinach or onion/pepper/spinach mixture has cooled, pour egg mixture over it, again making sure that the ingredients are evenly distributed. Dish can now be set aside, covered and refrigerated, for up to 8 hours before baking.

♦ When ready to bake, preheat oven to 450° F. Bake for approximately 15 to 20 minutes, or until the edges of the frittata are golden brown and the center is set but still slightly creamy. Do not overbake. (Cooking time will need to be adjusted if you are doubling or tripling the recipe.)

♦ Remove frittata to a rack and let cool approximately 15 minutes. Carefully loosen frittata from the pan with a long metal spatula. Slide out and continue to cool on rack. (You can serve double—or triple—versions directly from their baking dishes.) To serve either hot or at room temperature, slide frittata onto a flat surface and cut into wedges.

Serves 6 as an appetizer, 4 as an entrée

soups

O F ALL THE FOODS WE COOK, SOUPS ARE THE EASIEST TO PREPARE WITH LESS FAT. PURÉED VEGETABLES, GRAINS, AND LEGUMES READILY DOUBLE FOR HEAVY CREAM. INSTEAD OF BEING SAUTÉED IN FAT, INGREDIENTS CAN SIMPLY "SWEAT" IN THEIR OWN JUICES. GOOD-QUALITY, READY-MADE VEGETABLE STOCKS (PAGE 40) EASILY CONVERT MANY A SOUP INTO VEGETARIAN FARE.

French Green Lentils

We now have a domestic source for the French *lentilles verts du puy* (green lentils): our own Eastern Washington Palouse country. These lentils are very different from commonly available red or brown lentils. They cook up firm and meaty. Use them in any recipe where the lentils are *not* puréed (they have marvelous texture but resist all efforts to make them creamy).

To cook green lentils, rinse and pick them over for any debris. Place in saucepan. Cover with salted water, bring to a boil, reduce heat, and simmer until tender (15 to 25 minutes). When cooked, season, dress with oil (extra virgin olive oil or walnut oil) or a vinaigrette, and serve at room temperature. Or cook the lentils in a flavorful broth and serve hot as a side to roasted meats and vegetables. They make an inspired change from potatoes, rice, or pasta. Like all other lentils, green lentils are high in fiber, vitamins, and minerals.

Baby Garbanzo and French Lentil Soup

This Yellow Line soup is typical of how absolutely marvelous and uncompromising low-fat eating can be. There are only 3 grams of fat per cup, and only 14 percent of the soup's 160 calories per cup come from fat.

The recipe takes advantage of the firm texture of baby garbanzo beans and French green lentils (both available at Pasta & Co. stores). Combining these two legumes with rice gives us a soup that is high in low-fat protein. You can make the soup vegetarian or not, depending on your choice of stock. With so little fat, you might want to top the soup with a bit of crumbled feta cheese.

PREPARE-AHEAD NOTES:

The soup keeps well for at least five days refrigerated and can be frozen very successfully. You can cook the baby garbanzos or white beans days ahead (and even freeze them) before making the soup.

INGREDIENTS:

½ cup dried baby garbanzos (chana dal), or ½ cup dried small white beans
1 ½ teaspoons salt
1 ½ teaspoons extra virgin olive oil
1 onion, peeled and coarsely chopped
6 large cloves garlic, peeled and finely chopped
1 tablespoon ground cumin
1 teaspoon dried oregano
½ teaspoon dried basil
½ teaspoon salt (depending on saltiness of your stock)
⅛ teaspoon ground allspice
⅛ teaspoon cayenne

1 ½ cups crushed tomatoes in purée (we prefer
    Paradiso or DiNola brand)
7 cups vegetable stock or defatted chicken stock, more
    if needed
½ cup uncooked green lentils (page 37)
½ cup uncooked white rice

♦ Cook baby garbanzos according to the directions on page 87. Add the 1½ teaspoons of salt when the garbanzos are almost tender. Finish cooking (they should be very creamy), rinse, drain, and reserve.

♦ In a large kettle, heat the olive oil. Add the onions and sauté over medium-low heat until soft. Add the garlic, cumin, oregano, basil, ½ teaspoon salt, allspice, and cayenne. Cook just until the garlic is golden but not browned. Add the tomatoes, stock, lentils, and rice. Simmer until the lentils and rice are tender. Stir in the cooked baby garbanzos and simmer just to heat through. If soup seems too thick, add water or additional stock to thin (it may need another cup or two of liquid). Remove from heat and taste for salt and pepper.

Makes 8 to 10 cups

White Bean, Carrot, and Roasted Garlic Soup

Lisa Szkodyn, one of our store managers, brought this delicious recipe to us. It uses puréed beans and roasted garlic to create the illusion of creaminess in a soup with barely any fat in it. Once again, you have the choice of making it vegetarian or not.

Freezing Cooked Legumes

Many of our low-fat recipes depend on cooking dried beans and other legumes—a fairly easy but time-consuming task. What is often overlooked, however, by cooks who claim they don't have time to deal with the likes of dried beans is that once cooked the legumes (and many grains, for that matter) can be successfully stored frozen. Store them in cup or pint portions in airtight containers. Adding them to dishes is just a matter of stirring them—thawed or frozen—into whatever you are making and allowing a little extra cooking time for the beans to marry with the dish.

YELLOW LINE

PASTA & CO

for more about

**PASTA & CO.
YELLOW LINE
DISHES**

turn to page xv.

Like all of our soups, this one keeps well for at least five days refrigerated and can be successfully frozen. The soup is easy to make, but allow plenty of time for the beans to cook.

INGREDIENTS:

> 1 ½ cups dried white beans
>
> 1 large sprig fresh rosemary or ½ to 1 teaspoon dried rosemary
>
> 2 to 4 teaspoons salt (depending on saltiness of your stock)
>
> 1 ½ teaspoons extra virgin olive oil
>
> ½ large yellow onion, peeled and cut into ½-inch dice
>
> 2 cloves garlic, peeled and put through a press
>
> 2 ¼ cups peeled, coarsely chopped carrots
>
> 2 average-size heads roasted garlic (page 23)
>
> 3 cups vegetable stock or defatted chicken stock, more if needed
>
> ½ to 1 ½ teaspoons Tabasco sauce

◆ Cook beans with the rosemary according to the directions on page 87. Add the salt when the beans are almost tender. Continue cooking until they are very tender. Drain the beans and reserve. If using fresh rosemary, remove the leaves from the stem and return them to the beans, discarding the stem.

◆ Place olive oil, onion, and garlic in another kettle over medium-low heat. Cover and let onions slowly "sweat" (give off moisture) until they are golden (do not burn), about 15 minutes. Add carrots and just enough water to cover. Cover and boil until carrots are very tender, about 15 minutes. Remove from heat.

◆ While carrots are cooking, squeeze the meat from each clove of roasted garlic. Reserve.

◆ Place carrots and their cooking liquid, the meat from the roasted garlic, and half the cooked beans in a food processor bowl equipped with a steel blade. Purée the mixture until quite smooth. Return the mixture to the kettle.

Whisk in stock, Tabasco to taste, and remaining beans. Add salt and pepper to taste.

♦ If the soup is too thick, add stock or water. Taste for seasoning.

Makes 9 cups

Winter Squash Soup

Consider this low-fat soup as an alternative to some of the more typical winter soups that are laden with heavy cream. It is light and brothy yet rich with the velvety texture of cooked squash—a perfect case of cutting fat and fooling the palate. There are 3 grams of fat per cup with only 20 percent of the 160 calories per cup from fat.

PREPARE-AHEAD NOTES:

The soup keeps well in the refrigerator for at least five days. It can also be frozen.

INGREDIENTS:

> 1 ½ teaspoons extra virgin olive oil
> ½ large onion, peeled and cut into ½-inch dice
> 1 ½ teaspoons sweet paprika
> 1 ½ teaspoons brown sugar
> ¼ teaspoon dried sage, crumbled
> ¼ teaspoon dried thyme
> ⅛ teaspoon cayenne
> 2 medium carrots, peeled and cut into ½-inch dice
> 7 ½ cups vegetable stock or defatted chicken stock,
>   more if needed
> 1 ½ large white rose potatoes (about ¾ pound),
>   washed and cut into ½-inch dice
> 1 butternut squash (about 1 ½ pounds), peeled (use a
>   carrot peeler), seeded, and cut into ½-inch dice

Stock Options for Trimming Fat

Very early in our low-fat efforts, we learned Fat-Trimming Tip No. 1 (page xvi): "Substitute good-quality defatted stock or broth for part or all of the fats called for in savory recipes." Fortunately, several high-quality, commercially made meat and vegetable broth products are now available.

♦ Swanson's Vegetable Broth, from the Campbell Soup Co., which has given us tasty chicken broth for years, is now commonly available at grocery stores and is a fine way to convert many a recipe to vegetarian with no loss of flavor. It is available at grocery stores.

♦ Perfect Additions is a line of frozen, salt-free stocks: chicken, beef, veal, fish, and vegetable. It's tough to beat these premium-priced products, especially the vegetable and fish stock. They are available at Pasta & Co.

♦ Organic Gourmet is a shelf-stable line of two vegetarian stocks—vegetable and wild mushroom—from Germany. The products have only trace amounts of fat, relatively little salt, and because they are concentrated and inexpensive, they're ever so handy to keep ready for use in your refrigerator. We use these products in our kitchens for almost all our vegetable stock needs. They are excellent but need to be used with discretion. When used in too high a proportion in a recipe, they impart a sort of "instant onion soup" taste. They are available at Pasta & Co.

♦ Demi-Glace, that culinary elixir that hardly any home cook has time to make, is now available in several commercial forms. Three we like are Demi-Glace Gold (a four-times reduction of veal stock, flavored with red wine, tomato paste, vegetables, herbs and spices), Glace de Poulet Gold (a ten-times reduction of chicken stock, vegetables, and wine), and Veggie-Glace Gold, a vegetarian demi-glace substitute. The great thing about these demi-glace products is that they contain very little fat and carry a real flavor wallop when added full strength to almost any savory dish (see Oven-Roasted Onion and Fennel Sauce, page 185). All three of these

½ teaspoon salt (more or less, depending on the
    saltiness of your stock)
10 grinds black pepper
¼ head white cabbage (about 2 cups), cored and
    sliced ⅛ inch thick
3 tablespoons finely chopped parsley

♦ In a large kettle, heat the olive oil over medium-low heat. Add the onion, paprika, sugar, sage, thyme, and cayenne. Cook until onion begins to soften, about 5 to 8 minutes. Add the carrots, cover, and cook another 5 minutes.

♦ Add the stock, potatoes, squash, salt, and pepper. Bring to a simmer and cook, covered, until squash and potatoes are tender, about 15 minutes. Add the cabbage and parsley. Cook another 5 minutes to soften cabbage. (Do not overcook the soup, or the potatoes and squash will become too soft.) Taste for seasoning. You may also want to thin the soup with more stock or water.

Makes 11 cups

Lisa's Vegetarian Chili

This is another invention from manager Lisa Szkodyn. *It is low-fat, vegetarian, and just about as hearty as our old-time, meat-loaded chili recipe (page 171). This zesty meal of a soup holds a mere 2 grams of fat in a 1-cup, 120-calorie serving. Only 16 percent of those calories are from fat.*

PREPARE-AHEAD NOTES:

The chili can be made days before serving. Don't hesitate to double the recipe and pop leftovers away in the freezer.

INGREDIENTS:

¾ cup dried black beans

1 tablespoon salt

1 ½ teaspoons extra virgin olive oil

1 onion, peeled and cut into ¼-inch dice

1 zucchini, cut into ¼-inch dice

½ red bell pepper, cored and cut into ¼-inch dice

1 small carrot, peeled and cut into ¼-inch dice

½ rib celery, cut into ¼-inch dice

3 cloves garlic, peeled and finely minced

1 to 2 tablespoons mild chili powder

2 ¼ teaspoons ground cumin

1 ½ teaspoons dried oregano

½ teaspoon ground black pepper

½ teaspoon salt

⅛ to ¼ teaspoon dried red pepper flakes

2 cups crushed tomatoes

¾ cup vegetable stock, more if needed

¾ cup frozen corn, thawed but not cooked

1 teaspoon freshly squeezed lemon juice

¼ cup chopped parsley

products are available at Pasta & Co. (See also Reducing Stock, page 82, and Don't Forget to Skim, page 48.)

♦ Presoak and cook the beans according to the directions on page 87. When almost done cooking, add the tablespoon of salt. When beans are done, drain and reserve.

♦ Heat the olive oil in a large kettle over medium heat. Add onions, zucchini, red pepper, carrot, celery, and garlic. Cover and cook over medium heat until soft, about 7 minutes. Mix together the chili powder, cumin, oregano, pepper, ½ teaspoon salt, and red pepper flakes. Add the mixture to the softened vegetables along with the tomatoes and their juices and the stock. Simmer for 15 minutes, then add the corn, lemon juice, parsley, and reserved beans. Simmer another 10 minutes. Adjust seasoning and, if the chili is too thick, add extra stock.

Makes 7 cups

for more about

**PASTA & CO.
YELLOW LINE
DISHES**

turn to page xv.

Black Bean Chowder

Black Bean Chowder is a customer favorite that was introduced long before the concern about dietary fat. Originally, the soup was made with 3 tablespoons of olive oil and chicken stock. We have eliminated the olive oil and substituted vegetable stock for the chicken. The result is a vegetarian, low-fat Yellow Line product—as popular as ever—that has only 3.12 grams of fat and 148 calories per cup— 19 percent of the calories from fat.

PREPARE-AHEAD NOTES:

The soup keeps well for a week refrigerated and for a couple of months frozen.

INGREDIENTS:

⅔ pound (11 ounces or about 1 ½ cups) dried black beans, well-washed and picked over for foreign matter

1 ¾ quarts vegetable or defatted chicken stock, more if needed

2 cups coarsely chopped yellow onion

3 cloves garlic, peeled and put through a press

¾ teaspoon dried oregano

½ bunch cilantro, stemmed and thoroughly washed

1 to 2 small-sized jalapeño peppers, tops cut off, but not seeded

1 16-ounce can (2 cups) whole tomatoes, coarsely chopped, and their juice (Paradiso or DiNola brand is a good choice)

2 ½ tablespoons dark rum

2 tablespoons freshly squeezed lime juice

Salt and pepper to taste

TO TOP:

Red onion, finely chopped
Optional: sour cream (if you're not watching fat)

◆ Cook beans according to directions on page 87, but in this case, after the initial presoaking, use the stock instead of water and cook the beans until they fall apart, about 2 hours. Stir vigorously now and then with a whisk to break up the beans. After 40 minutes of cooking, add the onions, garlic, and oregano. Stir well. As the beans begin to break apart, lower the heat and stir frequently so that no sticking occurs.

◆ Purée the cilantro and jalapeños in a food processor bowl equipped with a steel blade. Remove the mixture and reserve. When the beans have cooked until there are only a few whole ones left, add the puréed cilantro and jalapeños and the tomatoes, rum, and lime juice. Stir well and return to a simmer. In the same processor bowl, purée about 2 cups of the soup and then return the soup purée to the kettle. Stir and check for seasoning and consistency. Add salt and pepper to taste. If the soup is too thick, thin with additional stock. Serve topped with red onion and the optional sour cream.

Makes 7 cups

Quinoa and Cabbage Soup

A simple cabbage broth is the base for this wonderfully comforting soup that's a snap to put together. For meat eaters, the bacon not only flavors the soup but adds heft. However, skip the bacon and you have not only a tasty vegetarian soup but a lower-fat one as well, one that qualifies as Yellow Line. The addition of quinoa illustrates the versatility of this "miracle grain" (page 101) and increases significantly the soup's nutritional value. However, if quinoa is not available to you, substitute another grain, such as cooked brown rice, and you will still have a fine soup.

PREPARE-AHEAD NOTES:

This recipe makes a lot of soup. It can be halved, but then you're left with half a head of cabbage. Since the soup can be frozen, it seems a shame not to make a whole-head batch. The soup keeps well refrigerated for at least five days.

INGREDIENTS:

4 quarts water

2 tablespoons salt

1 small head cabbage

½ pound bacon, diced (about 2 cups), or 1 scant tablespoon extra virgin olive oil if making the lower-fat vegetarian version

1 yellow onion, peeled and coarsely chopped

9 cloves garlic, peeled and finely chopped

1 can (28 ounces) whole tomatoes, drained and cut into 1-inch pieces (we prefer Paradiso, DiNola, or San Marzano brand—page 178)

1 cup chopped parsley

1 ¼ cups (½ pound) raw quinoa, prepared according to directions on page 102

Additional salt and freshly ground black pepper to taste

◆ In a large kettle, bring water and salt to a boil. Meanwhile, cut the cabbage into quarters. Cut out core pieces and discard. Chop cabbage into 1- to 2-inch pieces. Add cabbage to the boiling salted water and simmer for about 5 minutes. Remove from heat.

◆ In a large skillet, fry the bacon until golden. (If making the soup low fat and vegetarian, use a nonstick skillet and a scant tablespoon of extra virgin olive oil for cooking the onion.) Drain off all but a tablespoon of the fat. Add onion and cook about 10 minutes, or until golden brown. Add garlic and cook for a couple more minutes, being careful not to burn the garlic. Add onion mixture to cabbage along with the tomatoes and parsley. As soon as the quinoa is cooked, drain it and add it to the soup. Return the soup to medium heat and simmer about 5 minutes to blend flavors. Taste for salt and pepper and adjust if necessary.

Makes about 16 cups

Red Gazpacho

Longtime staffer and Pasta & Co. friend Judy Birkland invented this recipe for warm-weather eating. It has always been a summertime favorite—even more so today because of its exceedingly low fat content.

Serve icy cold. If not counting grams of fat, accompany it with lots of freshly toasted croutons or Pasta & Co. Cheesed and Herbed Breadsticks, purchased or made according to the recipe on this page. Substitute garden-ripe fresh tomatoes—peeled but with all their juices—when available.

Great Soup Accompaniment: Cheesed and Herbed Breadsticks

For years, Pasta & Co. has made a plain breadstick of which we are shamelessly proud. Some customers prefer an embellished version gilded with a mixture of olive oil, cheese, and dried herbs. We sell hundreds of both types of breadstick every day. Making the cheese version at home is a simple way of quickly creating the welcoming aroma of fresh baking when you are short on time. You and guests will love the smell, as well as the taste.

◆ 10 Pasta & Co. breadsticks
◆ 2 tablespoons freshly grated Romano cheese
◆ 2 tablespoons freshly grated Parmesan cheese
◆ 1 teaspoon Pasta & Co. House Herbs (page 166), or a mixture of dried basil and oregano
◆ 1 tablespoon extra virgin olive oil

◆ Preheat oven to 375° F. Place breadsticks close together—almost touching—on a cookie sheet. Mix together the cheeses and herbs. Brush the breadsticks with the oil. Sprinkle the cheese mixture over the top.

♦ Bake approximately 8 minutes, or until cheese melts.

♦ Cool just long enough for cheese to firm. Then cut or break apart into individual breadsticks.

♦ Serve warm or at room temperature.

♦ Use any of the cooked cheese mixture that breaks off to sprinkle over a green salad or a soup.

Allow plenty of time for the soup to chill: three hours is optimum. The gazpacho keeps refrigerated for at least five days.

INGREDIENTS:

2 cups canned crushed tomatoes in juice (use whole San Marzano tomatoes, page 178, if possible; chop coarsely in a food processor before adding with all their juices to soup)
2 cups cold water
1 cup canned tomato juice
2 cloves garlic, peeled and put through a press
3 tablespoons freshly squeezed lemon juice
2 tablespoons white wine vinegar
1 tablespoon extra virgin olive oil
1 teaspoon ground coriander
¾ teaspoon dried thyme
½ teaspoon salt
1 scant teaspoon Tabasco sauce
1 tablespoon finely chopped cilantro
Optional: 2 sprigs fresh thyme
½ cup peeled, seeded, and cubed cucumber (¼-inch cubes)
¼ heaping cup seeded and cubed green bell pepper (¼-inch cubes)
¼ cup thinly sliced green onions
¼ cup cubed celery (¼-inch cubes)
¼ cup finely chopped parsley

♦ In a large bowl, whisk together the tomatoes, water, tomato juice, garlic, lemon juice, vinegar, olive oil, coriander, thyme, salt, and Tabasco. Add cilantro and optional thyme sprigs. Stir in remaining ingredients and chill. After 2 to 3 hours, remove the thyme sprigs, if used, and serve.

Makes 6 ½ cups

Black-Eyed Pea and Lentil Soup

*T*his brothy soup, originally made with vegetables sautéed in olive oil, is now created with vegetables simply simmered in the soup's liquid. You will find that cooking the vegetables this way gives a meaty, chewy texture that lends welcome substance to a soup that does not have the richness that comes from using fat.

In this recipe, wine—a low-fat ingredient—gives the soup depth of flavor. Use the best dry red wine you have available.

A flourish of your best olive oil right before serving (page 77) could add a well-deserved fillip to this spartan soup, which otherwise is frugal in fat.

PREPARE-AHEAD NOTES:

If you are concerned about having sufficient time to cook the black-eyed peas, remember that legumes can be cooked well ahead of time and frozen (page 38). Actually, compared to other dried legumes, black-eyed peas are relatively fast-cooking. They are usually tender within 40 minutes after soaking. Once the soup is assembled, it keeps well for up to a week refrigerated and also freezes well.

INGREDIENTS:

⅓ pound (5 ounces) dried black-eyed peas
    (about 1 cup)
1 tablespoon salt for peas
¾ cup dry red wine
7 cups defatted chicken or vegetable stock,
    more if needed
½ cup dried lentils (do not use French green lentils—
    page 37)
½ teaspoon salt for lentils
1 medium yellow onion, peeled and cut into ¼-inch
    crescents (page 22), then cut in half again

Don't Forget to Skim

*I*f you're making your own stock, don't forget that it needs to be "defatted" if you are watching fat intake. Otherwise, you're adding fat at the same time you're replacing it. The best way to defat stock is to refrigerate it overnight; the next day, skim off the layer of fat that will have formed on the top.

If you're using canned broth, you may find a glob of fat on top. Dispose of it before using the broth.

for more about

**PASTA & CO.
YELLOW LINE
DISHES**

turn to page xv.

2 carrots, peeled and cut into ½-inch dice
1 celery stalk, cut into ½-inch dice
1 tablespoon finely chopped garlic
1 bay leaf
¾ teaspoon dried thyme
¾ teaspoon ground coriander
¾ teaspoon ground cumin
⅛ teaspoon cayenne
1 cup canned whole tomatoes, cut into ¼-inch dice,
*   with all the juices (Paradiso or DiNola brand is*
*   a good choice)*
1 tablespoon balsamic vinegar

♦ Cook black-eyed peas according to the directions on page 87. Add the tablespoon of salt when the peas are almost tender. When finished cooking, drain peas and place in a bowl.

♦ Meanwhile, combine wine and 3 cups of the stock in another saucepan. Bring to a boil, add lentils and ½ teaspoon salt, and cook until tender, about 30 minutes. Remove from heat and reserve.

♦ In the pot used to cook the black-eyed peas, place 1 cup of stock. Add onions, carrots, celery, garlic, bay leaf, thyme, coriander, cumin, and cayenne. Cover and cook over medium-high heat until the vegetables soften, about 15 minutes. Add the remaining 3 cups stock, tomatoes, and vinegar, and simmer uncovered another 10 minutes. Stir in the reserved black-eyed peas and the lentil mixture. Simmer until heated through and flavors are blended. Taste for salt and pepper. Thin with additional water or stock, if desired.

Makes 9 cups

Fresh Cilantro and Rice Soup

H*ere is another case of simmering rather than sautéing the soup vegetables in order to eliminate fat and produce a hefty mouth-feel in this otherwise light-textured soup. It is our low-fat answer to tortilla soup. Add all the high-fat condiments—tortilla chips, avocado, and sour cream—only if you wish.*

PREPARE-AHEAD NOTES:

The soup keeps well for several days and rewarms perfectly. It is also a good candidate for the freezer.

INGREDIENTS:

½ cup uncooked rice
1 cup coarsely chopped yellow onion
2 large cloves garlic, peeled and put through a press
1 teaspoon ground cumin
Optional: 1 teaspoon salt (depending on saltiness of your stock)
⅛ teaspoon dried red pepper flakes
8 cups defatted chicken stock
Juice of 1 lemon
1 ½ cups diced tomatoes, fresh or canned, including their juice (recommended: San Marzano brand— page 178)
16 whole sprigs fresh cilantro, tied together with kitchen string
½ cup chopped cilantro
Additional salt to taste

♦ Cook rice according to package directions, making sure it is quite dry when cooked. Reserve.
♦ Place onion, garlic, cumin, optional salt, and red pepper flakes in a large saucepan and ladle in enough of the

chicken stock to cover the vegetables. Cover and cook over medium heat until onion begins to soften, about 10 minutes. Remove lid. Add remaining stock, lemon juice, tomatoes, and cilantro sprigs, and continue to simmer until onions are very tender, about 30 minutes. Remove the cilantro sprigs. Stir in the reserved rice and the chopped cilantro, and season with salt to taste.

Makes 8 cups

Three Soups After Fat-Trimming Tip No. 13

The next three recipes (Chicken Senegalese Soup, Wild Mushroom Soup, and Cream of Tomato and Cauliflower Soup) are for classic cream soups—big and rich, based on a butter and flour roux and a whole lot of heavy cream and half-and-half. We have revised each of them, using Fat Trimming Tip No. 13 (page xvii): "Become fat-conscious in your cooking. Look before you cook. Not every recipe can be converted to low-fat, but almost every recipe can stand some fat-trimming."

In all three of these recipes, we have slashed cups of cream and table-spoons of butter and increased the amount of

Chicken Senegalese Soup

Use this very substantial and pretty soup as an entrée or as a soup course for a formal dinner.

PREPARE-AHEAD NOTES:

While the soup keeps well refrigerated for several days, re-warming needs to be done gently, as with all cream soups. This soup requires even more care to keep the chicken meat from becoming dried out. Freeze as a last resort.

INGREDIENTS:

½ to ¾ pound boneless, skinless chicken breasts
2 ¾ cups defatted chicken stock, more if needed
¾ cup dry sherry
2 tablespoons butter
5 shallots, peeled and finely minced
3 celery stalks, finely chopped
1 ½ teaspoons curry powder
1 teaspoon dried dill weed
1 teaspoon freshly ground black pepper
¾ teaspoon salt
½ teaspoon ground nutmeg
¼ to ½ teaspoon cayenne
½ cup flour

¾ cup apple cider
2 cups half-and-half, heated
1 cup heavy cream, heated
1 large, tart apple (preferably Granny Smith), peeled,
  cored, and finely minced

◆ Cut chicken into ½-inch pieces. Reserve. Place chicken stock and sherry in a saucepan and bring to a boil. Remove from heat. Reserve.

◆ Melt butter in a soup kettle. Add shallots and celery and cook until soft, stirring occasionally, about 10 minutes. Add curry powder, dill, pepper, salt, nutmeg, and cayenne, and cook another 2 minutes, stirring constantly. Do not brown. Add flour. Cook another 2 minutes, continuing to stir. Gradually whisk in the reserved hot chicken stock and sherry. Add the apple cider and cook about 8 minutes over medium heat. Add the heated half-and-half, heated cream, apples, and reserved chicken. Simmer just until the chicken is cooked, stirring occasionally and being careful not to burn the soup on the bottom. Taste for texture and seasoning. If too thick, add more chicken stock. Taste again for seasoning and adjust to taste.

Makes 10 cups

stock with no noticeable change in quality. Rest assured, however, that although the recipes are now fat-conscious, the soups remain far from low-fat and are luxuriously delicious.

Wild Mushroom Soup

Here is another fat-reduced version of a roux-based soup (page 51)—still so luscious, it's a clear candidate to start a celebratory meal.

A word about the Wild Mushroom Powder. We love the heady flavor of wild mushrooms but not their high cost or the special handling they require. In many recipes, such as this one, you can get much of the quintessential flavor of wild mushrooms by using a product called Woodland Pantry Wild Mushroom Powder from Forest Foods, Inc., in River Forest, Illinois. Our stores have sold the product and our kitchens have used it for years. It's especially good for boosting mushroom flavor in soups, sauces, and stews.

PREPARE-AHEAD NOTES:

The soup keeps well refrigerated for up to five days and freezes well.

INGREDIENTS:

2 tablespoons butter

1 small leek, cut in half the long way, rinsed under running water to remove grit, and cut (using about half the green) into ½-inch slices

1 tablespoon finely minced garlic

½ pound mushrooms, cleaned and finely chopped (about 2 cups)

1 ½ tablespoons fresh sage, or 1 ½ teaspoons dried sage

1 tablespoon Woodland Pantry Wild Mushroom Powder (see note above)

½ teaspoon salt

½ teaspoon dried thyme

4 grinds black pepper (we recomment Pasta & Co. No. 4 Pepper Blend with Whole Allspice)

Pinch of cayenne

3 tablespoons flour

3 ½ cups vegetable or defatted chicken stock,
    heated (we use Organic Gourmet Wild Mushroom
    Stock Base)
1 ¼ cups half-and-half, heated
⅓ cup dry sherry
3 tablespoons finely chopped parsley

◆ Melt butter in a large saucepan over medium heat. Add
leeks and cook a few more minutes. Add garlic and continue cooking until leeks are soft but not browned. Add
the chopped mushrooms and cook about a minute more.
Add the sage, mushroom powder, salt, thyme, black pepper, and cayenne. Stir. Add the flour. Stir and cook 1
minute, being careful not to brown the roux. Add 1 cup
of the hot stock and cook over medium heat, whisking
until well blended. Add remaining stock, heated half-and-
half, and sherry. Raise heat and bring soup to a boil.
Lower heat and simmer until flavors are well blended. Stir
in parsley and serve.

Makes 7 cups

Cream of Tomato and Cauliflower Soup

This is a lovely cream soup—just a touch lighter than
when it was made with more cream and less stock. It
is beautifully scented with tarragon. When you have fresh
tarragon in your garden, substitute it generously for the dried
tarragon.

PREPARE-AHEAD NOTES:

The soup holds well for three days refrigerated and can be
frozen. Reheat gently.

2 tablespoons butter
¾ cup diced onion (¼-inch dice)
¾ cup diced celery (¼-inch dice)
¾ cup diced carrots (¼-inch dice)
1 ½ teaspoons dried tarragon
1 ¼ teaspoons finely minced garlic
¼ cup flour
3 ¾ cups defatted chicken stock or vegetable stock
1 cup dry white wine
1 small to medium head cauliflower, cut into
  small florets
2 cups whole canned tomatoes and their juice,
  chopped briefly in food processor (Paradiso or
  DiNola brand is a good choice)
1 cup half-and-half, heated
½ cup heavy cream, heated
1 teaspoon salt
Pinch ground nutmeg
½ cup sour cream
Freshly cracked pepper to taste

◆ In a 4-quart saucepan, melt butter and add onion, celery, carrots, and tarragon. Cook over medium heat until vegetables are tender, about 5 minutes. Add garlic and cook 3 more minutes. Add flour and stir to make a roux. Do not brown. Remove from heat.

◆ In another saucepan, boil stock and wine together for 3 minutes. Whisk a small amount of the hot stock mixture into the roux. Place roux mixture over medium heat and stir in the rest of the stock mixture. Add the cauliflower and simmer until it is tender, stirring frequently, about 10 minutes. Add tomatoes, heated half-and-half, heated cream, salt, and nutmeg. Continue to cook, stirring, until thickened. Remove from heat.

◆ Place sour cream into a medium-sized bowl or measuring cup. Stir in 4 ladlefuls of the hot soup to blend. (Do not cheat on this step and stir the sour cream directly into the hot soup. It will most certainly curdle.) Then stir sour cream mixture into soup. Simmer 5 minutes. Do *not* boil. Season to taste with black pepper and serve.

Makes 12 cups

South American Summer Soup

I n contrast to the rich cream soups, this chilled soup is rich in a completely different way. Here, olive oil makes the soup succulent while at the same time its texture stays extremely light.

PREPARE-AHEAD NOTES:

This soup is quick to make and keeps well refrigerated for two days. Be sure to allow adequate time for chilling—three hours should do.

INGREDIENTS:

1 cup finely diced onion (small onions can be cut into crescents, page 22); Walla Walla Sweets or Maui onions are preferred

2 tablespoons cider vinegar

½ pound best-quality cooked and peeled shrimp (ask for Chilean shrimp or use cooked prawns, tails removed, cut into ½-inch pieces)

1 jar (16 ounces) Pasta & Co. Marinara Sauce, or 2 cups Basic Marinara Sauce (page 180)

1 cup cold water

½ cup freshly squeezed orange juice (approximately 1 orange)

¼ cup extra virgin olive oil

2 tablespoons freshly squeezed lime juice
¼ cup finely chopped cilantro
½ teaspoon finely minced garlic
½ jalapeño pepper, seeded and finely minced
½ teaspoon Worcestershire sauce
¼ teaspoon Tabasco sauce
⅛ teaspoon ground cumin
½ to 1 teaspoon salt, or to taste
Freshly ground pepper to taste

♦ Marinate the onion in the cider vinegar for 15 minutes and reserve. Rinse shrimp in cold water and drain well.

♦ While onions marinate and shrimp drain, stir together in a large bowl the marinara sauce, water, orange juice, olive oil, lime juice, cilantro, garlic, jalapeño, Worcestershire sauce, Tabasco sauce, and cumin. Add the onions along with their vinegar and the drained shrimp. Season with salt and pepper to taste. Refrigerate and serve well chilled, tasting for seasoning just before serving. If soup seems too thick or intense in flavor, thin with a small amount of cold water.

Makes 4 cups

room temperature foods

PASTAS, GRAINS, BEANS,
VEGETABLES, AND MEATS
FOR FIRST COURSES,
ENTRÉES, AND SIDE DISHES

THE RECIPES IN THIS CHAPTER REPRESENT QUINTESSENTIAL PASTA & CO. FOOD: UNPRETENTIOUS DISHES WITH FLAVORS SO ROBUST THAT THEY CAN BE PREPARED HOURS—IF NOT DAYS—BEFORE SERVING. THEY CAN BE STORED REFRIGERATED BUT ACHIEVE THEIR FULL GLORY IF ALLOWED TO SIT AT ROOM TEMPERATURE FOR AN HOUR OR SO BEFORE SERVING.

More Ideas

For more room-temperature pasta dishes, see Pasta and Poquitos (page 83), Barley and Bowties (page 98), and Tortellini with Barley (page 99).

What Is "Squeaky Cheese"?

Squeaky cheese is what we call dry-curd cottage cheese—the little chalky white curds used in making cottage cheese. It is sold in nondescript plastic bags labeled "0 grams of fat"; you'll find them in your grocer's dairy case. If you eat them right from the bag, you'd never imagine that the curds could be the basis for such tasty recipes as Sumac Spiced Cheese and Tomato Salad (page 10), Southwest Curd and Corn Salad (page 116), and our top-selling pasta salad, Rotini with Squeaky Cheese, Cucumber, and Green Onion (this page).

ROOM-TEMPERATURE
PASTAS

Although these dishes are most commonly called "pasta salads," the term has become so hackneyed, so suggestive of overcooked, under-flavored, careless concoctions, that we try to avoid it. Instead, we prefer to imply glorious dishes with provocative ingredients, dishes that are a joy to serve and to eat. We think of them simply as pasta dishes meant to be served at room temperature—as appetizers, side dishes, or entrées. Among these recipes you will find some of our most popular lower-fat dishes.

YELLOW LINE

Rotini with Squeaky Cheese, Cucumber, and Green Onion

This dish is proof that unexpected or unusual texture combined with high flavor can compensate for a lack of fat. In it, the "squeaky" mouth feel of dry-curd cottage cheese combines with pungent vinegar and a large dose of garlic to make this dish the quintessential pasta salad for the nineties.

PREPARE-AHEAD NOTES:

The dressing can be prepared a day ahead. Toss with pasta and other ingredients within a few hours of serving.

INGREDIENTS:

1 tablespoon salt for pasta water
2 cups dry-curd cottage cheese
½ cup nonfat Quark (page 62)
½ cup white wine vinegar

2 tablespoons extra virgin olive oil

1 ½ tablespoons finely minced garlic

1 ½ teaspoons salt

Cracked pepper to taste

⅔ pound (11 ounces) fresh rotini or ½ pound dried

1 ½ cups thinly sliced green onion, including green tops

1 cup diced, seeded, unpeeled cucumber (¼-inch dice)

TO TOP:

16 cherry tomatoes, quartered

¼ cup white wine vinegar

Salt

2 tablespoons finely chopped parsley

♦ Bring 4 to 6 quarts of water and the 1 tablespoon of salt to a boil. Meanwhile, in a large bowl, fold together 1 ½ cups of the cottage cheese (reserving the remaining ½ cup), the Quark, the ½ cup vinegar, olive oil, garlic, the 1 ½ teaspoons salt, and pepper to taste.

♦ Cook the rotini in the boiling salted water until barely tender. Rinse with cold water, drain well, and fold into cottage cheese mixture. Let sit 15 minutes to absorb dressing. Fold in green onions and cucumber.

♦ For the topping, toss tomatoes with the ¼ cup white wine vinegar and salt to taste. Set aside.

♦ Place rotini mixture in a large serving dish. Top with the seasoned tomatoes. Sprinkle with the remaining ½ cup cottage cheese and the parsley. Serve at room temperature.

Makes 11 cups

Tossed with a lot of vinegar, garlic, and salt, the initially bland little pellets turn into lively pouches of taste and texture. We call them "squeaky cheese" because of the slight squeaky sensation they cause in the mouth. Remember, when you cut fat, you need new sources of interest for the palate.

Product Spotlight: Quark

Quark is a spreadable cheese that we suggest substituting for sour cream or yogurt. It is sold in both low-fat and nonfat varieties; we recommend the nonfat one. Four ounces of nonfat Quark contain only 4.8 milligrams of cholesterol and 71 calories (compared to sour cream's 14 milligrams of cholesterol and 243 calories). Yogurt is lower in calories but thinner in flavor and texture than Quark.

Some grocery stores, such as QFC in the Seattle area, sell Quark. If you have difficulty obtaining it, contact Appel Farms in Ferndale, Washington, (360) 384-4996.

Best Pasta Cooking Instructions

◆ For optimum cooking, do not cook more than 2 pounds at a time. Do not crowd the pasta.

◆ Allow 4 to 6 quarts of water per pound of pasta. Bring water and 1 tablespoon of salt to a boil.

◆ Add pasta to boiling water. Stir and begin timing immediately.

◆ Pasta needs to move while it cooks so that it will cook evenly and not stick together. Stir frequently until the boil itself is vigorous enough to move the pasta.

◆ The only sure way of knowing whether the pasta is done is to taste it. Keep in mind that fresh pasta cooks much faster than dried.

◆ Once pasta is tender, drain very well and toss immediately with sauce or dressing, coating pasta evenly.

◆ Do *not* rinse pasta *unless* specifically instructed to do so in a recipe or unless you suspect you have overcooked it (rinsing with cold water will halt cooking).

◆ Pasta needs to be thoroughly dressed with a liquid (olive oil, sauce, butter, salad dressing, or broth) immediately after draining; otherwise it sticks together, as one Seattle restaurant reviewer once put it, like "impassioned night crawlers."

◆ **A little pasta cooking water can help you use less fat:** We always stress thorough draining of the pasta after cooking so as not to dilute sauces and dressings. In some cases, however, especially with hot pastas and sauces, you will find that a little of the starchy cooking water clinging to the pasta actually helps you use less sauce and can add a creamy texture. Use your best cook's judgment.

◆ **Pasta cooking times for high-acid dishes:** As you will see, most of the lower-fat dressings for pasta are highly acidic—so much so that they literally "cook" (or at least continue to soften) the pasta after the dish is assembled. Guard against pasta becoming unpleasantly soft in these dishes by slightly undercooking it. We use the term "barely tender." Keep in mind, too, that cooking time should be slightly reduced if you plan to serve the dish hours after it is made rather than immediately, since the longer the pasta is in the dressing, the softer it will become.

◆ **On the other hand, there's tortellini:** Do *not* be tempted to undercook tortellini. Even in high-acid dressings, they will firm up as they cool down. For our fresh tortellini, we suggest a cooking time of 14 minutes if it is going to be used in a room-temperature dish, 12 minutes if it is to be served hot.

Santa Fe Pasta

Here we use a whoppingly acidic dressing and take advantage of the intense flavor of sun-dried tomatoes (reconstituted only with boiling water, not oil) to add a hefty flavor to room-temperature pasta. Be sure to use pasta made with 100 percent semolina flour to stand up to this high-acid dressing. Olives and feta cheese add token fat, but the dish qualifies for the Pasta & Co. Yellow Line, with 29 percent of its calories coming from fat. There are 7 grams of fat and 210 calories per cup—no room to cheat by adding more than the ½ cup of feta called for as a garnish.

PREPARE-AHEAD NOTES:

The sun-dried tomatoes and dressing can be prepared several days ahead of serving. Toss with pasta and other ingredients no more than a few hours before serving.

INGREDIENTS:

1 tablespoon salt for pasta water
1 cup sun-dried tomatoes (not *packed in oil*)
½ cup red wine vinegar
½ cup freshly squeezed lemon juice
¼ cup extra virgin olive oil
2 tablespoons pressed garlic (use a garlic press)
2 teaspoons salt
1 teaspoon freshly ground black pepper
¾ pound fresh egg rotini
½ pound fresh red chile rotini (if red chile rotini is not available, use a total of 1 ¼ pounds egg rotini)
1 cup diced red bell pepper (¼-inch dice)
1 cup pitted black olives, rinsed, well drained, and quartered
1 cup thinly sliced green onions

Sun-Dried Tomatoes: A Big Flavor Booster for Low-Fat Dishes

How deplorable when a great ingredient becomes a cliché. That is certainly what happened to sun-dried tomatoes in the 1980s. They became so overused in recipes and on menus that they became a culinary embarrassment. For years, we avoided them in new recipes. Then we discovered their value as a low-fat ingredient—low-fat, that is, if you eliminate the olive oil traditionally used to rehydrate and preserve the tomatoes. Buy dried tomatoes in bags and rehydrate them yourself, using only boiling water or stock. These morsels are not as rich tasting as their succulent, oil-laden cousins, but their concentrated flavor is tailor-made for lower-fat cooking, as in Santa Fe Pasta (this page).

TO TOP:

½ cup crumbled feta cheese
¼ cup finely chopped parsley

♦ Bring 4 to 6 quarts of water and the tablespoon of salt to a boil. Meanwhile, reconstitute the sun-dried tomatoes by soaking them in boiling water for 3 minutes, or until tender. Rinse with cold water and drain well. Cut into thin strips and set aside.
♦ In a large bowl, whisk together vinegar, lemon juice, olive oil, garlic, salt, and pepper. Reserve.
♦ Cook rotini in the boiling salted water, until barely tender—about 4 minutes. Rinse with cold water and drain well. Toss with the reserved dressing and the reconstituted tomatoes. Let sit for 15 minutes to absorb dressing. Then fold in the bell pepper, olives, and green onions.
♦ Place in serving bowl and top with the feta and parsley.

Makes 11 cups

Thai Shrimp and Rice Stick Pasta

Asian cooking is replete with low-fat possibilities. Lura Throssel, our prepared foods manager, combines several Asian elements, including rice stick noodles and sweetened cucumbers, to give us this Yellow Line dish.

PREPARE-AHEAD NOTES:

The dressings can be prepared a couple of days ahead, but the dish should be served the same day it is assembled.

CUCUMBER DRESSING:

½ cup white wine vinegar
¼ cup sugar
¼ teaspoon salt
⅛ teaspoon dried red pepper flakes

SALAD DRESSING:

¼ cup sugar
¼ cup boiling water
¼ cup white wine vinegar
1 ½ tablespoons freshly squeezed lime juice
1 teaspoon pressed garlic (use a garlic press)
Scant ½ teaspoon salt
⅛ teaspoon dried red pepper flakes

NOODLES:

8 ounces rice stick noodles (we like Elephant brand)
1 ½ tablespoons vegetable oil

TO ASSEMBLE:

1 large bunch cilantro, washed, dried, and finely
    chopped
1 bunch green onions, sliced
1 pound peeled, cooked shrimp, well rinsed and
    drained (we prefer Chilean shrimp)
2 cucumbers, cut in half, seeded, and cut into ¼-inch
    slices
½ medium red onion, peeled and cut into thin
    crescents (page 22)

♦ To make cucumber dressing, whisk together white wine vinegar, sugar, salt, and red pepper flakes in a small saucepan. Heat just until sugar dissolves. Set aside to cool.
♦ To make salad dressing, whisk together sugar, boiling water, vinegar, lime juice, garlic, salt, and red pepper flakes in a large measuring cup. Continue mixing until sugar has dissolved.

for more about
**PASTA & CO.
YELLOW LINE
DISHES**
turn to page xv.

Serving Temperature: It Counts for a Lot

Serving temperature is easily as important to good food and drink as ingredients or preparation. Any connoisseur of fine wines or cheeses will agree. A serving temperature that is too hot or too cold can mean death to the very precious flavors that elevate drinking and eating from mere sustenance to sheer pleasure.

This is especially true with low-fat foods. Since cold typically subdues flavor, serving a low-fat dish at room temperature rather than right from the refrigerator can be the flavor builder that makes it work.

◆ Soak noodles in hot tap water for 30 minutes. Meanwhile, bring 6 quarts of water to a simmer. At the end of 30 minutes, drain the noodles and immerse half of them in the simmering water for 5 seconds. Remove immediately and rinse with cold water (the noodles should feel like rubber bands). Repeat with the remaining noodles. Let the noodles drain well, then toss them with the vegetable oil, making sure each noodle is separate and well coated with oil.

◆ To assemble, toss the salad dressing with the noodles. Fold in cilantro, green onions, and shrimp. Toss cucumber and onion with the cooled cucumber dressing. Immediately remove half the cucumbers and onion from the liquid and reserve. Toss remaining cucumbers, onions, and dressing with the noodles. Place noodles in serving bowl and top with reserved cucumbers and onions.

Makes 11 to 12 cups

Tortellini in Paprika Garlic Sauce

Instead of tortellini, try using the dressing on a dried heavy pasta such as bucatini for a lighter side dish that is delicious with roasted chicken and blanched vegetables. (There will be enough dressing for 1 pound of dried bucatini or spaghetti.) We call this variation Moroccan spaghetti.

Assuming that you use Pasta & Co. Chicken Tortellini (which is our lowest-fat tortellini with only 4 grams of fat per serving), this dish gets 29 percent of its calories from fat and contains 6 grams of fat and 210 calories per 1-cup serving. With unfilled pasta, the fat drops to around 4 grams per serving.

Case Study: The Making of a Low-Fat Classic

Tortellini in Paprika Garlic Sauce is one of our best-selling Yellow Line products. To be Yellow Line, it requires a tortellini with no more than 4 grams of fat per serving, such as our Chicken Tortellini. The story of how the rest of the dish evolved, however, illustrates several key points in the crafting of lower-fat foods.

The dish is inspired by a Moroccan sauce called chermoula. Chermoula recipes vary widely, but all contain generous amounts of olive oil, lemon juice, garlic, cumin, and more sweet paprika than American cooks typically use in a lifetime. Depending on the cook, the sauce may also include cilantro, cayenne, oregano, and basil. It is precisely the kind of assertive flavor that low-fat cooking needs. One problem: Even a conservative rendition of the sauce required 1 cup of olive oil to dress 2 pounds of pasta.

We did some quick calculations. To bring the dish down to less than 30 percent calories from fat would allow only ¼ cup of olive oil. It was time to apply some of our Fat-Trimming Tips (pages xvi–xvii).

We started with Tip No. 1: Substitute good-quality, defatted stock for part or all of the fats called for in recipes. We replaced ¾ cup of the olive oil with ¾ cup chicken stock (chicken because it accents the flavor of the tortellini filling). As good a fat substitute as stock is, however, it's no match for fat in texture. Unless greatly reduced by boiling, stock is very thin compared to olive oil.

We then moved on to Tip No. 8; we needed a low-fat thickener. Tomato paste was the choice. We added 2 tablespoons to the stock. The remaining traditional ingredients—hefty amounts of sweet paprika and cumin, and touches of salt and cayenne—were easy to honor.

The amount of lemon juice, however, became problematic (Tip No. 2). With so little fat (only ¼ cup of olive oil, instead of 1 cup), we had to reduce the lemon juice to prevent the dish from becoming unacceptably acidic. We started with ¾ cup lemon juice but reduced it to ⅔ cup. Still, when there is more acid than fat in a recipe, the resulting dressing can "cook" other ingredients, making chicken and seafood taste dry, grains and pastas, too soft. In this case, the solution was to choose a sturdy ingredient—tortellini. (For an unfilled pasta, we recommend bucatini—see page 67.) If using a more fragile pasta, you might slightly undercook the pasta and keep in mind that the dish will have a shorter shelf life, since the longer the pasta is in the sauce the softer it becomes.

Garlic: The Ingredient Fat-Slashers Can't Live Without

One of the best ways to build flavor without fat is to increase the amount of garlic in a recipe. As you will see, we make liberal use of garlic in all its guises, from mellow-flavored roasted cloves to high-powered raw ones.

Find our garlic usage packs too big a wallop? Feel free to adjust to your taste. Keep in mind, however, that in the rush to healthier eating, garlic is a welcome spur.

PREPARE-AHEAD NOTES:

The dressing can be made a day ahead of serving. Once you have added the pasta, serve the dish within 24 hours, as the highly acidic dressing will continue to soften the pasta. Remember to allow enough time for the pasta to be in the dressing at least one hour before serving. If you find that, after a few hours, the dish has lost its shine, toss the pasta with an additional ½ cup chicken stock mixed with 1 teaspoon olive oil. Making the dish with tortellini gives it about twice the shelf life of one made with a less sturdy pasta.

INGREDIENTS:

> 1 tablespoon salt for pasta water
> 1 ⅓ cups defatted chicken stock
> ⅔ cup freshly squeezed lemon juice
> ¼ cup extra virgin olive oil
> 2 tablespoons sweet (not hot) paprika
> 2 tablespoons tomato paste
> 1 tablespoon plus 2 teaspoons pressed garlic
>   (use a garlic press)
> 1 teaspoon salt
> ½ teaspoon ground cumin
> ¼ teaspoon cayenne
> 2 pounds fresh chicken tortellini
> OR: another tortellini with no more than 4 grams of
>   fat per serving (if you are not watching fat grams,
>   any tortellini of your choice will work)

TO TOP:

> 2 cups thinly sliced green onions
>   (slice on the diagonal)

♦ Bring 4 to 6 quarts of water and the tablespoon of salt to a boil. Meanwhile, in a large stainless steel bowl, whisk together the chicken stock, lemon juice, olive oil, paprika, tomato paste, garlic, the 1 teaspoon salt, cumin, and cayenne.

♦ Cook tortellini in the boiling salted water until tender (about 14 minutes—see page 63). Drain well (do *not* rinse) and toss immediately with dressing. Allow the tortellini to sit in the dressing for at least 1 hour before serving. During the first hour, it is important to turn the pasta over in the dressing several times so that they absorb the dressing evenly.

♦ After about an hour, place in a serving dish and top with the green onions.

Makes 8 cups

Pasta Salad con Salami

For 15 years, this has been our top-selling room-temperature pasta salad. Originally, we used thinly sliced salami. Recently, we have used a mild pepperoni called kabonossi that our stores sell. If you can't find fresh spinach and red pepper rotini, substitute fresh egg rotini, using a total of 1 pound.

PREPARE-AHEAD NOTES:

The ingredients may be prepared a day ahead of serving. Once assembled, the dish is best served within a couple of hours. If you hold it longer, you may want to toss it with a little additional olive oil and vinegar.

INGREDIENTS:

1 tablespoon salt for pasta water
½ cup extra virgin olive oil
½ cup vegetable oil
1 cup white wine vinegar
1 teaspoon pressed garlic (use a garlic press)
10 grinds black pepper

Fresh Pasta Versus Dried

Pasta & Co. makes and sells over a ton of fresh pasta products a week. We make a dozen different shapes of fresh pasta and supplement them with top-quality dried pasta in the shapes that are not feasible for us to produce.

In short, we use both fresh and dried pasta. And we hasten to point out that fresh does not automatically mean better. There are now a slew of mass-produced fresh pasta products on the market that are no better than, and in some cases not as good as, dried pasta. To be of superior quality, pasta must be made with premium ingredients, and moisture and other variables must be controlled. Fresh, good-quality pasta offers obvious advantages over dried, especially for basic long noodles, lasagne, and filled pasta. If the shape of pasta you want is not available fresh, look for top-quality dried pasta made with 100 percent semolina flour.

Note: If a recipe calls for 1 pound of fresh pasta, you can substitute ⅔ pound (11 ounces) of dried pasta. As a general rule, the cooking time for dried pasta is approximately four times that of fresh pasta.

1 pound fresh pasta, preferably:
  ⅓ pound (5 ounces) egg rotini
  ⅓ pound (5 ounces) spinach rotini
  ⅓ pound (5 ounces) red pepper rotini
OR: ⅔ pound (11 ounces) dried pasta, preferably a short, curly cut
⅓ pound (5 ounces) salami, thinly sliced and cut into ¼-inch-wide strips or 6 kabonossi, sliced ¼-inch thick on the diagonal
1 green bell pepper, cored and cut into ¼-inch-wide strips no longer than 2 inches
½ red bell pepper, cored and cut into ¼-inch-wide strips no longer than 2 inches
2 cups California pitted black olives, well drained and quartered
1 cup sliced green onions (¼ inch slices)
½ to ⅔ cup freshly grated Parmesan cheese
½ to ⅔ cup freshly grated Romano cheese
½ cup finely chopped parsley

♦ Bring 4 quarts of water and the tablespoon of salt to a boil. Meanwhile, in a large bowl, whisk together olive oil, vegetable oil, vinegar, garlic, and pepper. Reserve.

♦ Cook each type of pasta separately in the boiling salted water until tender. Lift pasta out, drain well, and immediately toss with the dressing. When all three pastas have been cooked and added to the dressing, set aside to cool for 30 minutes, tossing the pasta with the dressing occasionally. When cool, add the salami (be sure to separate the slices; they tend to stick together), peppers, olives, green onions, cheeses, and parsley. Toss again until all ingredients are well coated with the dressing. Place in a serving dish and serve at room temperature.

Makes 12 cups

Tortellini with Peppers and Pine Nuts

This is another top-selling Pasta & Co. classic.

PREPARE-AHEAD NOTES:

This dish can be made several hours ahead, but do not add the vegetables until shortly before serving.

INGREDIENTS:

> 1 tablespoon salt for pasta water
> 1 cup extra virgin olive oil
> 1/3 cup white wine vinegar
> 1 teaspoon pressed garlic (use a garlic press)
> 10 grinds black pepper
> 1 teaspoon dried basil, or 1/4 cup fresh basil leaves, washed, dried, and finely chopped
> 1 pound fresh tortellini
> 1/2 cup finely chopped fresh parsley
> 1/2 red bell pepper, cored and cut into 1/2-inch diamonds
> 1/2 green bell pepper, cored and cut into 1/2-inch diamonds
> 1/2 cup freshly grated Romano cheese
> 1/4 cup pine nuts, lightly toasted

TO TOP:

> 1/2 cup sliced green onions (slice 1/8 inch thick on the diagonal)

♦ Bring 4 to 6 quarts of water and the tablespoon of salt to a boil. Meanwhile, in a large bowl mix together the olive oil, vinegar, garlic, pepper, and basil.
♦ Cook the tortellini in the boiling salted water until tender, about 13 to 14 minutes. Drain well and toss immedi-

Recommended Equipment: The Pasta Cooker

While not essential, a pasta cooker (a kettle that has a colander insert for cooking and draining pasta) is a boon for cooking pasta, especially if you are cooking several batches. If you don't have a pasta cooker, you can handle small batches simply by scooping out the cooked pasta with a large sieve. Either way, you need only one kettle of boiling water. Note: Four quarts of water will cook up to two 1-pound batches of pasta before starch buildup necessitates fresh water.

ately with the dressing. Let cool for about 30 minutes, tossing occasionally.

♦ When cool, toss with parsley, red and green bell pepper, cheese, and pine nuts. Taste for seasoning. If not using within an hour, refrigerate. When ready to serve, bring the dish to room temperature, spoon into a shallow serving dish, and top with the green onions.

Makes 8 cups

Pasta Brutta:

TORTELLINI WITH SUN-DRIED TOMATOES AND KABONOSSI

*W*e have been making this dish several times a week for over a decade. When we first perfected it, we said, "Great taste, but it's ugly." Hence the name "Pasta Brutta"—brutta meaning ugly in Italian. Recently, we stepped up the seasoning by about a third, a testament to our customers' preference for ever zestier foods.

Note that since the dressing is a thick paste and clings well to the pasta, it turns the tortellini into bite-sized morsels very suitable for appetizers. Just serve with toothpicks and cocktail napkins for catching any drips.

PREPARE-AHEAD NOTES:

The dressing can be prepared several days before combining with the cooked tortellini. The assembled dish holds well refrigerated for a couple of days. Add the green onions just before serving.

1 tablespoon salt for pasta water

1 cup sun-dried tomatoes in olive oil

Extra virgin olive oil

¼ pound kabonossi (this is a pepperoni-like product that is made for our stores by a San Francisco sausage maker; if necessary, substitute another good-quality pepperoni), cut into 1-inch pieces

3 cloves garlic, peeled

4 teaspoons grainy mustard

4 teaspoons freshly squeezed lemon juice

¾ teaspoon dried red pepper flakes

1 ½ pounds fresh tortellini—cheese, veal, pesto, or chicken

TO TOP:

1 ½ cups sliced green onions (sliced ⅛ inch thick on the diagonal)

◆ Bring 4 to 6 quarts of water and the salt to a boil. Meanwhile, drain olive oil from tomatoes into a measuring cup. Reserve tomatoes and add extra virgin olive oil to the measuring cup to total ⅔ cup plus 1 tablespoon. Reserve.

◆ In bowl of food processor equipped with steel blade, place the kabonossi and garlic. Process about 1 minute. Add reserved sun-dried tomatoes, mustard, lemon juice, and red pepper flakes. Process until ingredients form a finely ground paste. With the processor still running, add the olive oil in a steady stream.

◆ Cook the tortellini in the boiling salted water until tender, about 13 to 14 minutes. Drain well and immediately toss with dressing. Set aside to cool. To serve, spoon into shallow platter and top with the green onions.

Makes 8 cups

When to Use What Oil

For the purposes of this book, we use a simple system of referring to culinary oils. We specify four different categories of oil:

♦ **Vegetable oil**: Any of the commonly available oils such as canola, soybean, corn, or grapeseed. These are called for when a dish needs a flavorless or neutral oil.

♦ **Extra virgin olive oil**: Less expensive extra virgin olive oils (under $15 a liter) that are suitable for either cooking (i.e., heating) or for dressings. These will tend to be mild-flavored oils.

♦ **Best-quality extra virgin olive oil**: More expensive extra virgin olive oils that we classify as condiment oils—oils that should be reserved for room-temperature applications, definitely for the "final flourish" we recommend for finishing off certain dishes (page 77). These oils will tend to have fuller, more complex flavors.

♦ **Exotic oils**: Almond oil, macadamia nut oil, hazelnut oil, and so on. As a general rule, these are also condiment oils—not to be heated but rather used straight out of the bottle to enhance the

Jade and Ivory

Its sharp, clean taste and its versatility keep this dish popular with Pasta & Co. customers. It's an excellent side to almost any entrée. For a vegetarian meal, we suggest coupling it with Couscous and Black Beans (page 92), another Pasta & Co. classic.

The myzithra cheese (also spelled "mitzithra") is a goat or sheep's milk cheese of Greek origin. We use it as a grating cheese to give Jade and Ivory its pungent, distinctive flavor. You can substitute Romano cheese, but the dish's taste will be much less distinguished.

PREPARE-AHEAD NOTES:

Although the dressing can be made a couple of days ahead, the dish should be served the same day it is assembled.

INGREDIENTS:

1 tablespoon salt for pasta water

1 cup extra virgin olive oil

¼ cup freshly squeezed lemon juice

3 tablespoons heavy cream

3 large cloves garlic, peeled and put through a press

½ teaspoon dried red pepper flakes

¼ teaspoon salt

20 grinds black pepper

1 pound fresh Pasta & Co. pescine, or ⅔ pound (11 ounces) any short dried pasta

⅓ cup freshly grated myzithra cheese

¼ cup freshly grated Parmesan cheese

1 cup sliced green onions (¼ inch thick—use both white and green parts)

½ cup finely chopped parsley

2 cups frozen peas, thawed, rinsed, and drained but not cooked; or 2 cups blanched asparagus tips, no longer than 2 inches

½ cup sliced green onions (sliced ⅛ inch thick on
   the diagonal)

♦ Bring 4 to 6 quarts of water and the tablespoon of salt
to a boil. Meanwhile, in a large bowl, whisk together olive
oil, lemon juice, heavy cream, garlic, red pepper flakes,
the ¼ teaspoon salt, and pepper. Reserve.
♦ Cook the pasta until tender (about 2 minutes). Drain,
rinse with cold water, and drain again. Immediately toss
the pasta with the dressing, using a large rubber spatula,
until well coated. Let cool to room temperature (up to
1 hour), then fold in the cheeses, green onions, and
parsley. Add the peas or asparagus just before serving.
Place in serving dish and top with the additional green
onions. Serve at room temperature.

Makes 9 cups

Pasta with Chicken, Feta, and Roasted Peppers

Normally, we prefer a more substantial, easier-to-serve
pasta than fettuccine for a room-temperature dish.
*Certainly, you can substitute a short, light-textured pasta,
but the heft of fettuccine is just right in this dressing.
Consider it a warm-weather lunch or supper entrée. It's a fine
way to use up leftover grilled chicken meat.*

PREPARE-AHEAD NOTES:

This dish holds well for a couple of days. You will want to
toss it a few times and then top it with the peppers and
parsley immediately before serving.

flavor of dishes. We have
had especially exciting
results using porcini oil,
walnut oil, and truffle oil
(page 191).

Which Type of Olive Oil?

Olive oil termino-
logy is a source
of great confusion for just
about everyone. Keep the
following in mind:
♦ The best olive oils are
labeled "extra virgin,"
implying that they have
come from the first pressing of the olives and that
no heat or chemical
extraction methods have
been used. Within the
"extra virgin" category,
however, there is a wide
range of quality and taste.
♦ Olive oil is the juice of
the olive, just as wine is

the juice of the grape. Accordingly, olive oils at any price will vary greatly in their flavor profiles. Personal taste and how an oil complements a particular dish are the deciding factors.

Olive Oil as a Final Flourish

A single tablespoon of olive oil adds 14 grams of fat to a recipe. At Pasta & Co., while we have drastically reduced our use of olive oil, we like to think of it as a sort of "final flourish" for some dishes. Drizzling on a tablespoon of extra virgin olive oil right before serving allows you to optimize the shine and flavor that the oil gives a dish.

½ tablespoon salt for pasta water
½ cup extra virgin olive oil
2 tablespoons freshly squeezed lemon juice
1 ½ tablespoons heavy cream
¼ teaspoon dried red pepper flakes
⅛ teaspoon salt
10 grinds black pepper
½ pound fresh egg fettuccine (or Pasta & Co. pescine—a short cut of pasta that is similar in texture to fettuccine) or ⅓ pound (5 ounces) dried pasta
4 cups cooked boned, skinned chicken (preferably grilled), cut into bite-size pieces
½ cup crumbled feta cheese

TO TOP:

½ cup roasted red peppers, cut into ¼-inch dice (jarred are fine)
1 tablespoon finely chopped parsley

◆ Bring 4 quarts of water and the ½ tablespoon of salt to a boil. Meanwhile, in a large bowl, whisk together olive oil, lemon juice, heavy cream, red pepper flakes, the ⅛ teaspoon salt, and black pepper.

◆ Cook the pasta in the boiling salted water until tender. Rinse with cold water and drain well. Immediately toss with the dressing. (Nothing works better to accomplish this than hands. If you're not up to this, then you'll need a sporkit or two—page 198—to properly toss the fettuccine with the sauce.) Fold in chicken and feta cheese. If the mixture seems dry, add a small amount of extra olive oil. Place in serving dish and top with the roasted peppers and parsley. Serve at room temperature.

Makes 7 ½ cups

White Truffle Oil on Cappellini

The following recipe puts truffle oil to good use on pasta, but the sauce is also superb on salad greens, grilled seafood, or smoked salmon on a bed of frisée. This pasta is best served as a side dish to seafood or roasted chicken.

PREPARE-AHEAD NOTES:

The pasta can be left for an hour or two at room temperature in the sauce (any longer and you begin to lose the aromatic qualities of the truffle oil). Right before serving, re-toss with the sauce and top with the chives.

INGREDIENTS:

>   1 tablespoon salt for pasta water
>   ¼ cup Agribosco white truffle oil (or a mixture
>   of truffle oil and mild extra virgin olive oil
>   to equal ¼ cup)
>   1 tablespoon freshly squeezed lemon juice
>   ¼ cup very finely minced shallots
>   2 to 4 premium-quality anchovy fillets, such as
>   Rusticella or Bel Aria brand, very finely minced
>   2 tablespoons very finely minced chives
>   ⅛ teaspoon salt
>   Freshly ground black pepper to taste
>   ⅓ pound (5 ounces) Rusticella brand dried cappellini
>   (page 79)

TO TOP:

>   2 tablespoons very finely minced chives

◆ Bring 4 quarts of water and the tablespoon of salt to a boil. Meanwhile, whisk together the truffle oil, lemon juice, shallots, anchovy, chives, ⅛ teaspoon salt, and pepper. Cook cappellini in the boiling salted water until tender (about 5 minutes). Drain well and immediately toss with the truffle oil mixture (as inelegant as it sounds, the

Recipes with Caviar and White Truffle Oil

The recipes for White Truffle Oil on Cappellini (this page) and Cappellini with Caviar (page 79) are the most extravagant in this book. They demonstrate how you can best include truffle oil and caviar in your cooking. If you cook to entertain, you will thank us for this information. These are exquisite tastes worthy of letting up on both the fat-watch and the grocery budget.

White Truffle Oil

With the retail price of fresh white truffles running to $200 an ounce (when and if you can even obtain them), white truffle oil (the best alternative to the fresh funghi itself) at about $6 an ounce seems an indisputable culinary value. Although there are several brands of white truffle oil on the market, the best we have found and the one that our stores sell is Agribosco. The Italian producer does a superb job of infusing a light extra virgin olive oil with the aroma and taste of fresh white truffle trimmings. The result is an oil scrumptiously pungent with the famous subterranean funghi: uniquely and characteristically earthy, a taste quite beyond words. Once opened, the truffle oil will keep for months in the refrigerator, but with a gradual reduction in its aroma. It's best to use the oil soon after opening it: make the recipes on these pages and use up any remaining truffle oil by brushing it on thin slices of warm toasted baguette as an easy and most distinctive appetizer.

Choosing Cappellini

Known as "angel's hair," it is the thinnest cut of long pasta, and it is exquisite in such dishes as Cappellini with Caviar. Keep in mind that the cappellini you choose needs to be very sturdy in order to stand up to cooking. Be sure to select a brand made with 100 percent semolina. We use and sell Rusticella brand cappellini.

best way to do this is to "scrub up" and use your hands to combine the pasta with the sauce, being sure to swab up all of the shallots and chives with the pasta as you lift it onto the serving plate). Place on serving dish and top with remaining chives. Serve at once or let cool to room temperature.

Serves 2 to 4 as a side dish

Cappellini with Caviar

If you should ever want to pair pasta with caviar, the way to do it is this variation on our recipe for White Truffle Oil on Cappellini (page 78). We developed the recipe for a series of caviar and champagne tastings held at our stores in the fall of 1995.

While you can substitute mild-flavored olive oil for some or all of the very aromatic truffle oil (page 78), the dish loses some interest with the change.

USEFUL, BUT NOT ESSENTIAL, EQUIPMENT:

♦ A kitchen scale
♦ Disposable rubber gloves (since the best way to combine the pasta with the sauce and then serve it is with your hands)
♦ Don't want to use your hands? Then you need a sporkit (page 198)

PREPARE-AHEAD NOTES:

Same as for White Truffle Oil on Cappellini (page 78). Place the pasta on serving plates and top it with the caviar right before serving.

INGREDIENTS:

>   1 tablespoon salt for pasta water
>   ¼ cup Agribosco white truffle oil (or a mixture of
>   truffle oil and mild-flavored extra virgin olive oil
>   to equal ¼ cup)
>   1 tablespoon mild-flavored extra virgin olive oil
>   1 tablespoon freshly squeezed lemon juice
>   2 tablespoons very finely minced shallot
>   2 premium-quality anchovy fillets, such as Rusticella
>   or Bel Aria brand, very finely minced
>   ⅛ teaspoon salt
>   ⅓ pound (5 ounces) Rusticella brand dried cappellini
>   (page 79)

TO TOP:

>   Fresh caviar
>   Finely snipped chives
>   Tiniest diced red bell pepper and tiniest diced
>   lemon zest (by "tiniest" we mean that the size of
>   these toppings should be nearly as small as the
>   individual beads of caviar)

◆ Bring 4 quarts of water and the 1 tablespoon of salt to a boil. Meanwhile, whisk together the truffle oil, olive oil, lemon juice, shallot, anchovy, and the ⅛ teaspoon salt.

◆ Cook cappellini and toss with the truffle oil mixture according to directions in White Truffle Oil on Cappellini (page 78). The pasta can be served immediately or left for several hours at room temperature in the sauce. When ready to serve, place the pasta on a serving dish or distribute it evenly among serving plates. Hands are best for this. (If you are doing a large number of 1-ounce appetizer portions for a dainty hors d'oeuvre, a kitchen scale is invaluable. Don't forget to deduct the weight of the plate before placing the sauced pasta and garnish on it.) Top each serving of pasta with a little of the caviar, a light sprinkling of chives, and tiny specks of the red bell pepper and lemon zest around the edges.

Makes about 4 cups

How Much Caviar for How Much Pasta?

Use as much caviar as you can afford. As a small hors d'oeuvre, we get 18 one-ounce servings out of the recipe for Cappellini with Caviar, and like to top each with ½ teaspoon sevruga caviar. This proportion highlights the caviar.

For a sit-down first course, however, you could double or triple the amount of pasta per serving (getting 9 or even just 4 servings) and top with as little as ½ teaspoon of the caviar.

Wines for Dishes with Truffle Oil

Carefully choose your wines to accompany such a very distinctive and aromatic dish as one containing truffle oil. A dry, crisp sparkling wine is a reliable choice, but an earthy still wine, such as a Meursault or a Hermitage Blanc (earthy but floral as well), will greatly enhance the dish's appeal.

for more about

**PASTA & CO.
YELLOW LINE
DISHES**

turn to page xv.

ROOM-TEMPERATURE
BEANS

With their jubilant colors and shapes—which seem more varied every year—beans are a kick to cook with. They also lend themselves especially well to room-temperature dishes. Over and over, we have found beans to be invaluable for combining with pasta or rice to produce a source of lower-fat protein. And they always add visual interest to our recipes.

South American
Beans and Rice

T*he* Seattle Times *chose this vegetarian Yellow Line dish as one of the top 10 recipes it published in 1995. It combines a legume (beans) with a grain (rice), and nearly every step, from the toasting of the rice to the use of reduced stock, involves building flavor to make up for lack of fat. The result is a robust dish with high fiber, 28 percent of the calories from fat, and 230 calories and 7.41 grams of fat per cup.*

You can substitute brown rice for the white rice in this dish. If you do, increase both the cooking time and the amount of stock.

PREPARE-AHEAD NOTES:

The dish keeps well for up to four days, except that the flavor of the fresh cilantro will fade. A good idea is to add the cilantro just before serving. You can also add extra cilantro before serving a batch that has been refrigerated for a few days.

INGREDIENTS:

⅓ pound (about ¾ cup) uncooked dried beans—
   use a small red bean, such as poquitos (page 83)
   or appaloosas
1 tablespoon salt
2 ¼ cups vegetarian stock or defatted chicken stock
   (see Stock Options for Trimming Fat on page 40)
1 tablespoon vegetable oil
1 cup uncooked long-grain white rice
1 onion, peeled and cut into ¼-inch dice
½ teaspoon liquid garlic (page 150), or use ½ teaspoon finely chopped fresh garlic, being very careful
   not to burn the garlic when cooking
¼ teaspoon salt
½ cup vegetable or defatted chicken stock, boiled until
   reduced to ¼ cup (see this page)
3 tablespoons freshly squeezed lemon juice
3 tablespoons sherry vinegar
½ teaspoon garlic, finely minced
1 ½ tablespoons olive oil
1 tablespoon dried oregano
1 teaspoon dried thyme
½ teaspoon hot paprika
1 small bunch cilantro, washed, dried, and finely
   chopped

TO TOP:

2 or 3 Roma tomatoes or 6 cherry tomatoes, cut into
   ¼-inch dice

♦ Cook the beans according to the directions on page 87.
When the beans are almost tender, add the tablespoon (or
more, depending upon the saltiness of your stock) of salt,
and continue cooking until beans are very creamy. Drain
off cooking water, rinse, drain again, and reserve.
♦ Bring the 2 ¼ cups of stock to a boil, remove from
heat, and reserve.
♦ In a large skillet (preferably nonstick), heat vegetable oil
until nearly smoking. Add rice, lower heat to medium-

Reducing Stock

To "reduce" stock, boil until it is half its original volume. The liquid will not only intensify in flavor but will also become almost syrupy in texture. Since reduction intensifies saltiness, you will want to adjust recipe seasonings, depending upon the particular stock you use.

high, and toast until it is the color of dark straw, being careful not to burn the rice. Add half the diced onion and the ½ teaspoon of garlic (liquid or fresh), and cook a few more minutes. If substituting fresh garlic, be careful not to burn it. Add the hot stock and ¼ teaspoon salt. Stir, cover, lower heat, and simmer until liquid is absorbed, about 10 minutes. Cover and let stand for about 10 minutes. Fluff the rice with a fork and reserve.

♦ In a measuring cup, whisk together the reduced stock, lemon juice, sherry vinegar, and the second ½ teaspoon garlic. Reserve.

♦ Heat olive oil in another skillet over medium heat. Add the remaining onion, oregano, thyme, and paprika. Sauté until golden. Add reduced stock mixture. Remove from heat and toss with the reserved rice. Fold in reserved beans.

♦ Just before serving, toss cilantro with rice and beans. Spoon into serving dish. Top with tomatoes. Serve at room temperature.

Makes 7 cups

Pasta and Poquitos

This is another Yellow Line dish that takes advantage of Fat-Trimming Tip No. 4 (page xvi): Combine legumes (dried beans) and grains (pasta) for lower-fat recipes. The number of grams of fat per serving is high in this dish—11.14—but the percentage of calories from fat comes in at 27, and the dish is an extremely tasty vegetarian entrée that can be served either at room temperature or hot off the stove.

PREPARE-AHEAD NOTES:

The beans can be cooked three to four days before serving and then brought back to room temperature or reheated in the sauce. The sauce can also be made days ahead and

Our Favorite Little Red Bean: Poquitos

As far as we know, poquitos are grown and marketed only by one farmer in Santa Maria, California. For many California cooks, they are a grocery store staple. Our stores sell poquitos under our own label. What's so great about them? They're one of the few beans that cook up creamy and tender without splitting their skins, making them much superior to the average pinto bean or even many of the so-called heirloom beans that have come on the market in recent years.

reheated. That leaves only the pasta to be cooked within hours or minutes (depending on whether you want to serve the dish hot or at room temperature) of serving.

INGREDIENTS:

½ cup dried poquitos (page 83) or other small
   red beans
2 teaspoons salt for beans
½ tablespoon salt for pasta water
2 tablespoons extra virgin olive oil
4 ½ teaspoons finely minced garlic
1 teaspoon Pasta & Co. House Herbs (page 166)
   or other dried herbs of your choice
¼ to ½ teaspoon salt, depending on the saltiness
   of stock
⅛ teaspoon dried red pepper flakes
1 ½ cups vegetable stock (page 40)
1 tablespoon plus 1 teaspoon tomato paste
2 tablespoons capers, well rinsed and drained
⅔ pound (11 ounces) Pasta & Co. Little Hats
   or other short dried pasta

TO TOP:

2 tablespoons grated feta or Romano cheese
1 tablespoon finely chopped parsley

♦ Cook beans according to directions on page 87. Add the 2 teaspoons salt only when the beans are almost tender. When beans are creamy and a few are just beginning to split their skins (if you're using poquitos, hardly any will have split their skins by the time they are tender), drain, rinse with cold water, and reserve.
♦ Bring 4 quarts of water and the ½ tablespoon of salt to a boil.
♦ Meanwhile, place olive oil, garlic, herbs, the ¼ to ½ teaspoon salt, and red pepper flakes in a large sauté pan over medium heat. Cook until garlic is barely golden (do not brown). Add stock and simmer for 5 minutes. Add tomato paste and continue to simmer 2 more minutes; do

YELLOW LINE
PASTA & CO

for more about
**PASTA & CO.
YELLOW LINE
DISHES**
turn to page xv.

not allow the mixture to cook longer or you will not have enough sauce. Fold in reserved beans and the capers. Remove from heat.

♦ Cook the pasta in the boiling salted water until barely tender—about 8 to 9 minutes. Drain and rinse well with cold water. Shake out any excess water, then toss with the bean mixture. If serving hot, top immediately with the cheese and parsley. If serving at room temperature, let cool, tossing several times with the sauce, before topping with cheese and parsley.

Makes about 8 cups

Southwest White Beans

For cilantro lovers, this is one of our most popular low-fat Yellow Line dishes. Cooked dried beans hold up well to high-acid dressings (unlike fresh pasta, vegetables, seafood, and chicken—see page 63). In fact, the dressing is made only with vinegar, garlic, and seasonings; there is no oil whatsoever.

PREPARE-AHEAD NOTES:

The beans and dressing can be made and assembled up to two days ahead. Add the vegetables within eight hours of serving. The cilantro itself is best chopped and added at the last minute.

INGREDIENTS:

1 ½ cups dried small white beans (our favorite is the tiny rice bean, but any small white bean will do)
3 large cloves garlic, peeled
½ teaspoon whole cumin seed
2 bay leaves
1 tablespoon salt

DRESSING:

> 5 tablespoons red wine vinegar
> 2 large cloves garlic, peeled and put through a press
> 1 jalapeño pepper, seeded and minced
> ¾ teaspoon salt
> ¼ teaspoon ground cumin

TO ASSEMBLE:

> 2 cups frozen corn, thawed, rinsed, and drained but
>   not cooked, or fresh corn cut from the cob and
>   briefly blanched and drained (page 120)
> ½ pound (3 large) Roma tomatoes, cut into ¼-inch
>   dice and seasoned with ¼ teaspoon salt
> 1 bunch green onions, cleaned and thinly sliced
>   (use both white and green parts)
> ⅔ cup minced red onion
> ½ cup pitted black olives, rinsed, well drained, and
>   quartered
> 1 large bunch cilantro, washed, dried, and chopped

♦ Cook beans according to directions on page 87, adding the whole garlic cloves, cumin seed, and bay leaves after the beans have presoaked. Add the 1 tablespoon salt when beans are almost tender. Cook until the beans are very tender. (Note: Rice beans typically take about twice as long to cook as other white beans.) While beans are cooking, whisk together vinegar, garlic, jalapeño pepper, the ¾ teaspoon salt, and cumin in a large bowl. When beans are cooked, rinse with cold water, drain very well, discard bay leaves and garlic, and immediately fold into dressing.
♦ Shortly before serving, fold in corn, tomatoes, green onions, red onion, black olives, and cilantro.
♦ Place in serving dish. Serve at room temperature.

Makes 10 cups

Cilantro: The Fat Trimmer's Herb

The last few years have seen cilantro run the cycle from discovery to cliché, along with sun-dried tomatoes, balsamic vinegar, goat cheese, and arugula. Food fashion aside, cilantro is a valuable flavor builder for low-fat dishes. One tip: Cilantro's strong flavor fades quickly; it is best chopped and added to dishes shortly before serving.

Best Bean Cooking Instructions

As Jefferey Steingarten, *Vogue*'s food editor, wrote some years back, "Beans are too important to be left languishing in a state of intellectual confusion." If you are one of the many who are still unfamiliar with cooking dried beans, here are the instructions; follow them precisely. Properly cooked dried beans are creamy on the inside, neither crunchy nor mushy; they are ready to pop their skins but are still mostly intact.

♦ Sort through beans and discard any debris. Be thorough. Rinse.

♦ Place beans in a saucepan large enough to hold them after they have cooked (they usually expand to two to three times their dried volume). Add warm water to cover the beans by about 3 inches. Cover the pan and bring the beans to a boil over low heat (this will take approximately 30 minutes). Boil for 1 minute. Remove from heat and let rest, covered, for 1 hour.

♦ After this presoak, drain beans and add enough fresh water to cover them by 1 inch. With lid ajar, bring beans to a boil over medium-high heat. For even cooking, keep beans at a low boil for the entire cooking time. (If water level drops below beans, add more water.)

♦ Do *not* add salt to the cooking liquid when you first put the beans on to cook, since it toughens the beans and inhibits their cooking. Rather, add salt after approximately 45 minutes of cooking (or when beans are almost tender). Use 1 tablespoon salt per cup of dried beans. This seems like a lot, but beans are stubbornly bland.

♦ The only way to tell whether beans are done is to taste them periodically during cooking. The cooking time will depend upon their age and size. Most dried beans will take at least an hour to cook; some will take much longer. The beans should feel creamy on your tongue and a few in the pot will begin to split before the batch is done.

♦ When the beans are done, drain well, rinse in cold water, and proceed with your recipe.

White Beans with Low-Fat Greek-Style Dressing

*H*ere you have it: a tasty bean dish that has only trace amounts of fat and only 200 calories per 1-cup serving. The trick is dressing white beans with classic Greek tzatziki—nonfat yogurt with cucumber and lots of garlic and fresh mint. Pair the dish with blanched vegetables (no fat added, of course—page 114) and warm pita bread for a delicious, low-fat meal, especially refreshing for summertime eating.

PREPARE-AHEAD NOTES:

The dressing uses yogurt that has been partially drained of whey—similar to Nonfat Yogurt Cheese (page 6) but not as thick. You will need to allow eight to ten hours for the yogurt to drain. Add the remaining ingredients as close to serving time as possible. Once assembled, the dish will keep well for a couple of days. And don't forget that you can cook up a large batch of beans and keep them in your freezer. For this recipe, let the beans thaw (and drain off any liquid) before folding them into the yogurt.

INGREDIENTS:

 2 cups plain nonfat yogurt
 1 ⅛ cups dried small white beans (or try a really big
    white bean such as Gigantic Runners, using about
    1 ½ cups)
 1 tablespoon salt for beans
 2 small cucumbers, peeled, seeded, and coarsely
    chopped (about 2 ½ cups)
 2 to 3 cloves garlic, peeled
 2 tablespoons freshly squeezed lemon juice
 ¼ teaspoon salt

for more about
**PASTA & CO.
YELLOW LINE
DISHES**
turn to page xv.

Pinch cayenne
¼ cup fresh mint leaves
2 cups canned tomatoes, diced and very well drained
  of all juice
Salt and freshly ground black pepper to taste

TO TOP:

Quartered cherry tomatoes or diced Roma tomatoes
Finely chopped fresh mint

◆ Make Nonfat Yogurt Cheese following the instructions on page 6, allowing yogurt to drain for only 8 to 10 hours.
◆ Meanwhile, cook beans according to the directions on page 87. Add the tablespoon of salt when the beans are almost tender. Be sure the beans are tender and sufficiently seasoned. Reserve.
◆ Place cucumbers in a food processor equipped with a steel blade and pulse until finely chopped; be careful not to purée. Place chopped cucumber in a sieve to drain for 15 minutes, then wring out extra liquid with your hands. Reserve cucumbers.
◆ In same food processor bowl, place garlic, lemon juice, the ¼ teaspoon salt, cayenne, and mint leaves. Process until garlic and mint leaves are finely chopped. Remove to a large mixing bowl. Stir in reserved beans, drained yogurt, reserved cucumbers, and drained canned tomatoes. Season to taste with salt and pepper.
◆ Place in serving dish and top with the fresh tomatoes and chopped mint.

Makes 6 to 7 cups

Salt—Regrettably Indispensable to Fat-Slashers

When Pasta & Co. first opened in 1981, there was a great deal of interest in reduced-salt cooking. So, in formulating many of our early products, we were very conservative in adding salt. What we conveniently overlooked was the fact that so many of our popular ingredients, such as cheeses, cured meats, and olives, were not only high in fat but also high in salt.

When we started concentrating on lower-fat foods, these ingredients—at least in the amounts we were accustomed to—were no longer available for our use. What we found was that when fat is at a minimum and taste is not to be compromised, dishes usually need generous salting.

On the other hand, preferences for more or less salt are at least partially learned. While some consider less salty foods a compromise, others may not. If you need to watch salt intake, vinegar, citrus juices, and spices—the same assertive ingredients that help us cut fat—can help to compensate for the reduction in salt.

We would also make a case for the principles of good salting:

♦ Think of salt not so much as a flavoring in itself but as a switch to turn on or even moderate other seasonings. For instance, experts on highly spiced cuisines such as Thai or Cajun point out that salt is essential for mellowing the pungency of many hot ingredients.

♦ Concentrate, too, on progressive salting, adding it throughout the cooking process rather than just at the end, which tends to give a dish a salt overlay, like salt crystals sparkling on hot french fries. (There is one exception to progressive salting: beans. See page 87.) As a general rule, salt added during cooking contributes complexities that are impossible to achieve when salt is merely dashed over the top of the finished dish.

♦ Experiment with different types of salt. Both iodized and plain salt give a sharp salt flavor; sea salt (the unrefined salt crystals left when seawater evaporates) is milder, and kosher salt (which contains no additives and has larger crystals) is somewhere in the middle.

Our favorite sea salts: Maldon Sea Salt, from Maldon, England, has unique coarse, flat crystals that are so soft they require no grinding. The salt contains no additives and lends a pure salt flavor with no bitter aftertaste. Its fans claim that the quality of this salt enables them to use less of it and that it is particularly good for making last-minute adjustments to the taste of a dish. We think the salt's distinctive crystals suit it especially well for topping baked goods, such as focaccia.

Another premium sea salt, called Fleur de Sel (flower of salt), comes from Guérande, a French coastal town south of Brittany. It is harvested by hand between late June and early September, only in sunny weather and only when an easterly wind is blowing. The grains are light gray in color and quite moist, almost like wet sand. Experimenting with it, we have come to love this salt for the clean sparkle it brings to food. For us, it is more distinguished than any other salt we have used. Unfortunately, this salt is very expensive and difficult to obtain.

Both Maldon Sea Salt and Fleur de Sel are available at Pasta & Co. stores.

The Making of Stunning Foods

Successful garnishing is more a matter of mastering a few simple concepts than of making radish roses, carving carrots, and laboring over other such seemingly awkward touches.

◆ Sometimes it is nothing more than keeping the food looking shiny. Food that is old usually appears dry. Food that has sat untouched for even as little as 30 minutes can acquire a pallor. All the shine literally drops to the bottom of the dish along with the juices. To make the food look fresh, turn it over in its juices so that the top shines once again. This is all the "garnishing" that dishes like Pasta Salad con Salami (page 70), Tortellini with Peppers and Pine Nuts (page 72), and Tuscan Vegetables (page 123) need to look their best.

◆ When shine alone is not enough, use clean, "redundant" garnishes to top the dish. Ever notice that when you fold the ingredients of a dish together, visually they blur? The result is that even the tastiest dish may have no eye appeal. We have learned that if you repeat a few key ingredients on

East Indian Bean Salad

This is a delicious room-temperature bean dish. Making it visually appealing is a challenge we meet by blanketing the beans with chopped fresh tomatoes and cilantro—a common technique from our theory of "The Making of Stunning Foods" (see this page).

PREPARE-AHEAD NOTES:

The salad keeps well refrigerated for a couple of days. Bring it back to room temperature and top with the tomatoes and cilantro or parsley just before serving.

INGREDIENTS:

> 1 cup dried black-eyed peas (or other small white or brown bean)
> 1 tablespoon salt for peas
> ¼ cup vegetable oil
> 2 tablespoons seeded, minced jalapeño peppers
> 2 ½ teaspoons whole cumin seed
> 10 grinds black pepper
> ¼ teaspoon ground cloves
> 2 bay leaves
> 2 ¼ cups coarsely chopped onion
> 2 cups coarsely chopped Roma tomatoes (use juice as well as pulp)
> 1 ½ teaspoons salt
> 4 to 5 heaping tablespoons sour cream
> ¼ cup finely chopped cilantro

TO TOP:

> Coarsely chopped Roma tomatoes
> Finely chopped cilantro or parsley

◆ Cook the black-eyed peas according to the directions on page 87. When almost tender, add the 1 tablespoon salt and finish cooking. Drain well and reserve.

♦ While peas cook, heat oil in a large sauté pan over medium heat. Stir in jalapeño peppers, cumin seed, black pepper, cloves, and bay leaves. Stir for 1 minute, then add onions. Lower heat and cook slowly until onions are very well browned, about 30 minutes. Add tomatoes and their juices, the 1 ½ teaspoons salt, sour cream, and reserved black-eyed peas or beans. Cook over low heat for just a couple of minutes.

♦ Place in serving dish to cool. When cooled to room temperature, fold in the cilantro and top with the tomatoes and cilantro or parsley.

Makes about 5 ½ cups

Couscous and Black Beans

Couscous and Black Beans was our first couscous dish. After all these years, it is still one of the most dependably attractive buffet dishes in our product line. We now make it with vegetable stock instead of chicken stock but point out that since the recipe calls for Worcestershire sauce, which contains anchovy, it is not truly vegetarian. We are not willing to strike this ingredient, but depending upon dietary preferences, you may.

PREPARE-AHEAD NOTES:

Allow plenty of time for cooking the beans. The beans can be cooked and marinated two days before assembling the final dish, as can the couscous mixture. The dish can be assembled several hours before serving.

BEANS:

> 1 ¼ cups dried black beans, picked over for stones
> and rinsed
> 2 cloves garlic, peeled

top of a dish, as we do with the tomatoes on top of the East Indian Bean Salad (page 91) and the green onions on top of Jade and Ivory (page 75), the dish retains a clean, lively look.

♦ Sometimes a dish needs contrasting, rather than redundant, garnishing, both for taste and for appearance. A case in point are the vinegar-doused tomatoes in Rotini with Squeaky Cheese, Cucumber, and Green Onion (page 61). Another example: the green onions used on top of both the Pasta Brutta (page 73) and the Tortellini in Paprika Garlic Sauce (page 67).

1 bay leaf
1 tablespoon salt for beans
⅓ cup extra virgin olive oil
¼ cup sherry wine vinegar
1 teaspoon salt
1 teaspoon ground cumin
¼ teaspoon freshly cracked black pepper
1 ½ teaspoons Worcestershire sauce
1 clove garlic, peeled and put through a press

COUSCOUS:

½ cup extra virgin olive oil
3 tablespoons sherry wine vinegar
2 tablespoons freshly squeezed lemon juice
1 clove garlic, peeled and put through a press
1 ½ teaspoons ground cumin
½ teaspoon dried oregano
½ teaspoon salt
⅛ teaspoon black pepper
1 ½ cups vegetable or defatted chicken stock
2 tablespoons extra virgin olive oil
1 ½ cups uncooked couscous (the package will
    probably say "quick-cooking" or "instant")

TO ASSEMBLE:

⅔ cup (about half a small pepper) diced red bell
    pepper (¼-inch dice)
⅔ cup (about half a small pepper) diced green bell
    pepper (¼-inch dice)
⅔ cup (about half a small pepper) diced yellow bell
    pepper (¼-inch dice)
¾ cup finely chopped parsley
½ cup sliced green onions (slice ⅛ inch thick on
    the diagonal)

♦ Cook the beans according to the directions on page 87, adding the whole garlic cloves and bay leaf to the cooking water. When the beans are almost tender, add the tablespoon of salt and finish cooking.

♦ While beans cook, whisk together in a large bowl the ⅓ cup olive oil, sherry wine vinegar, 1 teaspoon salt, cumin, pepper, Worcestershire sauce, and pressed garlic. As soon as the beans are cooked, rinse thoroughly with cold water. Drain beans very well. Remove garlic cloves and bay leaf, and toss the beans with the dressing. Reserve.

♦ For the couscous, whisk together the ½ cup olive oil, sherry wine vinegar, lemon juice, garlic, cumin, oregano, the ½ teaspoon salt, and pepper in a large bowl. Reserve.

♦ In a 1-quart saucepan or skillet, heat stock and 2 table-spoons olive oil until simmering. Stir in couscous, cover pan, and remove from heat. Let stand 3 to 5 minutes, then stir well with a fork to remove any lumps in the couscous. Stir couscous into the reserved dressing and let cool to room temperature.

♦ To assemble, toss marinated beans with couscous. Add peppers and parsley, reserving a third of each for topping the dish. Place in serving dish, top with the remaining peppers and parsley and the green onions. Serve at room temperature.

Makes 10 cups

Master Recipe for Cooking Barley

Barley is not exactly an exotic ingredient. Anyone can cook it. That must be why there are dozens of methods, each one posing a slightly different pitfall for the cook. After testing dozens of batches, we have come up with what we believe to be a foolproof method that produces flavorful, fluffy barley every time.

INGREDIENTS:

1 cup pearl barley
3 cups stock or water
(if you are concerned about saltiness, use half stock, half water)

♦ In a heavy-bottomed sauté pan or saucepan, toast the barley over medium-high heat for about 5 minutes, stirring frequently to prevent scorching. The barley should become golden brown and aromatic. Pour in stock or water and bring to a boil. Cover, reduce heat to low, and cook for 35 to 40 minutes. Check after 30 minutes to make sure that the barley is not sticking to the bottom of the pan. If necessary, you can add a very small amount of additional liquid to finish the cooking.

ROOM-TEMPERATURE
GRAINS

For intriguing, varied textures and tastes, it is hard to beat grains for their adventuresome room-temperature menu possibilities. We turn to them frequently to add lower-fat interest to dishes. In doing so, we have richly expanded our culinary repertoire.

Bumpy Barley

Dry-toasting the barley helps make this a high-flavor, good-textured dish with only 4 grams of fat per cup and 21.5 percent of calories from fat.

PREPARE-AHEAD NOTES:

The dish holds well for a day in the refrigerator. Return to room temperature and add the topping just before serving.

INGREDIENTS:

1 cup barley, preferably pearl
3 to 4 cups vegetable or defatted chicken stock
¾ cup finely minced onion
2 teaspoons dried thyme
1 ½ teaspoons dried oregano
1 teaspoon finely minced garlic
3 tablespoons white wine vinegar
1 ½ tablespoons vegetable oil
½ teaspoon salt
¼ teaspoon freshly cracked black pepper
3 Roma tomatoes, seeded and cut into ¼-inch dice

1 cup frozen corn, thawed, rinsed, and drained but
    not cooked
¼ cup finely chopped parsley

TO TOP:

½ cup diced red onion (¼-inch dice)
¼ cup finely chopped parsley

♦ When the barley is tender, remove from heat and fluff with a fork. It is now ready to eat or to be incorporated into other dishes.

♦ Cook the barley in the stock according to the directions on page 95, adding the onion, thyme, oregano, and garlic after the initial toasting and right before adding the 3 cups of stock. Add some or all of the remaining cup of stock if barley becomes dry before it is done cooking. When barley is done, fluff with a fork and cool to room temperature.

♦ Meanwhile, whisk together the vinegar, vegetable oil, salt, and pepper in a large bowl. When the barley is cool, toss with the dressing. Fold in the tomatoes, corn, and parsley. To serve, place the barley in a serving dish and top with the red onion and parsley. Serve at room temperature.

Makes 6 cups

for more about
**PASTA & CO.
YELLOW LINE
DISHES**
turn to page xv.

Grains: Another Texture Boon to Fat-Slashers

A good thing about altering eating habits is that it forces us to try new options. Think of it. With such favorite ingredients as salami, olives, nuts, and cheeses on the restricted list of possible ingredients, those who create recipes for a living could feel rather strapped for new sources of taste and texture.

One of the categories of food that is full of new possibilities is the broad category of whole grains. At Pasta & Co., we increasingly make use of grains, not so much for their well-publicized nutritional merits, but more because of their potential for adding texture to lower-fat recipes. Remember: One of the most common complaints about low-fat foods is that they are bereft not only of flavor but also of mouth feel. Grains can add invaluable low-fat interest to soups, salads, vegetables, pastas, and meats. For instance, in crafting a low-fat alternative to our original room-temperature tortellini dish, we used toasted barley to replicate pine nuts (page 99). In Barley and Bowties (page 98), we found another good marriage between barley and pasta.

The merits of another grain, bulgur, are known to most cooks. Not only does it blend well with room-temperature vinaigrettes, it is an excellent substitute for meat, as in Bulgur with Two Beans (page 149). Less known is quinoa's unique texture (page 101). It has proved an especially attractive counterpoint to low-fat dressings. In addition, we've just begun to explore other grains such as amaranth (which has pilaf possibilities), buckwheat (with a flavor so strong that it needs to be combined with a more neutral grain such as brown rice), millet, farro, and wheat berries.

Definition: Grains are the seeds and fruits of cereal grasses and are the most widely consumed staple foods in the world. Since they contain protein, carbohydrates, fiber, fatty acids, vitamins, and minerals, they have been called the most nutritious of all foods. We include couscous (made much like pasta with semolina flour and water) in this grain section because its texture is more akin to grains than to pastas.

Storage: Whole grains are best stored refrigerated or frozen to keep them from becoming rancid. Under these conditions, they will keep for at least a year.

General Rules for Preparing Grains:
♦ Sloppy cooking can spoil the texture of grains. Cooked grains should be tender, fluffy, and sometimes just a touch crunchy. Follow the cooking procedures, which vary from one grain to another, precisely.
♦ As a general rule, start with a minimum quantity of liquid and add more only if needed.
♦ To amplify the nutty flavor of most grains, toast them in a dry skillet before cooking.
♦ To further build flavor, cook grains in strong-bodied stocks rather than water.

Barley and Bowties

*F*at watchers love this dish: only 3 grams of fat and 180 calories per cup. Fifteen percent of its calories come from fat. Best of all there is something inexplicably appealing in the combined textures of the barley and the bowtie pasta used in this dish. Notice that since we use only ¼ cup of cheese, we suggest a fairly pungent one. Romano is more easily available, but an aged goat cheese delivers more flavor to the dish.

PREPARE-AHEAD NOTES:

The barley and pasta mixture can be prepared a day ahead. Fold in vegetables and top with cheese right before serving.

INGREDIENTS:

½ cup barley, preferably pearl
1 ½ cups vegetable or defatted chicken stock
½ cup minced onion
1 teaspoon dried thyme
¾ teaspoon dried oregano
½ teaspoon minced garlic
1 ½ tablespoons white wine vinegar
1 ½ teaspoons vegetable oil
¼ teaspoon salt
⅛ teaspoon freshly ground pepper
½ tablespoon salt for pasta water
⅓ pound (5 ounces) dried bowtie pasta
½ cup diced green or red bell pepper (⅛-inch dice),
   or ½ cup diced Roma tomatoes (⅛-inch dice)
½ cup frozen corn, thawed, rinsed, and drained
   but not cooked
2 tablespoons finely chopped parsley

TO TOP:

¼ cup freshly grated Romano cheese or aged goat
   cheese

Barley: Pearl or Hulled?

*U*ndoubtedly, you will have easiest access to pearl barley—the most processed form of barley in which the bran has been entirely removed and the grain has a smooth, uniform pale cream color. Hulled barley, which is less refined, will work but will probably require up to 1 ½ cups more liquid and may need to cook almost twice as long.

Cheese: Bane of Fat-Trimmers

Cheese is so tasty but so high in fat. The trick is to make a little cheese go a long way. Grating, rather than crumbling, slicing, or cubing, for instance, best disperses the taste benefits of cheese. Also, don't overlook the option of substituting toasted bread crumbs (page 186) for cheese as a topping on pasta dishes.

◆ Cook the barley in the stock according to the directions on page 95, using the ½ cup barley and 1 ½ cups liquid called for in this recipe. Add the onion, thyme, oregano, and garlic after the initial toasting and right before adding the stock. Cover. Cooking time will be a little shorter, since it is a half batch. When barley is done, fluff with a fork and cool to room temperature. Reserve.

◆ Meanwhile, whisk together vinegar, vegetable oil, the ¼ teaspoon salt, and pepper in a large bowl. Reserve.

◆ Bring 4 quarts water and the ½ tablespoon salt to a boil. Cook pasta until barely tender. Drain well and toss gently with the dressing. Fold in reserved barley and let mixture cool before adding the peppers or tomatoes, the corn and the parsley, and topping with the cheese. Serve at room temperature.

Makes 6 ½ cups

YELLOW LINE

Tortellini with Barley

Here is a Yellow Line dish where sturdy tortellini holds its own against an acidic dressing consisting of both sherry vinegar and lemon juice offset by stock and only ¼ cup olive oil. Texture comes from using toasted barley to imitate the high-fat pine nuts in our original tortellini salad, Tortellini with Peppers and Pine Nuts (page 72). All in all, we use approximately one fourth of the fat called for in the original dish. To make the topping of feta cheese go farther, we grate the cheese rather than crumble it.

PREPARE-AHEAD NOTES:

All of the ingredients may be prepared a full day ahead of serving. Toss together and add the topping shortly before serving.

¼ cup extra virgin olive oil

¾ cup vegetable or defatted chicken stock

6 tablespoons sherry wine vinegar

6 tablespoons freshly squeezed lemon juice

1 tablespoon finely minced garlic

1 ½ teaspoons Pasta & Co. House Herbs (page 166)
or a mixture of dried basil and oregano

1 ½ teaspoons salt

½ teaspoon Tabasco sauce

1 cup barley, preferably pearl (page 98)

3 cups vegetable or defatted chicken stock

1 tablespoon salt for pasta water

1 pound fresh tortellini (we use Pasta & Co. Chicken
Tortellini)

1 ½ cups sliced green onions

1 yellow bell pepper, cored and cut into ⅛-inch dice

1 red bell pepper, cored and cut into ⅛-inch dice

½ cup finely chopped parsley

TO TOP:

½ cup grated feta cheese (page 99)

¼ cup finely chopped fresh parsley

♦ In a large bowl, make the dressing by whisking together the olive oil, stock, vinegar, lemon juice, garlic, herbs, the 1 ½ teaspoons salt, and Tabasco. Reserve.

♦ Cook the barley in the stock according to the directions on page 95, using the 3 cups of stock.

♦ While the barley cooks, bring 4 to 6 quarts of water and the tablespoon of salt to a boil. When salted water is at a rolling boil, add the tortellini and cook until very tender (about 14 minutes). Drain well (do not rinse) and toss with the reserved dressing.

for more about

**PASTA & CO.
YELLOW LINE
DISHES**

turn to page xv.

Quinoa: An Underutilized Source of Low-Fat, High-Fiber Protein

An underutilized ingredient in our culture's cuisine is quinoa (pronounced "keenwa"). This centuries-old food has been called a miracle grain, because it is a complete protein, containing an essential amino acid balance very similar to that of milk. (Legumes and other grains, in contrast, are incomplete proteins.) Quinoa grows mostly in Bolivia and Peru, where it has been a staple—along with potatoes and corn—ever since the time of the Incas. It is a source of high-fiber, low-fat protein with good-looking and good-tasting texture. Serve it hot or at room temperature. Since it can be easily rewarmed, cook a batch (using our master recipe, page 102), store it in your refrigerator, and experiment with it in all sorts of menu spots—perhaps reheated with a little olive oil and garlic or good stock, tossed with a room-temperature dressing (as we do in Quinoa Confetti, this page), added to soups (as in Quinoa and

♦ When the barley is tender, fluff with a fork and toss with the tortellini and dressing. Let cool to room temperature, then fold in the green onions, yellow and red peppers, and parsley. To serve, place in serving bowl and top with the cheese and parsley. Serve at room temperature.

Makes about 12 cups

Quinoa Confetti

Keep in mind that there are any number of high-fat dressings that could be used to turn cooked quinoa into very tasty room-temperature eating. We, however, were attracted to quinoa's unique texture and nutritional characteristics as a perfect foil for a low-fat dressing. This dish is the result.

The dressing is typically high in acid; the flavor is heightened by a large amount of garlic and the reduction of the stock. There are two ways to present the dish. One, with shallots or onions glazed in olive oil, brings the fat per cup up to 5.7 grams (though the percentage of calories from fat is still only 20 percent). The other keeps the dish strictly low fat by topping it simply with raw red onion and parsley. In this case, the dish contains less than 3 grams of fat per cup. The fat difference between the two garnishes illustrates quite dramatically what even a small amount of fat can do to the makeup of a dish.

PREPARE-AHEAD NOTES:

The dressing can be made several days ahead of serving and refrigerated. The quinoa itself can be cooked at least a day ahead, tossed with the dressing, and refrigerated. Bring it back to room temperature, add the vegetables, and top with the browned shallots or red onion and parsley right before serving.

⅓ cup plus 1 tablespoon freshly squeezed lemon juice

¼ cup vegetable or defatted chicken stock, boiled until reduced to 2 tablespoons (page 82)

2 tablespoons finely minced or pressed garlic

1 teaspoon salt

½ teaspoon Tabasco sauce

Pinch ground cloves

½ pound (1 ¼ cups) dried quinoa

½ red bell pepper, cut into ⅛-inch dice

½ yellow bell pepper, cut into ⅛-inch dice

1 carrot, peeled and grated

½ bunch green onions, very thinly sliced (use white and green parts)

2 tablespoons finely minced fresh parsley

To top (choose one):

Glazed Shallot/Onion Topping (recipe follows)
Or:
¾ cup red onion, peeled and cut either into crescents (page 22) or into ¼-inch dice
2 tablespoons finely chopped parsley

♦ In a large bowl, whisk together the lemon juice, reduced stock, garlic, salt, Tabasco, and cloves. Reserve.

♦ Rinse and cook quinoa according to directions on this page. After fluffing cooked quinoa, stir into dressing. When cool, fold in red pepper, yellow pepper, carrot, green onion, and parsley.

♦ To serve, place mixture in shallow bowl and top either with the Glazed Shallot/Onion Topping or with the raw red onion and parsley.

Makes 6 cups

Cabbage Soup, page 45), or tossed with a green salad. Surprisingly, it can be a very nice texture complement to pasta.

Special note to those with wheat and gluten allergies: One of the best wheat-free and gluten-free pastas we have discovered is made with a combination of corn and quinoa flour. Pasta & Co. stores sell Ancient Harvest brand quinoa linguine.

Master Recipe for Cooking Quinoa

As with all grains, careful cooking and handling are essential to preserving quinoa's unique texture. Over-cooked, it turns into a pale yellow mush. However, follow our directions exactly and you will have a dish notable for its high texture and numerous unusual menu possibilities.

♦ Pour 1 ¼ cups (½ pound) dried quinoa into a bowl of cold water. Swirl it around and pour into a fine strainer. Repeat this process at least three times, until the rinse water is clear. (This removes a bitter residue that is natural to quinoa and should be washed off before cooking.)

◆ Place rinsed quinoa in a large saucepan with 6 to 8 cups water. Bring to a boil, stirring now and then. As soon as it reaches a rolling boil, lower heat and simmer for about 5 minutes. The quinoa should be translucent and slightly crunchy. Drain quinoa, but do *not* rinse. Spread in a thin layer on a shallow baking sheet and fluff with a fork. Season to taste with your choice of salt, pepper, herbs, lemon juice, vinegar, olive oil, hot stock, and so on. Cooked quinoa keeps refrigerated for several days and rewarms well. *Makes about 4 cups*

GLAZED SHALLOT/ONION TOPPING:

> 2 tablespoons extra virgin olive oil
> 1 cup sliced shallots or red onion crescents (page 22)
> 1 teaspoon sugar
> 1 tablespoon finely chopped fresh parsley

◆ Heat olive oil in a skillet until nearly smoking. Add shallots or red onions and toss in the hot oil until they begin to brown. Lower heat, add sugar, and allow shallots to cook very slowly until glazed a shiny golden brown. This will take at least 20 minutes; do not rush the browning process. When done, spoon the glazed shallots or onions, including pan juices, over the top of the Quinoa Confetti. Sprinkle parsley over the entire dish and serve hot or at room temperature.

Couscous with Jicama

Enjoy this recipe for its fresh-tasting fragrance, its very pretty appearance, and the intriguing texture that comes from using crunchy jicama with the soft couscous. It can be prepared vegetarian or not.

PREPARE-AHEAD NOTES:

You can make the dressing and prepare the couscous up to three days ahead of serving. Assemble the dish up to eight hours before serving.

DRESSING:

> ½ cup mild-flavored extra virgin olive oil
> ⅓ cup white wine vinegar
> ¼ cup vegetable or defatted chicken stock
> 1 tablespoon ground cumin
> 1 ½ teaspoons chili powder
> 1 teaspoon salt

1 teaspoon black pepper

½ teaspoon finely minced garlic

Pinch cayenne

⅛ teaspoon Boyajian Orange Oil, or freshly squeezed orange juice to taste, about ¼ cup

2 ¼ cups vegetable or defatted chicken stock

1 ½ cups uncooked couscous (the package will probably say "quick-cooking" or "instant")

½ green bell pepper, cut into ¼-inch dice

½ red bell pepper, cut into ¼-inch dice

½ yellow bell pepper, cut into ¼-inch dice

½ jicama (about ½ pound), peeled and cut into ¼-inch dice

½ bunch cilantro, washed, dried, and finely chopped

Salt and pepper to taste

½ cup sliced green onions (slice ⅛ inch thick on the diagonal)

½ cup cherry tomatoes or quartered Roma tomatoes

◆ For the dressing, whisk together olive oil, vinegar, the ¼ cup stock, cumin, chili powder, salt, pepper, garlic, cayenne, and orange oil in a large bowl.

◆ For the couscous, in a large saucepan, heat the 2 ¼ cups stock until simmering. Stir in couscous, cover pan, and remove from heat. Let stand about 3 minutes, then stir well with a fork to remove any lumps. Fold couscous into dressing and let cool to room temperature. (Don't be concerned if couscous seems a bit heavy at this point.)

◆ When ready to serve, fold in peppers, jicama, and cilantro. Taste for salt and pepper. Place in serving bowl and top with green onions and cherry tomatoes.

Makes 10 cups

Food Find: Middle Eastern Couscous

Also known as Lebanese, Israeli, or Syrian couscous, Middle Eastern couscous is very different from the more commonly available fine-textured Moroccan couscous, used in Couscous with Jicama (page 103). The grains of Middle Eastern couscous are about four times larger than those of Moroccan couscous. The result is an ingredient with intriguing texture possibilities and a very different cooking method, which involves thoroughly toasting the couscous in hot fat (pilaf-style) before cooking it in hot stock. Do not substitute Moroccan couscous.

Maftoul

*T*his recipe turns Middle Eastern couscous into a versatile side dish of golden brown beads to be served either hot or at room temperature. It is also the basic cooking method for Middle Eastern couscous, which can be varied by combining with numerous dressings and other ingredients (see the recipe for Talid on page 106 or the recipe for Middle Eastern Couscous with Dwarf Gray Sugar Peas on page 108).

PREPARE-AHEAD NOTES:

The couscous can be cooked at least a day ahead of serving and brought back to room temperature or reheated. Add the topping of roasted peppers and parsley immediately before serving.

INGREDIENTS:

¼ cup extra virgin olive oil
1 ¼ cups finely minced onion
1 cup Middle Eastern couscous (available at
    Pasta & Co. stores—see this page)
2 teaspoons finely minced garlic
2 ⅓ cups boiling vegetable stock (we use Organic
    Gourmet's Pure Vegetable Broth—page 40)
    or defatted chicken stock
Salt and pepper to taste (depending on saltiness
    of stock)

TO TOP:

Finely diced roasted red bell peppers (fresh or jarred)
Finely chopped parsley

◆ In a heavy-bottomed pan that can be covered, heat the olive oil over medium-high heat and add the onion. Cook 5 to 7 minutes, stirring frequently. Just as the onion begins to brown, add the couscous. Cook, stirring frequently, until couscous is dark golden brown (4 to 5 minutes). Add the garlic, cook another minute, then pour in the boiling stock. Stir to blend. Reduce heat to low, cover, and cook (stirring occasionally) about 15 minutes, until couscous is very tender and most of the liquid is absorbed. (If couscous becomes dry before it is done cooking, add a tablespoon or two of water, re-cover, and continue cooking. A small amount of liquid remaining is desirable.) Add salt and pepper to taste. Place couscous and its cooking liquid in a serving dish. Top with the peppers and parsley. Serve hot or at room temperature.

Makes about 4 cups

Talid

T his is a traditional Lebanese treatment for Middle Eastern couscous. It is almost identical to Maftoul but is flavored with cinnamon and includes garbanzo beans. Together, the two elements turn the dish into a very attractive vegetarian entrée.

INGREDIENTS:

¼ cup extra virgin olive oil
1 ¼ cups finely minced onion
1 cup Middle Eastern couscous (available at
    Pasta & Co. stores—see page 105)
2 teaspoons finely minced garlic
2 ⅓ cups boiling vegetable stock (we use Organic
    Gourmet's Pure Vegetable Broth—page 40)
    or defatted chicken stock
1 teaspoon ground cinnamon
Optional: *½ teaspoon salt (depending upon saltiness*
    of stock)
5 grinds black pepper

1 tablespoon tomato paste
1 can (15 ounces) garbanzo beans, rinsed and well
   drained

TO TOP:

Finely diced roasted red bell peppers (fresh or jarred)
Finely chopped parsley

♦ In a heavy-bottomed pan that can be covered, heat the olive oil over medium-high heat and add the onion. Cook 5 to 7 minutes, stirring frequently. Just as the onion begins to brown, add the couscous. Cook, stirring frequently, until the couscous is dark golden brown (4 to 5 minutes). Add garlic and cook another minute. Pour in the boiling stock. Stir in the cinnamon, optional salt, pepper, and tomato paste.

♦ Reduce heat to low, cover, and cook, stirring occasionally, about 15 minutes or until the couscous is very tender. If liquid is absorbed too quickly, add water to keep from drying out. A small amount of liquid remaining is desirable. Fold in the drained garbanzo beans and cook for another couple of minutes. Place in serving dish and top with the roasted peppers and parsley. Serve hot or at room temperature.

Makes about 6 cups

Middle Eastern Couscous with Dwarf Gray Sugar Peas

Here we combine Middle Eastern couscous with a legume to produce a vegetarian protein dish. Dressing the combination with a zesty vinaigrette turns out lively room-temperature fare, rich with flavor and texture.

PREPARE-AHEAD NOTES:

The dish can be prepared and then refrigerated for up to two days. Bring to room temperature and add the garnish immediately before serving.

SUGAR PEAS:

¾ cup dried dwarf gray sugar peas or other small
    dried bean
1 tablespoon salt

COUSCOUS:

¼ cup extra virgin olive oil
1 ¼ cups very finely minced onion
¾ cup Middle Eastern couscous (available at Pasta
    & Co. stores—see page 105)
1 ½ teaspoons finely minced or pressed garlic
2 cups boiling vegetable stock (we use Organic
    Gourmet's Pure Vegetable Broth—page 40)
    or defatted chicken stock

DRESSING:

¼ cup plus 3 tablespoons extra virgin olive oil
¼ cup white wine vinegar
1 ½ teaspoons finely minced garlic
¾ teaspoon salt
½ teaspoon ground cumin
½ teaspoon pepper

¼ teaspoon dried oregano
¼ teaspoon dried basil

1 tablespoon finely minced parsley
¼ cup diced tomatoes, tossed with ¼ teaspoon salt

◆ Soak and cook dwarf sugar peas according to directions for cooking beans on page 87. When they are almost tender, add the 1 tablespoon salt. Dried sugar peas have very tough skins and can take 2 hours to cook. Do not undercook; the centers need to be very creamy.

◆ While the sugar peas cook, make the couscous. Place olive oil and onion in a heavy-bottomed saucepan. Sauté over medium-high heat. Just before the onion begins to brown, add the couscous. Cook, stirring frequently, until the couscous is dark golden brown. Add the garlic and cook another minute. Pour in boiling stock. Reduce heat to low, cover, and cook 15 to 20 minutes, until couscous is tender.

◆ While the couscous cooks, make the dressing. In a large bowl, combine the ¼ cup plus 3 tablespoons of olive oil, vinegar, garlic, the ¾ teaspoon salt, cumin, pepper, oregano, and basil. When the couscous is very tender and most of the liquid is absorbed, toss it (along with any remaining cooking liquid) with the dressing. When sugar peas are done cooking, drain them well and toss with the dressed couscous.

◆ Place the mixture in a serving bowl. Top with parsley and tomatoes. Serve at room temperature.

Makes 4 ½ cups

Shrimp and Rice in Garlic Mayonnaise

This shrimp and rice dish was originally created almost a decade before the Rice with Shrimp, Artichokes, Raisins, and Currants on page 112. And while neither of the recipes are low in fat, the contrast between the two is illustrative of two very different styles of eating. This one, with its aioli-style dressing, is deliciously rich, while the newer dish is deliciously light. Both are customer favorites.

Serve this substantial dish as a luncheon entrée. Present it on a chiffonade (page 132) of napa cabbage and accompany with some crusty bread or breadsticks. Note: This is one dish that because of the shrimp and the fresh mayonnaise, you'll want to serve slightly chilled (page 67).

PREPARE-AHEAD NOTES:

The dish holds well for up to three days refrigerated. Add garnish immediately before serving.

INGREDIENTS:

1 cup bottled clam juice
2 ½ cups water
2 teaspoons butter
1 ⅓ cups uncooked rice (we use Uncle Ben's)
1 whole egg
1 ½ tablespoons white wine vinegar
3 medium cloves garlic, peeled (the dish is meant to be garlicky, but adjust to your taste)
½ teaspoon salt
½ teaspoon pepper
½ teaspoon Tabasco sauce
1 cup extra virgin olive oil
¼ cup freshly squeezed lemon juice

⅔ pound (11 ounces) cooked, peeled shrimp, thawed, rinsed, and drained if frozen (we use Chilean shrimp; a good alternative is to buy cooked prawns, remove tails, and cut into ½-inch pieces)

¼ cup frozen peas, thawed, rinsed, and drained but not cooked

¼ cup thinly sliced celery

¼ cup finely chopped parsley

TO TOP:

Halved cherry tomatoes or quartered Roma tomatoes

♦ In a large saucepan, bring clam juice, water, butter, and rice to a boil. Reduce heat to low, cover, and simmer for 15 minutes (most of the liquid should be absorbed). Remove from heat and let sit, covered, for 15 minutes. Uncover and let cool to room temperature.

♦ Meanwhile, in the bowl of a food processor equipped with a steel blade, place egg, vinegar, garlic, salt, pepper, and Tabasco. Process until garlic is puréed. With the motor running, add the olive oil in a thin, steady stream. Next, slowly add lemon juice. The dressing should be a thick, creamy mayonnaise. If it is not thick enough, process a little longer. Place mayonnaise in a bowl large enough to hold the rice and other ingredients.

♦ When the rice reaches room temperature (no hotter or you will "cook" your mayonnaise; no colder or the rice will not properly absorb the mayonnaise), toss with the mayonnaise. Mix well. Add shrimp, peas, celery, and parsley.

♦ Place in serving bowl, top with tomatoes, and serve slightly chilled.

Makes 6 cups

Rice with Shrimp, Artichokes, Raisins, and Currants

For another rice dish that is good served at room temperature, see Easy Easy Risotto with Marinara Sauce, page 162.

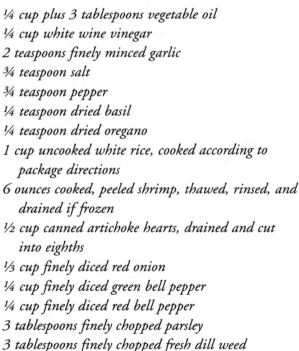

Don't miss trying this recipe. It is one of our new best-sellers from Lura Throssel's repertoire and has become a favorite among our catering customers, who like it served as a side dish to Lura's Stuffed Chicken Breasts (page 154).

While most of our dishes call for olive oil, in this one, Lura prefers using vegetable oil rather than an olive oil that would lend a heavier, more complex flavor to the dish.

PREPARE-AHEAD NOTES:

The rice can be cooked and tossed with the dressing up to three days before serving. Bring it back to room temperature and add the remaining ingredients shortly before serving.

INGREDIENTS:

¼ cup plus 3 tablespoons vegetable oil
¼ cup white wine vinegar
2 teaspoons finely minced garlic
¾ teaspoon salt
¾ teaspoon pepper
¼ teaspoon dried basil
¼ teaspoon dried oregano
1 cup uncooked white rice, cooked according to
    package directions
6 ounces cooked, peeled shrimp, thawed, rinsed, and
    drained if frozen
½ cup canned artichoke hearts, drained and cut
    into eighths
⅓ cup finely diced red onion
¼ cup finely diced green bell pepper
¼ cup finely diced red bell pepper
3 tablespoons finely chopped parsley
3 tablespoons finely chopped fresh dill weed

2 tablespoons capers, rinsed and drained

2 tablespoons golden raisins, plumped in hot water and drained

2 tablespoons currants, plumped in hot water and drained

To top:

1 tablespoon finely chopped parsley

♦ In a large bowl, whisk together vegetable oil, vinegar, garlic, salt, pepper, basil, and oregano.

♦ Toss the cooked rice with the dressing. Let cool.

♦ Add shrimp, artichoke hearts, onion, green and red bell pepper, parsley, dill weed, capers, raisins, and currants, tossing lightly to distribute evenly. Spoon into serving dish and top with additional parsley. Serve at room temperature.

Makes 6 cups

ROOM-TEMPERATURE
VEGETABLES

These are vegetable dishes that defy the notion that, to be stunning, vegetables must be piping hot. What an aid they are to a more relaxed dining style.

Great Vegetables

WITH OR WITHOUT FAT, ROOM TEMPERATURE OR HOT

Don't be put off by the lengthy instructions for this recipe. Integrate this method of preparing fresh vegetables into your cooking and you will thank us. The simple process of blanching vegetables hours or even days ahead of serving ensures gorgeously fresh vegetables with no last-minute hassle. The color and texture are set by plunging the hot vegetables into a bath of icy water, draining well, covering, and refrigerating until near serving time.

You then have numerous easy options, spelled out below. Almost all vegetables prepared this way can either be served at room temperature or reheated, with or without the addition of fat.

PREPARATION FOR BLANCHING:

◆ Green or wax beans, snow peas, sugar snap peas, and asparagus—trim ends and rinse with cold water.
◆ Brussels sprouts—trim loose outer leaves and tough stems; cut an "x" in stem ends or halve or quarter them; rinse with cold water.
◆ Carrots—peel and cut to desired size; rinse with cold water.
◆ Cabbage—trim outer leaves, quarter, and core; rinse with cold water.

for more about
**PASTA & CO.
YELLOW LINE
DISHES**
turn to page xv.

♦ Spinach, chard, kale (page 189), and other bitter greens, such as beet greens, mustard greens, and collards—cut away any tough spine that runs down the middle of each leaf; wash in several changes of water to remove sand; after blanching, you will want to "wring" handfuls of the greens, then coarsely chop them.

♦ Broccoli raab/rapini—trim tough ends and any yellowed leaves from stems; leave stalks intact or cut into 2-inch pieces on the diagonal; rinse with cold water.

BLANCHING INSTRUCTIONS:

♦ In a kettle large enough to hold the vegetables loosely (if necessary, you can cook in batches; a pasta cooker with a lift-out insert is handy for this), bring 4 to 6 quarts of water to a boil. Fill a large, shallow bowl with ice water. Add a tablespoon of salt (probably twice that for green beans, since they typically require extra seasoning) to the boiling water. When the water has returned to a rolling boil, plunge in the vegetables. Cook until just barely tender (personal preference counts here: we avoid "crunchy" vegetables). Drain and immediately submerge cooked vegetables in ice water. When vegetables have cooled, lift them out of the ice water and drain them well in a thin layer on paper towels. If you will not be serving the vegetables immediately, layer them in a shallow container. Cover tightly with plastic wrap and refrigerate for up to two days.

SERVING BLANCHED VEGETABLES:

♦ To serve blanched vegetables at room temperature, simply season with salt and pepper. Lightly dressing them with good-quality olive or walnut oil gives the vegetables an attractive shine, but if you're watching fat, skip the oil. (If using a vinaigrette, add it immediately before serving, since the acid—either vinegar or lemon juice—in the vinaigrette will quickly turn green vegetables yellow.)

♦ To serve blanched vegetables hot, you have several possibilities. You can toss them in a sauté pan with hot olive oil just long enough to heat through and give them a shine.

Even better, sauté a little garlic and onion in the oil before adding the vegetables.

♦ To avoid adding oil, you can reheat the blanched vegetables in boiling water for just a minute, drain, and serve, or you can wrap them in foil and warm them in a 350° F oven for 10 to 15 minutes.

Southwest Curd and Corn Salad

T*his is a fun way to use dry-curd cottage cheese (page 61). The dish is impressively low in fat. To offset the distinctive texture of the cheese, we add homemade bread crumbs as well as corn, olives, tomatoes, and green onions. To build flavor, we toast the cumin before adding it to the vinegar.*

PREPARE-AHEAD NOTES:

The dressing can be made ahead. Assemble the dish within 8 hours of serving. The cilantro is best chopped and added at the last minute.

INGREDIENTS:

5 tablespoons red wine vinegar
2 large cloves garlic, peeled and put through a press
1 jalapeño pepper, seeded and minced
¾ teaspoon salt
¼ teaspoon ground cumin
2 cups dry-curd cottage cheese
Scant 2 cups frozen corn, thawed, rinsed, and drained but not cooked
1 cup homemade, lightly toasted, very coarsely ground

bread crumbs (page 186—do not substitute
commercial bread crumbs)
½ pound Roma tomatoes, cut into ¼-inch dice and
seasoned with ¼ teaspoon salt
1 bunch green onions, cut ¼ inch thick (use both
white and green parts)
⅔ cup minced red onion
½ cup pitted black olives, rinsed, well drained, and
quartered
1 bunch cilantro, washed, dried, and finely chopped

◆ Whisk together vinegar, garlic, and jalapeño pepper in
a large bowl. Place salt and cumin in a dry sauté pan over
medium-high heat and toast just until the cumin browns
slightly and gives off a slightly pungent aroma; be careful
not to scorch. Remove from heat and stir into vinegar
mixture.
◆ Fold in cottage cheese, corn, bread crumbs, tomatoes,
green onion, red onion, black olives, and cilantro.
◆ Place in serving dish and serve at room temperature.

Makes 9 cups

Marinated Vegetables

This is the third in a series of marinated mixed
vegetable dishes we have done. Each has successively
contained less oil. (The second—Tuscan Vegetables—has been
revised on page 123.) You'll find this recipe supremely simple
and low fat at 3.5 grams per cup. The vegetables are served
raw, the dressing is 2 parts vinegar to 1 part oil, and the dish,
being truly low fat, benefits from being topped with a small
amount of a full-flavored, aged grating cheese—the best you
can obtain (hopefully, Parmigiano-Reggiano or, as a second
choice, the Pasta & Co. House Cheese: dry Monterey Jack).

Allow two hours for the vegetables to marinate before serving. This dish holds well for at least two days. Top with the cheese right before serving.

INGREDIENTS:

- ¼ cup white wine vinegar
- 2 tablespoons vegetable oil
- Heaping ¼ teaspoon salt
- 1 large clove garlic, peeled and put through a press
- 4 grinds black pepper
- ⅓ pound (5 ounces) carrots (about 2 small), peeled and cut into matchsticks, about 2 inches long and ¼ inch thick
- ½ pound zucchini (about 2 small) cut in half, seeded, and sliced at an angle, ¼ inch thick
- ⅔ pound (11 ounces) yellow squash (about 2 medium) cut in half, seeded, and sliced at an angle, ¼ inch thick
- ¼ pound celery (about 2 medium stalks), ends trimmed, sliced ⅛-inch thick
- ¼ pound red bell pepper (about ½ pepper), cut into ¼-inch by 2-inch matchsticks
- ¼ pound green bell pepper (about ½ pepper), cut into ¼-inch by 2-inch matchsticks
- 2 tablespoons freshly grated aged cheese, preferably Parmigiano-Reggiano or Pasta & Co. House Cheese (dry Monterey Jack)
- 2 teaspoons finely chopped parsley

♦ In a large bowl, whisk together vinegar, vegetable oil, salt, garlic, and pepper. Fold prepared vegetables into the dressing. Allow to marinate a couple of hours before serving.

♦ To serve, place in a large shallow dish and top with the cheese and parsley.

Makes about 7 cups

The Freshest Corn

Use these pointers to tell whether corn is freshly picked:

♦ Husks should be bright green with a soft texture and should surround the kernels tightly. Dry or yellow husks indicate that the corn is old.

♦ Never buy corn that has already been husked.

♦ The silk sticking out from the top of the husk should be a pale greenish white in color.

♦ Kernels should be plump and filled with a milky liquid when tested with your fingernail.

Favorite Way to Cook Fresh Corn

Every cook probably has a favorite way to cook fresh corn. This is ours. First, since salt toughens the skins of the kernels, we do not salt the water for cooking corn. We think the briefer the dip into boiling water the better, since heat speeds the conversion of sugar to starch and the toughening of the kernels.

Use a large kettle with plenty of water so that the ears will have lots of room. Bring the water to a rolling boil, add the ears, and a minute or two later, lift them out.

Whether "dipping" the ears in water as above (hardly even cooking) or grilling the ears on a barbecue, we suggest cooking with the last layer of husks still attached. With the husks on, the kernels actually steam. Remove ears from the heat, peel back the husks, remove silks, and use the corn as you want. If serving, it is attractive to leave the husks peeled back and still attached to the ear.

Fresh Corn Salad

Fresh corn and vine-ripe tomatoes are a must with this recipe. If the task of husking corn and cutting it from the ears sounds burdensome, just make a small batch and use it as a low-fat sauce over grilled chicken or seafood. The sweetness of the fresh corn against the pungent dressing is delicious.

PREPARE-AHEAD NOTES:

Although the recipe calls for blanching the corn, grilling it is even better. Prepare the corn as below, but instead of cooking it in boiling water, toss the ears on a hot barbecue for a couple of minutes after doing other grilling. You can keep the grilled corn in the refrigerator and make the salad another day. Once assembled, the salad keeps well refrigerated for a couple of days.

INGREDIENTS:

10 ears sweet corn, the freshest possible, husks removed
   except for the very last layer
4 large cloves garlic, peeled
1 teaspoon salt
1 teaspoon dried oregano
½ teaspoon ground cumin
6 tablespoons red wine vinegar
3 large, very ripe tomatoes, cut into ¼-inch dice
   (about 2 cups)
1 jalapeño pepper, seeded and very finely minced
1 bunch green onions, thinly sliced (both green and
   white parts), about 1 cup
⅔ cup diced red onion (¼-inch dice)
Salt and freshly cracked black pepper to taste (Pasta &
   Co. No. 4 Pepper Blend with Whole Allspice—page
   53—is a good choice here)
2 tablespoons finely chopped cilantro or parsley

♦ Bring a large kettle of unsalted water to a rolling boil. Add half the corn and cook for about 1 minute—do not overcook (see Favorite Way to Cook Fresh Corn, page 119). Immediately rinse with cold water, drain well, and remove remaining husks and silks. Repeat process for remaining ears. Cut corn from ears (see Removing Corn from the Cob, this page). You need about 4 cups of corn. Reserve.

♦ Finely mince together the garlic, salt, oregano, and cumin. In a large bowl, whisk together the garlic mixture with the vinegar. Toss with the corn, tomatoes, jalapeño pepper, green onion, and red onion. Let stand for an hour or so to meld flavors before serving. Taste for salt and pepper. Right before serving, toss with the cilantro or parsley.

Makes about 8 cups

Oven-Roasted Eggplant Salad

Oven roasting can do wonders for vegetables (page 182). This dish is easy to prepare and marvelous at room temperature, either as a vegetable side dish or as an appetizer served with pieces of pita bread or crostini. With only 2 tablespoons of olive oil, it has less than 5 grams of fat per cup. For an even lower-fat version, substitute defatted stock for all or part of the olive oil. The amount of feta you use however, really determines how low fat the dish is. We like lots.

PREPARE-AHEAD NOTES:

Though easy, this is not quick. The eggplant bakes for approximately 2 ½ hours. The dish keeps well for at

Removing Corn from the Cob

This task is not as tough as it seems. To strip corn kernels from the cob, first remove the husk and silks from each ear. Hold each ear vertically over a large plate that can catch the kernels and the "milk" that will spurt when the kernels are cut. Cut down against the cob with a sharp knife (some cooks prefer a serrated knife for this process), releasing the kernels. Rotate the cob and repeat until all kernels have been removed. Some kernels will come off separately; others will be connected in big chunks. This is fine. The chunks break apart easily when eaten or tossed with other ingredients.

Eggplant: To Salt or Not to Salt

Most of us learned early in our cooking careers that eggplant needs to be salted to draw out bitter juices before cooking. In many recipes, we continue to do this, but increasingly, we find it unnecessary. It seems that over years of hybridization, eggplant's excessive bitterness has been reduced. Don't count on this with every recipe, but we know it works to skip the salting in Oven-Roasted Eggplant Salad (page 120), Oven-Roasted Eggplant Sauce (page 182), Roasted Eggplant and Pepper Purée (page 8), and Eggplant Wraps (page 157).

For another eggplant dish good at room temperature, see Eggplant Wraps, page 157.

least five days. Top with the feta cheese immediately before serving.

INGREDIENTS:

1 eggplant (about 1 ½ pounds)
16 large cloves garlic, peeled
2 tablespoons extra virgin olive oil
2 tablespoons ground cumin
1 ½ teaspoons dried oregano
1 teaspoon dried basil
1 teaspoon salt
¼ to ½ teaspoon cayenne
¼ teaspoon ground allspice
1 pound onions, coarsely chopped
1 ⅓ cups diced tomatoes in purée
   (we like Paradiso or DiNola brand)
¼ cup freshly squeezed lemon juice

TO TOP:

Crumbled feta cheese (about ½ cup)
¼ cup finely chopped parsley

◆ Preheat oven to 350° F. Slice eggplant about ½ inch thick.

◆ In bowl of food processor equipped with steel blade, place garlic, olive oil, cumin, oregano, basil, salt, cayenne, and allspice. Process until garlic is very finely chopped. Add onions and process until finely chopped; be careful not to purée. Place in a bowl and stir in the tomatoes.

◆ In a shallow baking pan, layer tomato mixture with eggplant slices, starting and ending with the tomato mixture. Cover with foil. Bake in preheated oven until the eggplant breaks into pieces when it is pierced with a fork. This will take about 2 ½ hours. Remove from oven and toss with a fork to break up eggplant. Let cool. Stir in lemon juice and taste for seasoning. Top with the crumbled feta cheese and parsley. Serve at room temperature.

Makes 6 cups

Harvest Salad

This vegetable and fruit side dish is at its prime when the apples are fresh from the orchard and the zucchini plucked tiny from the vine. It is perfect with roasted ham or grilled sausages.

PREPARE-AHEAD NOTES:

This salad should be served the same day it is made.

INGREDIENTS:

⅔ cup mild-flavored extra virgin olive oil
⅓ cup rice wine vinegar
¾ teaspoon dried basil, or ⅓ cup julienned fresh basil
½ teaspoon salt
1 Red Delicious apple, cored and sliced into ¼-inch wedges
1 Golden Delicious apple, cored and sliced into ¼-inch wedges
1 Granny Smith apple, cored and sliced into ¼-inch wedges
1 zucchini (1 inch in diameter), sliced into coins ¼ inch thick
2 tablespoons finely minced red onions
Freshly cracked pepper to taste

TO TOP:

⅓ cup finely chopped red onion

♦ In a large bowl, whisk together olive oil, vinegar, basil, and salt. Place apples in the dressing as they are sliced, to prevent browning. Toss with zucchini, red onion, and cracked pepper.

♦ Garnish with finely chopped red onion and serve at room temperature.

Makes 8 cups

For other vegetable
dishes good at
room temperature, see
Oven-Roasted Vegetables
(page 165) and Oven-
Roasted Bell Peppers
(page 164).

Tuscan Vegetables

This classic recipe now calls for more vegetables and less olive oil than it originally did. Fat is down by a third (herbs are up slightly to build flavor), but the dish is still not low fat. Further cuts, we feel, would compromise taste. In short, this recipe is at its "fat point" (page 188), even though it still has 11 grams of fat per cup (this, of course, assumes that you sop up all those good oils with bread, since they are not totally absorbed by the vegetables). Calories are low at 140 per cup, but then 100 of them come from the olive oil! You can see by this recipe that a little fat very definitely goes a long way.

PREPARE-AHEAD NOTES:

The vegetables hold well for at least two days. We suggest allowing them to marinate for at least one hour before serving. Bring to room temperature and add any garnish just before serving.

INGREDIENTS:

1 tablespoon salt
½ cup extra virgin olive oil
¼ cup white wine vinegar
3 cloves garlic, peeled and put through a press
1 teaspoon dry mustard
½ teaspoon dried basil
½ teaspoon dried oregano
½ teaspoon dried thyme
½ teaspoon salt
⅛ teaspoon dried marjoram
5 grinds fresh black pepper (such as Pasta & Co.
    No. 4 Pepper Blend with Whole Allspice, page 53)
1 cup sliced carrots (slice ¼ inch thick on the
    diagonal)
1 ⅔ cups cauliflower florets (1-inch florets),
    about ½ head

1 cup sliced celery (slice ¼ inch thick on the diagonal)

1 ⅔ cups seeded, sliced zucchini (slice ¼ inch thick on the diagonal)

1 ⅔ cups seeded, sliced yellow squash (slice ¼ inch thick on the diagonal)

1 cup imported black olives with pits, well drained of brine

½ green bell pepper, cut in ¼-inch-wide matchsticks

½ red bell pepper, cut in ¼-inch-wide matchsticks

TO TOP (CHOOSE ONE OR MORE):

½ red onion, cut in ¼-inch-thick crescents (page 22)

8 cherry tomatoes, cut in half

½ cup finely minced fresh parsley

♦ Bring 6 quarts of water and the tablespoon of salt to a boil. While waiting, whisk together in a large bowl the olive oil, vinegar, garlic, dry mustard, basil, oregano, thyme, salt, marjoram, and pepper. Reserve.

♦ When the water is at a full boil, add carrots. Blanch for 1 minute. Leave them in the boiling water and add cauliflower. Blanch 2 more minutes, then add celery and cook for an additional 15 seconds. Vegetables should be tender but crunchy. When done to your taste, rinse thoroughly with very cold water, drain well, and add to the reserved dressing. Fold in zucchini, yellow squash, olives, and peppers. Mix well. Allow to marinate an hour or so before serving.

♦ Serve at room temperature with garnish of your choice.

Makes 11 cups

Bitter Greens
with Olive Vinaigrette

Althought this recipe sounds complicated, it's not. Rather, it is a lifesaver vegetable dish for such cumbersome meals as Thanksgiving or Christmas (or any other large-group meal for that matter). The flavors are a welcome surprise in a seasonal menu that is all too often exceedingly predictable.

This is a Spanish-influenced recipe that originally called for ¾ cup olive oil. We cut the oil to ⅓ cup. You can also substitute fat-free dried figs (page 129) for the olives.

For the greens, our preference is (very roughly) equal parts spinach, chard, and savoy cabbage. Purchase a bunch of red chard, a couple bunches of spinach, and a savoy cabbage. Trim the chard and the spinach, weigh, and make up the remaining amount with the cabbage. You'll probably have extra cabbage. It's good in soup.

PREPARE-AHEAD NOTES:

The greens can be blanched, drained, and cut, and then refrigerated a couple of days before serving. Bring them back to room temperature or reheat them. Pour the vinaigrette over them shortly before serving. Once dressed, the dish holds well for several hours, and even next-day leftovers are quite acceptable, but the vinaigrette does yellow the greens.

INGREDIENTS:

> About 4 pounds (any combination of) red or white
>   Swiss chard, mustard greens, spinach, other bitter
>   greens, or savoy cabbage
> 1 tablespoon salt for blanching
> ¼ cup red wine vinegar
> ½ cup minced shallots

2 teaspoons finely chopped garlic, or 2 teaspoons
Dilijan Liquid Garlic (page 150)
1 jalapeño pepper, seeded and minced, or ¼ teaspoon
Tabasco sauce
¾ teaspoon ground ginger
½ teaspoon salt
⅛ teaspoon ground cloves
⅓ cup extra virgin olive oil
¼ cup water
⅓ cup pitted and coarsely chopped imported black
and green olives—about 20 (page 5) or 3 dried
figs, coarsely chopped
¼ cup coarsely chopped cilantro
Salt and pepper to taste

♦ Trim and wash greens, cutting off stems about an inch into leaves. If using cabbage, core and cut into 2-inch wedges. You need a total of about 3 pounds of trimmed greens and/or cabbage leaves.

♦ Bring a large kettle of water to a boil and add the tablespoon of salt. Add greens (if using more than one kind, you'll want to blanch each separately, doing red chard last and keeping it separate, since the red will bleed onto the other greens). Boil greens until tender, about 3 minutes. Lift greens out of water and immediately rinse with very cold water. Thoroughly wring water from greens. Cut into a coarse chiffonade (page 132). Place in a bowl and fluff with a fork. (If using more than one kind of green, keep each in a separate container.) To hold for several hours or even overnight, cover the greens with a layer of wet paper towels, wrung very dry, and then cover with plastic wrap and refrigerate.

♦ Make vinaigrette by mixing together vinegar, shallots, garlic, jalapeño pepper, ginger, salt, and cloves. Whisk in olive oil and water. Fold in olives or figs and cilantro. Taste for salt and pepper. Refrigerate if not using immediately.

♦ Shortly before serving, bring greens and the vinaigrette to room temperature. Arrange greens on a serving platter (ovenproof if you plan to heat the dish later). If you are

Greens Are Dirty

Almost all dark, leafy greens require very thorough washing to remove sand. The best way to do this is to fill a clean sink with cold water. Plunge in trimmed greens, swish them around in the water several times, and lift them gently out of the water so that any dirt drops to the bottom of the sink. Drain and repeat the process until the water appears clean. Do not be tempted to stop with one wash.

using two or more greens, you can either combine them or keep each separate on your serving platter. If you want the greens hot, cover with foil and heat in a 300° F oven for 15 minutes. Immediately before serving (either at room temperature or heated), spoon vinaigrette over the greens.

Serves 6 to 8

Carrots in Paprika Garlic Sauce

H*ere is another variation on Moroccan chermoula (page 68). To conserve fat, we use considerably less olive oil than is traditional, but we do not reduce it as much as we do in the recipe for Tortellini in Paprika Garlic Sauce (page 67). The sauce by itself is also good served over grilled chicken or seafood.*

PREPARE-AHEAD NOTES:

This dish can be served hot as soon as it is assembled or at room temperature. The carrots keep well in the sauce, absorbing the flavors, for at least three days refrigerated. Return to room temperature and top with the fresh cilantro right before serving.

INGREDIENTS:

1 tablespoon salt for cooking carrots
3 tablespoons extra virgin olive oil
2 tablespoons plus 1 teaspoon freshly squeezed lemon juice
1 tablespoon water
1 teaspoon sweet (not hot) paprika
½ teaspoon salt
¼ teaspoon ground cumin
⅛ teaspoon cayenne

1 teaspoon finely chopped garlic
1 ½ pounds carrots, preferably small, slender ones,
  peeled and sliced 1 inch thick on the diagonal

TO TOP:

½ cup finely chopped cilantro

♦ Bring a large pot of water to a boil and add the table-spoon of salt. Meanwhile, in a large bowl, whisk together the olive oil, lemon juice, water, paprika, ½ teaspoon salt, cumin, cayenne, and garlic.

♦ Cook the carrots until tender in the boiling salted water, about 5 minutes (carrots should not be crunchy). Drain and toss immediately with dressing. Serve hot or at room temperature. Right before serving, top with the cilantro.

Makes about 4 cups

for more about
PASTA & CO.
YELLOW LINE
DISHES
turn to page xv.

Nonstick Cookware: A Boon to Fat-Trimmers

Nonstick pans of varying quality have been around for years and were originally shunned by many "real chefs." Their quality now is much improved and, with the growing emphasis on limiting fat, nonstick cookware has become invaluable.

A few tips:

◆ Be warned: Prices vary widely. A 12-inch skillet can cost from $18 to over $100, depending upon the brand name and coating technology. Talk to a knowledgeable kitchenware retailer before buying nonstick cookware, especially if what you are looking for is durability and weight of pan. A good "starter" brand is DuPont's popularly priced SilverStone, which comes in several grades.

◆ Even with much improved surfaces, you will still want to use wooden, plastic, or coated utensils with your nonstick cookware to keep the surface from becoming scratched or chipped. The best utensils are the Exoglass flat spatulas from France. They come in six sizes and are extravagantly priced,

MEATS & SEAFOOD

Such ease of dining results when you realize that even your entrée need not be hot off the stove. Instead, it can be prepared hours—even days—ahead, and served at room temperature. These dishes will especially lend grand style to buffet meals.

Chicken and Figs with Orzo

Fat-Trimming Tip No. 5 (page xvi) talks about identifying the staples of low-fat cooking, including some ingredients that, up until now, you have not commonly used. Dried figs are probably one of those. In fact, almost all dried fruits can add valuable heft to a recipe without adding fat (an average dried fig contains only 0.164 gram of fat—a number low enough to make figs technically "fat-free"). Figs, however, have even more to recommend them: They are the highest in dietary fiber of any common fruit, nut, or vegetable; they contain more calcium than milk; and they are virtually sodium free. In this dish, we combine figs with chicken and pasta to get dazzling results. Fat accounts for only 20 percent of the calories.

PREPARE-AHEAD NOTES:

This dish keeps refrigerated for at least three days. Although we consider it a room-temperature dish, it also is excellent hot—either straight from the stove or rewarmed. The recipe doubles and triples well to serve large groups.

While perfectly poached chicken (page 136) is exquisite in many dishes, here we want the look and taste of browned chicken meat. Using a nonstick skillet helps us get that while still using a minimum of fat. (For tips on nonstick cookware, see page 129.)

INGREDIENTS:

½ tablespoon salt for pasta water

¾ cup dried orzo pasta

1 tablespoon extra virgin olive oil

1 ½ pounds skinless, boneless chicken breasts, cut into
   1 ¼-inch pieces (bite size, but not too small)

½ red bell pepper, cut into diamond shapes about
   ½-inch wide

½ yellow bell pepper, cut the same as the red bell
   pepper

½ yellow onion, peeled and cut into crescents
   (page 22)

3 cloves garlic, peeled and finely minced

1 teaspoon salt

1 teaspoon Pasta & Co. House Herbs (page 166), or a
   mix of dried basil and oregano

⅛ teaspoon freshly ground black pepper

5 ounces dried figs, cut into pieces the same size as the
   peppers

1 tablespoon finely chopped fresh parsley

¾ cup dry white wine

TO TOP:

1 tablespoon extra virgin olive oil

1 tablespoon finely chopped fresh parsley

♦ Bring 4 to 6 quarts water and the ½ tablespoon salt to a boil. Add orzo and cook until tender, about 10 minutes, stirring occasionally to keep orzo from sticking together. When tender, rinse well to remove all starch, drain, and set aside.

from about $5 to $15, but they are the only utensils we have found that neither damage nonstick surfaces nor melt eventually into your food. Pasta & Co. stores stock a modestly sized and modestly priced Exoglass spatula. It is a cook's treasure.

♦ Do not expect nonstick pans to totally eliminate the need for fat. A small amount—even a light spray—of oil is generally needed to keep foods from cooking up rubbery in texture.

♦ Do not overlook the fact that while a good nonstick pan can significantly reduce the need for fat and make for very easy cleanup, you do not get the caramelized drippings from a coated pan that you do from a noncoated one. No matter how married you become to cutting fat, a good cook can never overlook the fact that some of the best and richest flavors come from deglazing a pan crusted with the residue of sautéing meat or vegetables in fat.

Wine: Another "Tool" for Fat-Trimmers

Wine, of course, is used extensively in cooking but is often overlooked as a non-fat way to build flavor and add liquid (and thus shine) into a dish. In Chicken and Figs with Orzo (page 129), wine combines with other cooking juices to make just the right amount of richly flavored but low-fat sauce.

♦ Heat olive oil in a large nonstick skillet over medium-high heat and cook the chicken pieces, a few at a time, until golden but not quite cooked through. Remove from pan and reserve. When all of the chicken has been cooked, add peppers, onion, garlic, 1 teaspoon salt, herbs, and pepper to the same skillet. Cook for about 15 minutes, until onions are translucent. Add figs, parsley, and wine. Simmer for 2 minutes, add reserved chicken, and continue cooking just until chicken is completely cooked but not dry. Add orzo and toss. Place in serving dish. Drizzle with extra virgin olive oil and top with parsley.

Makes about 8 cups

Moroccan Chicken

Over the years, this recipe has had everything, from its ingredients to its name, altered. For instance, as part of our fat-cutting efforts, we reduced the amount of olive oil, olives, and pine nuts. Through it all, Moroccan Chicken has remained probably our most impressive room-temperature chicken dish.

The most difficult part of making this dish may be finding the green olives. Most canned pitted green olives taste like pallid versions of black ones, and you want pungent taste and firm texture. Look for Spanish or Greek olives, or ask for "pitted greens" at a Pasta & Co. store—we usually have them available. Failing that, you may need to do the pitting yourself (page 5).

PREPARE-AHEAD NOTES:

This is perfect party food because the completed dish will hold for at least five days refrigerated. Bring to room temperature to serve. Plan ahead for the three days that the olives and chicken need to marinate.

OLIVES:

> ½ cup red wine vinegar
> 1 teaspoon ground cumin
> 1 teaspoon dried oregano
> 1 teaspoon dried thyme
> 1 teaspoon dried red pepper flakes
> ½ teaspoon dried rosemary, finely crumbled
> ½ teaspoon fennel seeds
> 8 cloves garlic, lightly crushed and peeled
> 4 bay leaves
> 3 ½ cups green olives, well drained, pitted, and
>   cut in half

CHICKEN:

> 2 ½ pounds boneless, skinless chicken breasts
> 1 pound boneless, skinless chicken thighs
> 1 ¼ cups extra virgin olive oil
> 1 ¼ cups freshly squeezed lemon juice
> 6 tablespoons red wine vinegar
> 2 ½ tablespoons sugar
> 1 tablespoon salt, or to taste
> ½ to 1 teaspoon dried red pepper flakes
> ⅛ teaspoon ground cloves
> Cracked black pepper to taste
> 5 bay leaves
> ½ cup golden raisins
> ½ cup seedless raisins

TO ASSEMBLE:

> 1 tablespoon salt for pasta water
> 1 ½ cups dried orzo pasta
> ¾ cup pine nuts, lightly toasted
> Optional: 1 small head napa cabbage, cored, washed,
>   and cut into chiffonade (see this page)

♦ To prepare olives, whisk together vinegar, cumin, oregano, thyme, red pepper flakes, rosemary, and fennel seeds in a bowl large enough to hold olives. Add garlic, bay leaves, and green olives. Add just enough water to cover

Chiffonade

Chiffonade is the pretentious term for a ruffly pile of julienne-like strips of fresh greens such as spinach, chard, kale, napa cabbage, mustard greens, basil leaves, and even iceberg or romaine lettuce.

The greens can be cooked (usually blanched), but in most cases we suggest using chiffonades raw for the texture and color they bring to dishes. The crispness of a chiffonade of raw greens, for instance, adds desirable contrast to pasta and, used as a bed for the noodles, eliminates the need for an additional green vegetable. The same is true when a chiffonade is used along with grilled meats or fish. Best of all, chiffonades are low-calorie, no-fat entrée extenders—far better for fat and calorie watchers than a tossed green salad.

♦ *To make a chiffonade of leafy greens, such as spinach:* Make a stack of 6 to 10 washed and dried leaves. Fold them in half along their stems and cut across the stems every ⅛ to ¼ inch. Use the same technique for fresh leaves of herbs, such as basil.

the olives. Cover and let marinate at room temperature for 3 days.

♦ To prepare chicken, poach chicken breasts and thighs in water according to directions on page 136, being very careful not to overcook them. Cut the meat across the grain into pieces approximately ½ inch wide, place in a bowl, and reserve.

♦ In a medium bowl, whisk together olive oil, lemon juice, vinegar, sugar, salt, red pepper flakes, cloves, and black pepper. Add bay leaves and set aside. Plump both kinds of raisins by covering them with boiling water and letting them stand 30 minutes. Drain very well. Add to oil mixture and pour over the reserved chicken. Cover with plastic wrap and let marinate for up to 3 days in refrigerator.

♦ To assemble, bring 4 quarts of water and the tablespoon of salt to a boil. Add orzo and cook until tender, about 10 minutes, stirring occasionally to keep orzo from sticking together. When done, drain well and toss with the chicken mixture. Drain marinade from olives, discarding the garlic cloves if you prefer. Fold olives into chicken mixture along with the toasted pine nuts. Serve at room temperature over the optional napa cabbage.

Makes about 12 cups

Spice-Cured Pork Tenderloin

T his is another Lura Throssel recipe. While the pork is delicious hot out of the oven, the recipe also provides one of the loveliest ways to present a room-temperature meat—lean, moist, exotically seasoned yet neutral enough to accompany almost any other dish. It is especially good served with the Pasta with Walnut Oil Sauce (page 192).

Note that if you increase the recipe to double or more, you will need to reduce the amount of pepper. We suggest increasing the amount by half each time you double the recipe. For instance, for 5 pounds of pork, use only 1 ½ tablespoons, not 2 tablespoons.

F or another meat dish good served at room temperature, see Lura's Stuffed Chicken Breasts (page 154) or Second Skin Chicken (page 152).

PREPARE-AHEAD NOTES:

Be sure to allow for the overnight curing of the meat, since both the final flavor and texture depend on it. Once the pork has been cured and roasted, it can be refrigerated for up to three days before being reheated or served at room temperature.

INGREDIENTS:

2 tablespoons sugar

1 tablespoon plus 1 teaspoon coarse sea salt, crushed in a mortar and pestle

1 tablespoon freshly ground black pepper

1 tablespoon dried oregano

2 teaspoons ground coriander

1 teaspoon ground cloves

2 ½ pounds pork tenderloins, dried well with paper towels

2 tablespoons extra virgin olive oil

½ cup pure maple syrup

½ cup water

♦ Mix together sugar, salt, pepper, oregano, coriander, and cloves. On a baking sheet, coat each tenderloin with the spice mixture. Make certain the tenderloins are completely coated with the spices, rolling them on the baking sheet to pick up any excess. Finally, place all the coated tenderloins on the baking sheet, cover with plastic wrap, and store overnight in refrigerator. (Overnight curing is crucial.)

♦ The next day, preheat oven to 350° F. Heat olive oil in a large skillet over high heat until very hot but not smoking. Add enough of the tenderloins to fill the pan but not crowd it. Sear the tenderloins for 3 to 5 minutes, turning until well browned on all sides (do not scrape off the crusty skin that forms). Remove the tenderloins to a shallow, ovenproof baking pan that holds them in a single layer with little extra room to spare (this is important so the juices don't burn during roasting—cut tenderloins in half if necessary to make them fit). Brush the tenderloins with maple syrup, reserving any that is left over. Pour water around tenderloins. Bake 10 minutes. Brush tenderloins once more with any remaining maple syrup and the pan juices and return to oven. Watch closely. If pan juices begin to cook dry, immediately add a small amount of extra water to keep from scorching. When tenderloins are done (after about 25 minutes total; thickest part should read 150° F to 155° F on a meat thermometer), remove from oven. Reserve pan juices.

♦ If you are serving immediately, let meat sit for 10 minutes, then slice as desired. Place on serving platter. Taste pan juices for seasoning, adjust if necessary, and pour over meat. If meat appears dry, drizzle with extra virgin olive oil.

♦ If serving meat later, either rewarmed or at room temperature, place pan juices and cooled meat (best if left unsliced) in separate sealed containers and store in refrigerator. When ready to serve, bring meat to room temperature or wrap in foil and rewarm at 400° F for about 15 minutes. Then slice and pour pan juices, heated or at room temperature, over meat as directed in the previous paragraph.

Serves 6 to 8

Poaching Chicken and Fish

Over the years, we have done a lot of poaching. "Perfectly poached" meat is neither undercooked nor overcooked. It should be satiny in texture, never dry. Because pieces of chicken and fish do not come in uniform thickness, poaching is not a question of timing but rather of taking care.

Poaching whole pieces of fish or chicken:
♦ Thoroughly rinse fish or chicken pieces in cold water and drain well. Trim off any excess fat. Arrange pieces (skin side up, if there is skin) in a large skillet. For 1 pound of meat, add water just to cover, ¼ onion, ¼ stalk celery, 1 teaspoon dried basil or Pasta & Co. House Herbs (page 166), and 1 teaspoon salt. (If the chicken or fish is going into a strongly seasoned dish, you may choose simply to poach it in salted water. On the other hand, if the meat is going into a mildly seasoned dish, you may want to enhance the flavor by poaching in a good-quality chicken or fish stock, being careful to taste for saltiness before adding salt.)
♦ Place pan over medium heat. When the liquid comes to a low simmer (not even bubbling), turn meat over, reduce heat, and continue to poach gently until the chicken meat just barely loses its pink color or the fish is barely opaque. If you are using an instant-read thermometer, the chicken will be done at 165° F, the fish at 150° F. Immediately remove meat from the cooking liquid. Remember that the meat will continue cooking from its own retained heat even when out of the broth. (If you have seasoned the poaching broth, you may want to strain and freeze it for use in stocks and sauces.)

Poaching small pieces of fish or chicken:
♦ If you are going to eventually cut up the pieces of chicken or fish, do the cutting before poaching and the task will be easier to perfect. Cook only a few pieces at a time, checking each carefully for satiny texture and doneness. If you discover that you have removed a piece before it is cooked through, you can return it to the simmering water for a few seconds and then recheck.

For another seafood dish good served at room temperature, see Shrimp and Feta Bake, (page 139) or Second Skin Fish (page 152).

Poached Sea Bass with Fresh Fennel

This is an exquisite room-temperature fish dish that is especially suited for a casual, special summer meal. The flavors are delicate: the light licorice taste of fresh fennel and the slight sweetness of sea bass, all dressed with fresh lemon juice and olive oil and just barely spiked with capers and anchovy. We specify sea bass because its silky texture takes well to poaching. Here is definitely the place to use your favorite best-quality extra virgin olive oil, since the dish depends upon the olive oil not only for sauce but flavor. Serve the dish with seasonal vegetables (either hot or at room temperature—garden-fresh tomatoes, green beans, and little boiled potatoes are splendid accompaniments) and lots of bread to sop up the juices that float out of this wonderfully Mediterranean fish dish.

PREPARE-AHEAD NOTES:

The dish holds well for a couple of days refrigerated.

INGREDIENTS:

> 1¼ pound freshest possible sea bass, cut into
>   2-inch chunks
> ½ cup best-quality extra virgin olive oil
> ¼ cup freshly squeezed lemon juice
> 2 small fennel bulbs (about 1 pound when trimmed)
> 1 small yellow onion, peeled and cut into ¼-inch
>   crescents (page 22)
> ⅓ cup minced parsley or chives
> 2 tablespoons capers, rinsed and drained
> 1 tablespoon good-quality anchovies, rinsed, drained,
>   and very finely chopped (such as Rusticella or
>   Bel Aria brand)

1 to 2 teaspoons salt
Freshly ground black pepper to taste (Pasta & Co.
No. 4 Pepper Blend with Whole Allspice is a good
choice here, page 53)

To TOP:

Best-quality extra virgin olive oil (see Olive Oil as a
Final Flourish, page 77)

♦ Poach sea bass in water according to directions on page 136, using 2 teaspoons salt for the poaching water.

♦ Place the ½ cup olive oil in a bowl large enough to hold the completed dish. As each piece of fish is poached, remove any skin and bones, flaking the fish into smaller pieces (not too small, since the fish will continue to break apart as it is tossed with the remaining ingredients). Place fish into the olive oil and toss to coat. Reserve.

♦ Place lemon juice in a small bowl. Cut the fennel stalks off where they meet the bulb. Discard any bruised or tough outer layers. Slice off a thin piece of the root end of the bulb. Cut bulb vertically into very thin slices, trimming out tough pieces of core. As you are cutting, immediately place the fennel slices into the lemon juice to keep them from turning brown. When all the fennel has been cut and tossed with the lemon juice, add the fennel—including all the lemon juice—to the fish. Add onion, parsley or chives, capers, anchovies, and salt. Toss mixture together. Cover with plastic wrap and let sit at room temperature for a couple of hours before serving. If holding the dish longer, refrigerate and then return to room temperature.

♦ Just before serving, taste for salt and pepper and adjust if necessary. Place mixture on a serving plate and drizzle with the olive oil to taste.

Serves 4 to 6

A Very Abbreviated Version of Shrimp and Feta Bake

Pour 16 ounces (2 cups) of Pasta & Co. Marinara Sauce (purchased or made according to recipe on page 180) into a shallow, broiler-proof baking dish. Top with the same amount of shrimp and feta cheese as in Shrimp and Feta Bake. Place mixture under preheated broiler until cheese is lightly browned and shrimp are pink, about 8 to 10 minutes. Remove from broiler, sprinkle with parsley, and drizzle with a tablespoon of your best-quality extra virgin olive oil. Serve hot or at room temperature. This dish is easy to prepare and you will be proud to serve it with chunks of warm bread or on a bed of hot pasta.

Shrimp and Feta Bake

This is a stunning first course or light entrée, served hot or at room temperature, with crusty bread to sop up the sauce. Using ready-made Pasta & Co. Marinara Sauce cuts cooking time by at least half, and the abbreviated version (this page) is especially quick to prepare.

PREPARE-AHEAD NOTES:

The sauce can be prepared up to a week ahead. Return it to room temperature and add the shrimp and feta up to four hours before broiling and serving.

INGREDIENTS:

> 1 tablespoon extra virgin olive oil
> 1 cup coarsely chopped onion
> 1 jar (16 ounces) Pasta & Co. Marinara Sauce,
>   or 2 cups homemade Basic Marinara Sauce
>   (page 180)
> 1 tablespoon ground cumin
> 1 tablespoon dried oregano leaves
> 1 teaspoon salt
> ⅛ teaspoon dried red pepper flakes
> ⅛ teaspoon ground black pepper
> 2 tablespoons pressed garlic (use a garlic press)
> 1 ½ teaspoons honey
> 1 cup dry white wine
> 1 ½ pounds large shrimp, peeled, deveined, and with
>   tails either removed or left on
> ½ teaspoon salt for shrimp
> 4 ounces feta cheese, well drained and coarsely
>   crumbled (we prefer Galilee brand Israeli feta)

TO TOP:

> 1 tablespoon finely chopped fresh parsley
> Optional: 1 tablespoon extra virgin olive oil
> Lemon wedges

♦ Heat olive oil over medium heat in a large sauté pan. Add onion and sauté until almost tender, about 4 minutes. Add marinara sauce, cumin, oregano, salt, red pepper flakes, black pepper, garlic, and honey. Cook over low heat for about 10 minutes. Add wine and cook, uncovered, about 15 minutes. Pour into a shallow 1 ½ quart broiler-proof baking dish.

♦ Toss the shrimp with the ½ teaspoon salt. Place shrimp on top of the sauce and top with the feta cheese. Preheat broiler. Place shrimp mixture under preheated broiler until cheese is lightly browned and shrimp are pink, 8 to 10 minutes. Remove from broiler. Sprinkle with parsley. Drizzle with optional olive oil (page 77). Serve hot or at room temperature with lemon wedges.

Serves 6 to 8 as a first course

hot entrées
and
side dishes

ALMOST ALL OUR HOT FOODS HAVE ONE THING IN COMMON: WE DESIGN THEM TO GO INTO OUR REFRIGERATED DISPLAY CASES OR FREEZERS IMMEDIATELY AFTER PREPARATION AND THEN TO BE REHEATED OR BAKED BY CUSTOMERS HOURS OR DAYS LATER. THIS IMPLIES PARTICULARLY DURABLE FOOD WITH FULL FLAVORS THAT CAN STAND UP TO SUCH TREATMENT. AS A HOME COOK, YOU CAN BENEFIT FROM OUR EXPERIENCE BY PREPARING THESE DISHES AHEAD—ON THE WEEKEND, SAY—AND REFRIGERATING OR FREEZING THEM UNTIL NEEDED. CHECK THE PREPARE-AHEAD NOTES IN EACH RECIPE FOR SPECIFIC INSTRUCTIONS. THE RESULTS ARE SURE TO BE PLEASING.

Skinnystrada

*T*ypically, a strada (sometimes spelled "strata") is deliciously rich with eggs, cream, and cheese, as are most
baked casserole dishes. Skinnystrada is our defiantly lower-fat
version. It is soufflé-like in its texture and herbaceous in its
seasoning. There are 5 grams of fat per 1-cup serving, but it
qualifies for our Yellow Line since only 17 percent of its calories come from fat.

PREPARE-AHEAD NOTES:

This is definitely a candidate for your freezer. Pasta & Co.
sells Skinnystrada only frozen. If you don't need the
cook-ahead convenience, bake it immediately after it is
assembled.

INGREDIENTS:

1 pound yellow onions, peeled and cut into ¼-inch
crescents (page 22)
1 pound mushrooms, wiped clean and thinly sliced
¾ teaspoon dried thyme
¾ teaspoon dried basil
2 teaspoons balsamic vinegar
4 cloves garlic, peeled and put through a press
1 10-ounce package frozen chopped spinach, thawed
and squeezed completely dry
3 cups nonfat ricotta cheese
2 teaspoons salt
¼ teaspoon black pepper
½ teaspoon ground nutmeg
3 ½ cups No-Oil-No-Salt-Added Marinara Sauce,
purchased or made according to recipe on page 178
About 12 ounces of bread sliced ¼ inch thick (no need
to trim crusts), enough to make two layers in a
9-inch by 13-inch baking dish

*⅓ cup homemade bread crumbs, preferably garlic
    bread crumbs (page 186)*
¾ cup (6 ounces) low-fat mozzarella cheese, grated

for more about
**PASTA & CO.
YELLOW LINE
DISHES**
turn to page xv.

◆ In a large, nonstick sauté pan, cook the onions over medium-low heat until they soften, about 20 minutes. (Since you are adding no fat, be sure the heat is low and that you stir frequently; the onions will give off their own liquid.) Add the mushrooms, thyme, and basil and cook, stirring frequently until mushrooms are soft and all their juices have cooked away (about 15 minutes). Do not brown. Add the balsamic vinegar and garlic and cook, stirring, a couple more minutes. Remove from heat and cool.

◆ When the mushroom mixture is cool, add the chopped dry spinach. Mix well with hands, breaking up any clumps of spinach. Stir in ricotta, salt, pepper, and nutmeg. Combine thoroughly. Taste for seasoning, adding more salt and pepper if necessary.

◆ Preheat oven to 375° F. Spread 1 ¾ cups of the marinara sauce in bottom of a 9-inch by 13-inch baking dish. Lay about half of the bread slices on top of the sauce in a single layer (you can cut or tear bread to fit). Spread 2 ½ cups of the spinach mixture over the top of the bread. Make a second layer of bread and top with ¾ cup of the marinara sauce (if you have extra bread, reserve for another use). Spread on another 2 ½ cups of the spinach mixture and top with the mozzarella cheese. Drizzle the last cup of sauce over the top. Sprinkle with the bread crumbs.

◆ Bake in preheated oven for approximately one hour. When golden brown and bubbling, remove from oven and let stand 10 to 15 minutes before cutting.

Serves 6 to 8

Vegetable Ragout

H ere is a fat-watcher's vegetarian delight: only 1 tablespoon of oil in the entire dish and lots of good, hearty eating. Don't be tempted to cook all the ingredients together at the same time. While it may save you a couple of dirty pans, it will cost you valuable texture. If you cannot find baby garbanzo beans (chana dhal available at Pasta & Co. stores), substitute the smallest dried white bean you can get.

PREPARE-AHEAD NOTES:

The dish keeps refrigerated for up to five days.

INGREDIENTS:

1 cup dried baby garbanzo beans (chana dhal)
1 tablespoon salt for beans
1 cup dried French green lentils (page 37)
2 teaspoons salt for lentils
2 cups peeled, cubed white or red potatoes
    (¾-inch cubes)
1 cup peeled, cubed turnip (¾-inch cubes)
1 tablespoon salt for cooking potatoes and turnips
1 tablespoon extra virgin olive oil
1 yellow onion, peeled and coarsely chopped
5 cloves garlic, peeled and finely chopped
2 teaspoons salt
1 teaspoon ground cumin
½ teaspoon ground ginger
½ teaspoon ground cinnamon
½ teaspoon ground turmeric
2 ½ cups vegetable stock (page 40)
3 cups peeled, sliced carrots (sliced ½ inch thick
    on the diagonal)
¾ cup currants
1 tablespoon balsamic vinegar

Finely chopped parsley

♦ Cook garbanzo beans according to directions on page 87, 25 to 35 minutes. Be sure beans are very tender. When almost done, season with the 1 tablespoon salt, cook a few more minutes, then drain and set aside.

♦ Cook lentils in water to cover until tender, about 20 minutes. When almost done, season with the 2 teaspoons salt, drain well, and reserve.

♦ Meanwhile, place potatoes and turnips in a saucepan with the 1 tablespoon salt. Cover with water and bring to a boil. Cook until tender (about 10 minutes). Drain and reserve.

♦ In a large saucepan with lid, heat olive oil over medium heat. Add onion and sauté until translucent, about 2 minutes. Add garlic, salt, cumin, ginger, cinnamon, and turmeric, and cook for a few minutes more, being sure not to brown garlic. Add stock, carrots, and currants. Cover and let cook until carrots are tender.

♦ When carrots are tender, fold in reserved potatoes, turnips, lentils, and garbanzo beans. Season with balsamic vinegar. Place on serving platter and top with a generous amount of chopped parsley.

Makes 12 cups

for more about
**PASTA & CO.
YELLOW LINE
DISHES**
turn to page xv.

Asian Ragout
with Velvet Chicken

This recipe uses an Asian-influenced low-fat technique: Boneless, skinless chicken breasts are poached in a highly fragrant broth. The result is a mahogany-colored meat that has a velvety texture, a rich broth, and no added fat. Served over boiled white or brown rice, the dish is incredibly low in fat.

PREPARE-AHEAD NOTES:

♦ Allow one day for the meat to marinate and acquire its distinctive texture.
♦ The dish keeps well refrigerated for several days.

INGREDIENTS:

> 3 cups water
> ½ cup plus 2 tablespoons soy sauce
> ½ cup plus 2 tablespoons dry sherry
> ¼ cup plus 2 tablespoons honey
> 2 tablespoons finely minced fresh ginger
> 1 teaspoon salt
> ⅛ teaspoon dried red pepper flakes
> 1 or 2 star anise
> 1 piece (3 inches) cinnamon stick
> 1 strip (3 inches) orange zest
> 2 ½ pounds boneless, skinless chicken breasts
> ¾ pound yellow onions, peeled and cut into ¼ inch
>   crescents (page 22)
> ½ pound small carrots, peeled and sliced ⅛ inch thick
>   on the diagonal

TO TOP:

> ½ red bell pepper, cut into diamond shapes no larger
>   than ½ inch

*½ green bell pepper, cut into diamond shapes no
    larger than ½ inch*
½ cup green onions, thinly sliced on the diagonal

♦ In a large sauté pan, combine water, soy sauce, sherry, honey, ginger, salt, red pepper flakes, star anise, cinnamon stick, and orange zest. Bring mixture to a boil and then lower heat to a very low simmer. Very carefully poach chicken in the liquid until barely cooked through (the chicken will continue to cook as it cools—see Poaching Chicken and Fish on page 136). Remove chicken pieces as they are done and reserve.

♦ When all the chicken has been removed from the sauce, add the onions, raise heat to medium-high, and cook 5 to 8 minutes. Add the carrots and cook another 5 to 8 minutes, or until they are tender. Remove pan from heat and let mixture cool.

♦ When the chicken has cooled to the touch, cut into 1-inch pieces across the grain. When the sauce has cooled, return chicken to the sauce and allow to marinate for at least a day.

♦ To serve, reheat chicken and sauce mixture and serve over boiled rice. Top with the bell peppers and green onion.

Serves 6 to 8

Canned Beans

We prefer not to use canned beans, but for sundry reasons (usually the need to save time), they have slipped into a number of our recipes, including Bulgur with Two Beans. (We also call for canned beans in our Chili—page 171—and though our own kitchens do not use canned black beans when making Black Bean Lasagne—page 175—we specify them in the home version—again for ease.)

Remember, however, that cooked beans can be frozen. Next time you cook beans, make extra and tuck them away in your freezer as an alternative to the canned version.

Bulgur with Two Beans

*T*his recipe is quick to prepare and is as low in fat as you want it to be. It is a Lebanese dish, shared with us by a staff member years ago. Originally, it called for 1 ½ pounds of ground lamb and for the bulgur to be cooked in the lamb drippings. We have taken the lamb out of the dish, but offer it dressed with nonfat yogurt as an optional accompaniment along with feta cheese. To add flavor, we toast the bulgur before adding other ingredients.

The dish in its low-fat version is great, hearty daily fare. Adding all the accompaniments, however, makes it company-food caliber with all the fun of lively ethnic flavors and textures.

PREPARE-AHEAD NOTES:

The entire dish can be made and held in the refrigerator for up to three days. Just rewarm and serve topped with whatever accompaniments you choose. If the bulgur mixture has become dry, reheat it with a small amount of water or stock.

INGREDIENTS:

1 tablespoon extra virgin olive oil or Dilijan Liquid Garlic (page 150)
1 large yellow onion, peeled and coarsely chopped
1 cup dried bulgur (cracked wheat)
1 tablespoon finely minced garlic (omit if using liquid garlic)
2 ½ cups defatted chicken or vegetable stock, more if needed
¼ teaspoon ground cinnamon
¼ teaspoon ground allspice
1 teaspoon salt
Freshly cracked black pepper to taste
1 tablespoon tomato paste

1 can (15 ounces) black beans, rinsed and well
    drained (or 1 ½ cups home-cooked black beans)
1 can (15 ounces) garbanzo beans, rinsed and well
    drained (or 1 ½ cups home-cooked garbanzo beans)
Optional: freshly squeezed lemon juice to taste

TO TOP:

2 or 3 diced tomatoes, seasoned to taste with salt
2 tablespoons finely chopped parsley or mint

OPTIONAL FETA CHEESE ACCOMPANIMENT:

8 ounces feta cheese, drained of brine
    (we prefer Galilee brand Israeli feta)
⅓ cup coarsly chopped fresh mint, or a combination of
    fresh mint, fresh oregano, and parsley

OPTIONAL LAMB ACCOMPANIMENT:

3 cloves garlic, peeled
1 ½ teaspoons whole cumin seed
1 ½ teaspoons salt
1 teaspoon dried oregano
1 ½ pounds ground lamb
1 cup nonfat yogurt
Juice of 1 or 2 lemons
3 tablespoons finely chopped fresh mint

♦ In a large nonstick skillet, heat the oil or liquid garlic
over medium heat, add the onion, and cook until soft.
Add the bulgur and toast for about 5 minutes, being careful not to burn. If using fresh garlic, add it now and cook
a few minutes more. Meanwhile, bring the stock to a boil.
Add boiling stock, cinnamon, allspice, the 1 teaspoon salt,
pepper, and tomato paste to the bulgur, along with the
black and garbanzo beans. Lower heat to medium, stir to
blend, cover, and cook slowly until bulgur is tender and
liquid is absorbed, about 15 minutes. Do not overcook
the bulgur. Add small amounts of additional stock if necessary. When done cooking, taste for seasoning. You may

Product Spotlight: Dilijan Brand Liquid Garlic

Fresh garlic is always best—better than garlic salt, garlic powder, or garlic flakes. The only garlic product that we have found that comes close to the taste of fresh is Dilijan Brand Liquid Garlic—soy oil infused with an extract of fresh garlic. Substitute it for equal amounts of fresh garlic. If you need more than 1 tablespoon of gar-lic in an average-sized recipe, use fresh garlic for the remaining amount. (In large amounts, the liquid garlic may give an unpleasant aftertaste.) A big advantage to the liquid garlic is in sautéing: it does not burn as readily as fresh garlic. Since the liquid garlic is an oil, you may want to reduce amounts of other oils in a dish.

want to add the lemon juice, especially if not using the optional lamb.

♦ Mound mixture on serving plate and top with the tomatoes, parsley, or mint. Serve with the feta cheese or lamb accompaniments if you choose.

♦ For the feta accompaniment, coarsly chop feta and herbs together until herbs are well distributed through the pieces of feta.

♦ For the lamb accompaniment, finely mince the garlic with the cumin, salt, and oregano. Reserve. In a nonstick skillet, cook the lamb over medium-high heat until the pink is just barely gone, breaking up the meat as it cooks. Place the cooked meat in a strainer and let the fat drain off for at least 5 minutes. Meanwhile, in the same skillet, over medium heat, toast the reserved garlic mixture, being very careful not to burn the garlic. Return the drained lamb to the pan and mix well. Season to taste. Remove from heat and stir in yogurt with the lemon juice. Place in a serving dish, top with the fresh mint, and serve hot as an accompaniment to the bulgur and beans.

Serves 4 to 6

Second Skin Chicken

*T*he skin on chicken adds about 5 grams of fat per serving. The fat-slashing answer is easy: Use skinless chicken. The problem is that discarding the skin without replacing it with some silky olive-oil-laden marinade usually makes for leatherlike grilled meat. (If you want plain skinless chicken, poach it according to the method on page 136. Done with care, poaching yields silken meat with no addition of fat, and you get the bonus of a couple cups of good broth, which, when defatted, is invaluable to lower-fat, flavorful cooking.)

Here we use only 1 tablespoon of olive oil to marinate 4 pounds of boneless, skinless chicken breasts. Then, before grilling, we slather each piece of meat with Nonfat Yogurt Cheese (page 6)—literally giving the chicken a nonfat "second skin" to keep the meat moist during cooking.

PREPARE-AHEAD NOTES:

♦ Allow at least 24 hours for the Nonfat Yogurt Cheese to drain before grilling. Since the yogurt cheese keeps well for at least a week and has multiple uses, make extra and keep a supply in the refrigerator.

♦ The marinade can be made several days ahead.

♦ Allow chicken to marinate two to four hours before grilling.

SERVING SUGGESTIONS:

If you're inclined to indulge in a touch of fat, definitely try the Mango Sauce recipe that follows on page 154. Otherwise, a fresh salsa of tomatoes, peppers, and onions will provide a flavorful sauce for your low-fat chicken, with boiled rice and blanched vegetables alongside.

Second Skin Fish

*T*he "second skin" idea works equally well for fish—especially firm, meaty fish such as halibut, swordfish, sea bass, or tuna. The marinade adds upbeat flavor and the yogurt keeps the fish decidedly moist.

Follow the recipe for Second Skin Chicken, but substitute 4 pounds of your choice of meaty fish for the chicken. Since fish can be costly and 4 pounds would easily feed 8, you may want to halve the recipe or use part chicken and part fish. (Marinate the chicken in one dish and the fish in another.) Other than increasing the challenge for whoever mans the grill, serving the mixed grill of fish and chicken makes a marvelous menu, especially if you serve it with Mango Sauce (page 154).

YELLOW LINE

PASTA & CO

for more about

**PASTA & CO.
YELLOW LINE
DISHES**

turn to page xv.

NONFAT YOGURT CHEESE:

> *2 cups plain nonfat yogurt*
> *2 teaspoons salt*

MARINADE:

> *¼ cup water*
> *1 tablespoon extra virgin olive oil*
> *12 cloves garlic, peeled*
> *1 tablespoon salt*
> *1 tablespoon sweet paprika*
> *1 teaspoon cayenne*
> *½ teaspoon ground cumin*
> *¼ teaspoon ground allspice*
> *¼ teaspoon ground cinnamon*
> *4 pounds boneless skinless chicken breasts*

◆ Prepare Nonfat Yogurt Cheese using the 2 teaspoons salt, according to directions on page 6. Reserve.

◆ Place water, olive oil, garlic, the 1 tablespoon salt, paprika, cayenne, cumin, allspice, and cinnamon in work bowl of food processor equipped with a steel blade. Process until garlic is minced very fine, scraping down sides of bowl several times during processing.

◆ Rub mixture evenly over chicken breasts. (This is most easily done with your hands. If you're squeamish about handling raw chicken, don some disposable rubber gloves.) Allow chicken to marinate, covered, in the refrigerator at least 3 or 4 hours. Turn the chicken in the marinade occasionally.

◆ About an hour before grilling, bring chicken to room temperature. Spread yogurt cheese on chicken pieces to coat both sides. Cook on a very hot, well-oiled grill (some of the yogurt coating may stick, but there will still be sufficient coating left on the chicken). Serve hot or at room temperature.

Makes 16 to 20 breast halves

Mango Sauce

Use this summery sauce to accompany grilled chicken, seafood, or pork. Vegetarians will love it for dressing up rice and bean dishes. Tossed with chunks of the season's best cantaloupe, it makes a dazzling fruit salad.

INGREDIENTS:

½ cup American Spoon Foods Mango Butter (see this page)
¼ cup finely chopped cilantro
3 tablespoons extra virgin olive oil
3 tablespoons very finely minced red onion
3 tablespoons very finely minced Anaheim pepper (or jalapeño if you wish extra heat)
4 teaspoons very finely minced garlic
4 teaspoons white balsamic vinegar or other mild white vinegar
Salt to taste

◆ Fold all the ingredients together, season to taste with salt, and serve at room temperature.

Makes about 1 cup

Lura's Stuffed Chicken Breasts

These chicken breasts are equally at home on a picnic or at a formal dinner party. They are splendid company fare, served hot or at room temperature, whole or sliced. No sauce or other trimmings are necessary.

Do not use store-bought bread crumbs in this recipe. The beauty of this dish is the texture of the coarse, freshly made bread crumbs (not the sandy-textured ones that are

Product Spotlight: Mango Butter

A small jam maker in Petroskey, Michigan, called American Spoon Foods, makes a mango butter that has become a Pasta & Co. staple. If you can obtain it, we're certain it will have a permanent place in your pantry as well. If you cannot find it, substitute up to a cup of coarsely chopped ripe mango. The sauce will be different in taste and texture, but will still be delicious for serving with grilled chicken or fish.

commercially available) against the chicken meat made rich and moist by the cream cheese filling.

PREPARE-AHEAD NOTES:

You can spread the preparation for this rather time-consuming recipe over several days. For instance, the stuffing can be made several days ahead of use (or can even be frozen). The chicken breasts can be stuffed and then refrigerated for at least 24 hours before you bread and bake them. Once they are cooked, they hold very well for a couple of days and can be rewarmed or served at room temperature.

STUFFING AND CHICKEN:

6 ounces cream cheese, at room temperature
6 tablespoons butter, at room temperature
¼ cup thinly sliced green onions
¼ cup grated Parmesan cheese
¼ cup sun-dried tomatoes packed in oil, drained and cut into julienne
2 tablespoons chopped fresh basil
1 tablespoon chopped parsley
2 large cloves garlic, peeled and put through a press
½ teaspoon salt
5 grinds black pepper
3 large boneless, skinless whole chicken breasts (about 2 ½ pounds)

BREADING:

¾ cup flour
¼ teaspoon salt
5 grinds black pepper
1 egg
¾ cup milk
4 cups freshly made bread crumbs (page 186)
¼ cup grated Parmesan cheese
¼ cup extra virgin olive oil
2 tablespoons finely chopped parsley

For the stuffing, use a wooden spoon to knead together the cream cheese and butter until completely smooth. Add the green onions, Parmesan cheese, sun-dried tomatoes, basil, parsley, garlic, salt, and pepper. Stir until well mixed. Refrigerate until ready to use.

♦ Trim chicken breasts of fat. Cut each whole breast into two halves, down the line separating the two sides. Using a very sharp knife, make a deep pocket in each of the halved chicken breasts by slicing horizontally from thick end to thin on the underside of the breast. Fill each pocket with up to ¼ cup (depending on the size of the breast) of the stuffing. With your hand, mold the chicken breast over the stuffing to seal the edges. Do not flatten the breast. Refrigerate the stuffed breasts until ready for breading and baking.

♦ For the breading, combine flour, the ¼ teaspoon salt, and pepper in a shallow bowl. Reserve.

♦ Whisk together egg and milk in another shallow bowl. Reserve.

♦ In a third shallow bowl, combine bread crumbs, Parmesan cheese, olive oil, and parsley until evenly mixed. Reserve.

♦ Preheat oven to 450° F.

♦ Dredge each chicken breast in the flour mixture, shaking off excess flour. Then, dip into the egg mixture. Lift chicken from egg mixture and place in bread crumb mixture, generously coating each breast with bread crumbs. Place breaded breast on a baking sheet. Repeat until all breasts are breaded. Bake on upper rack of preheated oven for 30 minutes, or until the bread crumb coating is golden brown and chicken is cooked through.

♦ Serve the breasts immediately, or let them cool and serve at room temperature, either whole or cut into thick slices. The cooked breasts will store refrigerated for up to 3 days. Either allow them to return to room temperature, or reheat them, covered, for 15 minutes in a 400° F oven, then remove cover and continue heating another 5 to 10 minutes before serving.

Makes 6 stuffed breast halves

For other meat dishes good served either hot or at room temperature, see Chicken and Figs with Orzo (page 129), Spice-Cured Pork Tenderloin (page 134), and Shrimp and Feta Bake (page 139).

Eggplant Wraps

O ne of the few vegetarian dishes that satisfies even
meat eaters, Eggplant Wraps make a good-looking
buffet dish and are as good at room temperature as they are
hot from the oven.

PREPARE-AHEAD NOTES:

The wraps can be assembled a day ahead of baking. Once
baked, they keep well for a couple of days.

INGREDIENTS:

2 medium-sized eggplants (about 2 ¼ pounds
    before trimming)
¼ cup extra virgin olive oil
1 teaspoon black pepper
About 1 ¼ pounds leeks (an average-size bunch)
1 tablespoon butter
⅓ cup sun-dried tomatoes, packed in oil, drained
1 clove garlic, peeled and put through a press
1 pound ricotta cheese
6 ounces mozzarella cheese, grated
1 cup grated Parmesan cheese
1 egg
1 egg yolk
¼ teaspoon salt
Pinch ground nutmeg
2 cups Pasta & Co. Marinara Sauce, purchased or
    made according to recipe on page 180

♦ Trim stem ends from the eggplants. Cut eggplants lengthwise into ¼-inch slices—you want at least 14 usable slices.
♦ Preheat oven to 400° F.
♦ Brush two cookie sheets with 1 tablespoon olive oil
each. Lay the eggplant slices next to each other on the prepared sheets and brush with the 2 tablespoons remaining
olive oil. Sprinkle with black pepper. Bake for 25 minutes,

or until eggplant is tender to the touch—not spongy or dried out. Remove from oven and cool. Reduce oven heat to 350° F.

♦ Trim the leeks, halve them lengthwise, rinse well in cold running water to remove all grit, and drain. Cut into ¼-inch slices. Melt the butter in a sauté pan over medium heat, add leeks, and sauté until wilted, but not browned, about 5 minutes. Remove from heat and cool.

♦ Chop the sun-dried tomatoes on a cutting board with the pressed garlic. Reserve.

♦ Combine ricotta, mozzarella, ½ cup of the Parmesan, egg, egg yolk, salt, and nutmeg in a medium bowl until well mixed. Stir in the sun-dried tomatoes and garlic and the sautéed leeks.

♦ Place ¼ cup of the ricotta mixture on the wide end of each eggplant slice and roll up. Place the rolls in a 9-inch by 13-inch ovenproof baking dish. Pour marinara sauce over the eggplant rolls. Sprinkle with the remaining ½ cup Parmesan cheese. Cover with a lightly oiled sheet of aluminum foil and bake for 35 minutes. Remove foil and serve immediately or let cool, re-cover, and store refrigerated. Bring to room temperature or reheat, covered, in a 400° F oven for about 15 minutes before serving.

Makes 14 to 16 Eggplant Wraps

Our Very Doable Polenta

Polenta has become a popular menu item in recent years. The problem with polenta is that the classic method of making it requires 40 to 45 minutes of constant stirring. From our earliest experiments with polenta, we were certain that there had to be an easier way to enjoy this marvel. To be sure, there are numerous alternative polenta methods that range from using a microwave to using a double boiler. After trying many of them, we came up with a shortcut to lumpless polenta that requires a maximum of eight minutes of stirring and yields a delectable—and only slightly untraditional—dish that you will want to use in myriad ways. Baked-Cheese Polenta (this page) is a firm-textured version of our very doable polenta; Cheese-Seasoned Polenta (page 161) is the soft-textured version. Either requires only eight minutes of stirring.

Baked-Cheese Polenta

(A FIRM POLENTA)

This firm-textured *polenta uses our eight-minute stir method.*

Unfortunately, "undressed" polenta (cooked classically with only cornmeal, water, and salt) can be as unappealing as unsauced pasta. It is, after all, a foil for the more complex flavors of sauces and cheeses. To formulate a basic firm polenta neutral enough to be served with any number of sauces and accompaniments, but still tasty on its own, we season the polenta with butter and cheese. Want it plain? See Polenta with Less Fat, page 161.

PREPARE-AHEAD NOTES:

The polenta can be baked, cooled, and stored refrigerated for a couple of days before reheating and serving.

INGREDIENTS:

5 cups whole milk
5 cups water
4 teaspoons salt
½ teaspoon ground nutmeg
3 ½ cups cornmeal (we mix together 2 cups white cornmeal and 1 ½ cups yellow cornmeal)
6 tablespoons butter
¼ cup finely chopped parsley
1 ½ cups freshly grated Parmesan cheese
1 cup grated cheese—sharp cheddar, fontina, or other cheese of your choice

TO TOP:

⅓ cup freshly grated Parmesan cheese

♦ Lightly butter a 9-inch by 13-inch baking dish. (Other shapes of shallow baking dishes—such as a round paella pan that allows the polenta to be cut into wedges—can make for more interesting presentation, but for ease of portioning, a basic 9-inch by 13-inch pan is best.)

♦ Place 2 ½ cups of the milk and all of the water in a large saucepan and bring to a boil. Add salt and nutmeg. Whisk the cornmeal together with the remaining 2 ½ cups milk (this step will prevent the cornmeal from forming lumps when it is added to the boiling liquid).

♦ When the milk/water mixture is at a boil, whisk in the cornmeal/milk mixture. Lower heat and cook for 5 to 8 minutes, whisking constantly. Add 4 tablespoons of the butter and stir until it has melted into the cornmeal. Stir in the parsley and remove from heat.

♦ Mix together the 1 ½ cups Parmesan with the other cup of cheese of your choice. Pour one-third of the cornmeal mixture into the prepared baking dish. Sprinkle with one-half of the cheese mixture. Repeat process until you have made three layers of polenta and two layers of cheese. Dot surface with the remaining 2 tablespoons butter and sprinkle with the ⅓ cup Parmesan. Cover with foil and let sit for 15 minutes while you preheat the oven to 400° F.

♦ Bake polenta, covered, for 30 minutes. Remove polenta from oven and uncover. Preheat broiler. Place polenta under broiler until top is well toasted—not burned, but dark golden.

♦ Let rest for about 20 minutes before serving hot. Or if serving later, let cool entirely, cover, and refrigerate. To serve, return to room temperature, cover with foil, and reheat at 400° F until warmed through, about 30 minutes. The polenta is also very good at room temperature. Either way, it can be served plain or with a sauce of your choice.

Serves 10 to 12

Polenta: Soft or Firm?

Basic polenta can be served two very different ways: soft or firm. When the polenta is served freshly cooked and hot off the stove, it is called a "soft" polenta, such as our Cheese-Seasoned Polenta (page 161). When the cooked polenta has been allowed to cool just long enough to congeal, it is called a "firm" polenta, such as our very doable Baked-Cheese Polenta (page 159). In this "firm" state, the polenta can be baked or grilled and served hot or at room temperature. Whichever you prefer, don't miss serving it with the Oven-Roasted Eggplant Sauce (page 182) or the Caprisi Sauce (page 189) ladled over it.

What Kind of Cornmeal?

You can use any kind of cornmeal for polenta, although we suggest coarse-ground cornmeal. For the very best results, use Italian cornmeal that has been especially grown and processed for making polenta.

Polenta with Less Fat

Y ou can omit the cheeses from either the Baked-Cheese Polenta or the Cheese-Seasoned Polenta for a lower-fat— and much blander— version of these dishes. To step up the flavor, substitute a good-quality vegetable or chicken stock for the water.

Without the cheeses, you can also skip the baking step for the firm version (the Baked-Cheese Polenta). Simply spread the warm polenta out on a board or in a shallow baking dish to a thickness of about 3 inches. Let sit until firm (an hour or two). The polenta can then be cut into slices and warmed in the oven, broiled, or grilled.

Cleaning the Polenta Pot

E ven with our easy method, you may end up with some polenta stuck to your cooking pot. After emptying the polenta from the pot, fill it with cold water and set aside to soak overnight. Most of the cornmeal film will then lift off easily.

Cheese-Seasoned Polenta

(A SOFT POLENTA)

H ere's the soft version *of our polenta recipe that takes only eight minutes of stirring.*

PREPARE AHEAD NOTES:

◆ Double this recipe and you can serve half "soft" right away and let the remainder firm up for baking and serving for another meal days later. Simply butter a shallow, ovenproof baking dish; pour, spoon, or pat (depending upon how firm the polenta has become) the polenta into the prepared dish; and follow the baking directions for Baked-Cheese Polenta on page 159. Reduce baking time relative to the amount of polenta you are baking.

◆ For easy, individual servings of firm polenta, spoon warm, soft polenta into nonstick muffin tins or oiled ramekins. No need to bake. When ready to use, unmold, reheat, and brown under a hot broiler.

INGREDIENTS:

2 ½ cups whole milk
2 ½ cups water
2 teaspoons salt
¼ teaspoon nutmeg
1 ¾ cups coarse-ground cornmeal
2 tablespoons butter
¾ cup freshly grated Parmesan cheese
½ cup grated cheese—sharp cheddar, fontina, or other
   cheese of your choice
2 tablespoons finely chopped parsley

◆ Place 1 ¼ cups of the milk and all of the water in a large saucepan and bring to a boil. Add salt and nutmeg. Whisk the cornmeal together with the remaining 1 ¼ cups milk (this step will prevent the cornmeal from forming lumps when it is added to the boiling liquid).

♦ When the milk/water mixture is at a boil, whisk in the cornmeal/milk mixture. Lower heat and cook for 5 to 8 minutes, whisking constantly. When cornmeal mixture is thick enough to cling to the whisk, add butter and stir until it has melted into the cornmeal. Stir in Parmesan, your choice of second cheese, and parsley. Serve immediately. The polenta sets up quickly and should be on the table within 5 minutes to be fully enjoyable.

Makes 4 to 6 servings

Easy Easy Risotto with Marinara Sauce

The rituals of risotto making are legendary: just the right Italian rice, the successive addition of small amounts of rich stock, the glory of the final creamy dish. Unquestionably, well-crafted risotto is a gastronomic pinnacle—just not one we want to scale after a long day at work.

If you love risotto but not the elaborate preparation, try this recipe. While it may not pass muster as legitimate risotto, it is a delicious rice dish that cooks almost unattended. Even the leftovers are superb, reheated or at room temperature. You can also form them into patties and brown them in a bit of hot butter. This recipe alone could be reason enough for keeping Pasta & Co. Marinara Sauce in your pantry.

PREPARE-AHEAD NOTES:

♦ The ingredients can be prepared early in the day for ease at mealtime.
♦ Since the risotto is equally good hot, at room temperature, or reheated, it is an excellent candidate when no one knows for sure when dinner will be served.

For other grain dishes excellent served hot or at room temperature, see Maftoul (page 105) and Talid (page 106).

2 cups Arborio rice

¼ cup extra virgin olive oil

2 cups minced onion

2 large cloves garlic, peeled and put through a press

2 cans (14 ½ ounces each) Swanson's Chicken Broth
(the fat-free, low-sodium variety is fine)

1 cup Pasta & Co. Marinara Sauce, purchased or
made according to recipe on page 180

1 ½ teaspoons salt (use less if you do not use
low-sodium stock)

Freshly ground black pepper

Pinch ground nutmeg

3 bay leaves

½ cup freshly grated Parmesan cheese

♦ Rinse the rice under cold running water and drain well (this violates a cardinal rule of good risotto making). In a large nonstick skillet, heat olive oil over medium-high heat. Sauté onion and rice until golden, about 10 minutes. Add garlic and cook for another minute. Add chicken broth, marinara sauce, salt, pepper, nutmeg, and bay leaves. Stir and cover tightly with lid or foil. Reduce heat to low and cook very slowly, without stirring, for about 30 minutes, or until rice is tender. The dish is meant to be a bit sticky. Fold in the Parmesan and taste for seasoning. Serve hot or at room temperature.

Serves 8 as a side dish

Oven-Roasted Bell Peppers

Agreat appetizer, vegetable side dish, or topping for pasta, this is one of our oven-roasted vegetable marvels (page 182), and it's easy to boot. The juices extracted by the high-temperature cooking combine with a little stock for deglazing the roasting pan, to make a sauce so good you'll want to use every drop. Unlike most roasted pepper dishes, this one, thankfully, does not require that you peel the peppers. Serve hot from the oven or at room temperature.

PREPARE-AHEAD NOTES:

The roasted peppers keep well refrigerated for up to five days.

INGREDIENTS:

> 4 green bell peppers (or any combination of red, green, yellow, or orange bell peppers), cored, and cut into strips 1 inch wide and about 2 inches long— be guided by the natural sections of the peppers and be sure to trim off all the white part inside the peppers
> 1 yellow onion, peeled and cut into ½-inch crescents (page 22)
> 8 cloves garlic, peeled and smashed with the side of a chef's knife
> ¼ cup extra virgin olive oil
> 1 teaspoon salt
> ¼ cup chicken or vegetable stock

♦ Preheat oven to 400° F.
♦ Place peppers, onion, garlic, and olive oil in a 9-inch by 13-inch baking dish. Sprinkle with salt and toss ingredients together until all are well coated with the oil. Place in lower third of preheated oven and bake 20 minutes. Stir vegetables and rotate pan. Return to oven for 10 to 15 minutes. Peppers should be fork tender. Remove from

oven and pour in stock. With a rubber spatula, scrape off any browned juices from edges of pan and incorporate into the peppers.

♦ Taste for salt and pepper. Adjust seasoning if necessary. Serve hot or at room temperature.

Makes 4 to 5 cups

Oven-Roasted Vegetables

*T*he minute these top-selling vegetables (another of our oven-roasted wonders—page 182) come out of the oven, you will be munching on their caramelized goodness. Serve them as a side dish to just about any meat or seafood. They also make a splendid vegetarian entrée served over rice.

If it's late spring or summer, you may find the quality of yams and sweet potatoes woody; if so, just substitute additional carrots, onions, or potatoes—or some of each.

PREPARE-AHEAD NOTES:

The vegetables hold well in the refrigerator for a couple of days. They can be reheated or served at room temperature. If they appear dull, drizzle them with a little extra virgin olive oil or good-quality stock before serving.

A NOTE ON CUTTING THE VEGETABLES:

Cut the vegetables into appropriately sized pieces so that they will get tender in the same amount of time. Carrots, for instance, tend to take longer to cook than potatoes, so cut them a little smaller. On the other hand, do not cut vegetables too small—they shrink a bit in the roasting.

INGREDIENTS:

1 pound red potatoes, trimmed and scrubbed (but not peeled), cut into 1 ½-inch cubes or wedges

For other vegetable dishes good served either at room temperature or hot, see Oven-Roasted Eggplant Salad (page 120), Bitter Greens with Olive Vinaigrette (page 125), and Carrots in Paprika Garlic Sauce (page 127).

*½ pound yellow onions, peeled and chopped into
1 ½-inch chunks*

*1 medium to large yam or sweet potato (about 12
ounces), peeled and cut in half lengthwise, then cut
crosswise into 1 ½-inch lengths*

*4 or 5 medium carrots (about 12 ounces), peeled and
cut into 1 ¼-inch lengths on the diagonal*

*3 cloves garlic, peeled and put through a press or finely
chopped*

3 bay leaves

2 teaspoons salt

*1 teaspoon Pasta & Co. House Herbs (see this page) or
your choice of dried herbs*

*1 tablespoon dark brown sugar, preferably Billington's
Premium Dark Brown (page 185)*

5 to 6 tablespoons extra virgin olive oil

TO TOP:

2 tablespoons chopped parsley

♦ Preheat oven to 400° F. Place the potatoes, onion, yam
or sweet potato, carrots, garlic, and bay leaves in a shallow,
ovenproof pan (a 9-inch by 13-inch baking dish works
fine). Sprinkle with salt, herbs, and sugar. Drizzle the olive
oil over all, and toss to coat thoroughly. Roast in upper
third of oven for about 45 minutes, rotating pan halfway
through baking time. To check for doneness, use a fork to
pierce a potato chunk and a carrot in the middle of the
pan. They should be tender, not crunchy. Stir the vegetables and continue roasting until they are fork tender and
nicely browned, another 15 to 20 minutes.

♦ If the vegetables are to be served immediately, remove
them to a serving dish and top with chopped parsley. If
you wish to serve them later, let them cool, cover, and
refrigerate. To serve, return them to room temperature or
reheat, covered, at 400° F for about 20 minutes. Top with
the parsley right before serving.

Serves 6 to 8

What Are Pasta &
Co. House Herbs?

A blend of basil,
oregano, marjo-
ram, rosemary, black pep-
per, and allspice, our dried
herb mix was originally
conceived to appeal to
customers who wanted
one multipurpose herb
blend to replace numerous
jars of aging herbs in their
spice cabinets. The prod-
uct has been so successful
that we have integrated it
into our own cooking,
using it in everything
from salad dressings to
pasta sauces.

encore

Why Do We Add Parsnips to Mashed Potatoes?

P arsnips have long been valued by cooks for the richness they add to the flavor of root vegetable purées. And that is precisely what they do to our mashed potatoes: along with the roasted garlic, they deepen the flavor of the puréed potatoes so that they can withstand refrigeration and reheating.

In shopping for this thick, long, ivory-colored root vegetable that is a close relative of the carrot, look for medium-sized parsnips that are firm, with a smooth skin.

Pasta & Co. Mashed Potatoes

W e sell mashed potatoes all year long, but they're especially popular at Thanksgiving and Christmas. The appeal of this recipe—in addition to its great taste—is that the potatoes can be made 2 or 3 days before serving and rewarmed with no harm. That can more than make up for the fact that the initial work dirties a total of two saucepans, a food processor work bowl, and a mixing bowl—about twice the amount of most mashed potato recipes. Leftover mashed potatoes make delightful-tasting dollops on top of a bowl of most any soup.

PREPARE AHEAD NOTES:

Roast the garlic ahead of time so that it will be ready to use. Once the potatoes and parsnips are cooked, it is critical to proceed with the recipe. Do not let them cool for more than 10 minutes before puréeing them with the other ingredients.

INGREDIENTS:

 1 pound parsnips, peeled and cut into fairly
  even pieces
 1 tablespoon salt for parsnips
 3 pounds baking potatoes, peeled and quartered
 1 tablespoon salt for potatoes
 1 to 2 large heads garlic, each roasted with 1
  tablespoon extra virgin olive oil until very soft
  (page 23) (include all pan juices)
 1 ⅓ cups heavy cream, heated if serving immediately
 6 tablespoons salted butter, at room temperature

OPTIONAL:

 ½ to 1 teaspoon salt, to taste
 Freshly cracked black pepper, to taste

Minced chives

♦ Place parsnips in a saucepan. Add cold water to cover the parsnips by an inch. Add the 1 tablespoon salt. Cook over medium-high heat until parsnips are very tender (about 45 minutes).

♦ While the parsnips are cooking, place the potatoes in another saucepan. Add cold water to cover them by an inch. Add the second tablespoon of salt. Cook over medium-high heat until potatoes are very tender (about 50 minutes).

♦ When the parsnips are done cooking, drain well and place in the work bowl of a food processor equipped with a steel blade. Slip roasted garlic cloves from their skins and add them to the food processor, along with their pan juices (you should have at least a tablespoon of garlic). Add ½ cup of the heavy cream and process until very smooth. Reserve.

♦ When the potatoes are done cooking, drain well and place them, along with the remaining cream, the butter, and the optional salt in a large bowl. Whip with an electric mixer for about 2 minutes (do *not* use a food processor for the potatoes). Add reserved parsnip mixture and continue to whip until light, fluffy, and fairly free of lumps (some prefer more lumps in their potatoes than others).

♦ Taste for salt and pepper. Serve immediately or cool, cover with plastic wrap, and refrigerate. Prior to serving, remove plastic wrap, cover with foil, and reheat in a 375° F oven for 30 to 45 minutes, or until warmed through. Right before serving, top with the chives.

Makes 8 cups

Gorgeous Dirty Rice

A Deep South specialty that we have adapted to our own taste, dirty rice is typically high on flavor (spicy to exceedingly fiery) and low on aesthetics (a mush of gray overcooked rice—unattractively delicious).

To improve appearance and texture, we call for our own House Blend Rice (a mix of wild rice, brown rice, and basmati). The mixture adds color, and the three rices together give a unique mouth feel because of their varied cooking times. We top the dish generously with a bright-colored garnish, sour cream, and cooked crabmeat. Skip the crabmeat and the dish is still great fare, but the cool sweetness of the seafood along with the sour cream is a good contrast to the dish's aboriginal heat. You can make this rice as hot as you like (even without the jolt of cayenne it has robust flavor).

A chiffonade of undressed raw greens (page 132) especially napa cabbage, or blanched, room-temperature asparagus (page 114) makes a great accompaniment to this dish.

PREPARE-AHEAD NOTES:

The dish holds well for two or three days. Just refrigerate and reheat, covered, in a 350° F oven. You may need to add a little stock if the mixture becomes dry. Remember it should be moist but not soupy. Top with the garnishes, sour cream, and optional crabmeat just before serving.

INGREDIENTS:

3 cups chicken stock, more if needed
½ to ⅔ pound ground pork (not sausage meat)
¾ cup diced yellow onion (¼-inch dice)
½ cup diced celery (¼-inch dice)
½ cup diced green bell pepper (¼-inch dice)
½ cup diced red bell pepper (¼-inch dice)
1 tablespoon finely minced garlic
1 teaspoon ground cumin
1 teaspoon salt
½ teaspoon freshly ground black pepper

¼ to ¾ teaspoon cayenne (depending on the strength
  of your cayenne)
½ teaspoon dried oregano
1 bag (16 ounces, heaping 2 cups) Pasta & Co. House
  Blend Rice, or 2 cups white or brown rice

TO TOP:

1 to 2 bunches green onions, cleaned and thinly sliced
  on the diagonal (use lots; they taste great with
  the rice)
½ cup diced red bell pepper (¼-inch dice)

OPTIONAL:

Cooked crabmeat—as much as you like
Dollops of sour cream

♦ Bring the stock to a boil in a saucepan and reserve. Meanwhile, in a large, heavy, flameproof casserole with lid, sauté pork over medium-high heat until it is no longer pink, breaking it into small pieces. Stir occasionally to prevent sticking. Remove pork and reserve. Pour off all but 2 tablespoons of pork fat (if the pork does not render this much fat, add a small amount of olive oil). Add onion, celery, and the ½ cup of each of the bell peppers. Sauté until the onion softens, about 5 minutes. Lower heat and add garlic, cumin, salt, pepper, cayenne, and oregano. Sauté briefly, taking care not to burn the garlic. Add the rice to the vegetable mixture and sauté an additional couple of minutes. Add the reserved hot stock and the reserved pork. Bring to a boil, reduce heat to very low, cover, and simmer for up to 70 minutes or until rices are tender and broth is almost, but not quite, absorbed. If the rice gets dry before it is tender, you can add more hot broth. Let sit, covered, for at least 15 minutes before serving. The final dish should be moist, but not soupy.
♦ Remove rice to a shallow serving dish (a paella pan is attractive) and top with the green onions, diced pepper, and optional crabmeat. Pass the optional sour cream separately.

Serves 6 to 8

Pasta & Co. Chili

We cut considerable fat from this classic recipe by eliminating the step of browning the meat in hot oil. To our surprise, the meat cooks down more tender and the flavor suffers not a bit. Just allow for three to four hours of unattended stove time.

Make this chili as hot as you like by altering the amount of red pepper flakes and jalapeños. Since it makes a very thick chili, we suggest serving it over rice with a bounty of condiments such as chopped fresh tomatoes, sliced green onions, diced avocado, grated cheddar or jack cheese, and dollops of sour cream. Or if you're not counting fat grams, try it French onion–soup style: in broilerproof bowls, topped with a thick layer of cheddar and jack cheeses, and broiled until the cheese topping is browned and bubbling. For a soupier chili, thin it with some stock.

Another chili option is Lisa's Vegetarian Chili, page 41.

PREPARE-AHEAD NOTES:

The chili keeps in the refrigerator for a week with no harm whatsoever. Store it in the freezer for two or three months and it's still suitable for party food. Just thaw, slowly reheat, and bring out the condiments.

INGREDIENTS:

Vegetable oil for sautéing (about 2 tablespoons, more
  if needed)
2 pounds onions (about 8 cups), peeled and cut into
  ½-inch dice
3 cloves garlic, peeled and put through a press

Spice mixture:
  ½ cup medium chili powder
  2 tablespoons cornmeal
  2 tablespoons sugar
  1 tablespoon plus 1 teaspoon ground cumin
  1 tablespoon salt

½ to 1 ½ teaspoons dried red pepper flakes
Scant teaspoon black pepper

2 ½ pounds beef stew meat, cut into pieces no larger
than ¾ inch
3 cups water
2 cans (28 ounces each) crushed tomatoes in purée
2 cans (15 ¼ ounces each) kidney beans, drained
Optional (depending upon how hot you want the
chili): 1 ½ teaspoons seeded and chopped jalapeños
Optional condiments such as those suggested above

◆ In a heavy, flameproof casserole with lid, heat a thin layer of oil over medium heat. Add onions and cook, stirring frequently to prevent burning, until golden brown (15 to 20 minutes). Add garlic and the spice mixture and cook until the mixture forms a paste (be careful not to scorch it), stirring frequently. Add the meat, water, tomatoes, and optional jalapeños. Bring to a boil, stir well, cover, lower heat, and simmer until meat is falling apart (about 3 ½ hours), stirring occasionally. Or bring to a boil, cover, and place in a 250° F to 300° F oven (whatever temperature keeps the chili at a very low simmer).

◆ At the end of the cooking time, roughly break the meat apart with a large fork until most of the chunks have been broken up. Stir in the drained beans and optional jalepeños. Bring to a simmer and taste for seasoning. To reduce fat further, refrigerate the chili until any fat congeals. Skim fat off the top and reheat and serve, skipping our favorite high-fat condiments and topping just with sliced green onions and chopped fresh tomatoes.

Makes nearly 14 cups

hot pastas
and sauces

PASTA, OF COURSE, IS OUR NAME. IT'S WITH PASTA THAT WE HAVE CREATED MANY OF OUR BEST-SELLING LOWER-FAT DISHES (SOME IN THIS SECTION, MANY MORE IN THE ROOM-TEMPERATURE FOODS CHAPTER). YET WE MUST STRESS THAT IT IS NOT EASY TO TAKE THE FATS OUT OF GOOD PASTA EATING. WHILE THE PASTA ITSELF IS LOW IN FAT, THE NOODLE FAMILY SEEMS TO CRAVE SUCH PARTNERS AS CREAM, BUTTER, OLIVE OIL, AND CHEESE. HERE ARE SOME OF OUR LATEST HOT PASTA DISHES—SOME REMARKABLY LOW IN FAT, OTHERS NOT.

FOR PASTA COOKING INSTRUCTIONS, SEE PAGE 63.

Pasta: Low Fat and Healthy

Even fresh pasta that is made with whole eggs gets only 10 percent of its calories from fat. Look for pasta made with 100 percent semolina flour, which contains the highest amount of complex carbohydrates of any wheat flour.

Concerned About Cholesterol in Pasta?

There is roughly ¼ of an egg in each main-course serving of Pasta & Co. fresh pasta. And even in cholesterol-controlled diets, the American Heart Association allows four eggs per week. At that rate, you could eat our pasta four times a week and still enjoy a three-egg omelet. (If you must avoid eggs entirely, most commercial dried pasta is egg-free.)

Black Bean Lasagne

This may be our masterpiece Yellow Line pasta dish. With only 26 percent of its calories from fat, Black Bean Lasagne has become our top-selling frozen entrée, unseating the previous front-runner, Beef Lasagne. A 1-cup portion contains 8 grams of fat and 310 calories.

PREPARE-AHEAD NOTES:

As with all lasagne recipes, the making of the component parts is tedious. This recipe makes one 9-inch by 13-inch lasagne. It takes very little additional effort to double the recipe and make a second lasagne. Since unbaked lasagne freezes well, why not?

The lasagne can also be assembled and left refrigerated a day or two before baking. Once baked, we suggest holding it no more than the 15 to 20 minutes recommended for cooling before serving.

A couple of other suggestions from Jenn McBride, a culinary student who for the last year has weekly made hundreds of this lasagne for us:

♦ For those who might like the dish more fiery, substitute a good-quality salsa for the No-Oil-No-Salt-Added Marinara.

♦ For those who cannot obtain Quark or who would like the dish richer, substitute sour cream (possibly low-fat) for part or all of the Quark.

RICE MIXTURE:

1 can (15 ounces) black beans
⅔ cup uncooked brown rice, or ⅔ cup Pasta & Co. House Blend Rice
1 teaspoon ground cumin
1 teaspoon ground coriander
Heaping ¼ teaspoon salt
Heaping ¼ teaspoon freshly cracked black pepper

1 cup frozen corn, thawed, rinsed, and drained but
    not cooked

½ cup plus 1 tablespoon vegetable stock

⅓ cup seeded and diced Anaheim peppers

1 can (4 ounces) Ortega chopped green chiles, well
    drained

3 tablespoons finely chopped cilantro

BEAN SAUCE:

¾ cup vegetable stock

2 tablespoons finely diced onion

2 teaspoons finely minced garlic

½ teaspoon ground cumin

½ teaspoon ground coriander

½ teaspoon chili powder

⅛ teaspoon pepper

1 ½ teaspoons dry sherry

½ teaspoon sherry vinegar

1 tablespoon tomato paste

2 tablespoons finely chopped cilantro

TO ASSEMBLE:

2 ⅔ cups Pasta & Co. No-Oil-No-Salt-Added
    Marinara, purchased or made according to recipe
    on page 178

6 sheets fresh lasagne (or enough cooked dried lasagne
    noodles to make three layers in a 9-inch by 13-inch
    pan)

1 cup Quark (page 62)

2 ⅔ cups grated low-moisture part-skim mozzarella
    cheese

¼ cup freshly made bread crumbs (page 186)

◆ For the rice mixture, drain the beans, reserving the liquid. Measure ⅔ cup of the beans for the rice mixture and reserve. Save the remaining beans and the liquid for the bean sauce.

◆ Cook the rice according to package directions until tender. In a dry skillet, roast the cumin and coriander,

for more about
**PASTA & CO.
YELLOW LINE
DISHES**
turn to page xv.

taking care not to burn them. Mix hot spices with cooked rice, stir in salt and pepper, and let cool. Stir in corn, vegetable stock, Anaheim peppers, chiles, cilantro, and reserved ⅔ cup black beans. Set aside.

♦ For the bean sauce, place 2 tablespoons of the vegetable stock in a saucepan. Add onion, garlic, cumin, coriander, chili powder, pepper, sherry, and sherry vinegar. Simmer for 3 minutes. Add tomato paste and the remaining black beans and their liquid and cook for another 8 minutes. Remove from heat. Place bean mixture in the work bowl of a food processor equipped with a steel blade. Process until almost smooth, leaving some pieces of bean intact. Add the remaining vegetable stock and cilantro. Reserve.

♦ To assemble, spread ⅔ cup of the marinara sauce in the bottom of a shallow 9-inch by 13-inch baking dish. Cover with one layer of uncooked fresh lasagne (or cooked dried) noodles. Spoon on half (about 2 cups) of the rice mixture and ¾ cup of the bean sauce. Top with ½ cup of the Quark and 1 ¼ cups of the mozzarella. Cover with another layer of lasagne noodles and 1 cup of marinara sauce. Follow with the same amounts of rice, black bean sauce, Quark, and mozzarella as before. Top with the last layer of noodles and press lightly with fingertips to distribute ingredients evenly in the layers. Top with the last cup of marinara sauce, the remaining mozzarella, and the bread crumbs.

♦ Preheat oven to 400° F. Bake lasagne for 35 minutes, or until sauce bubbles around the edge and top is nicely browned. If top browns too quickly, cover with aluminum foil during last 10 minutes of cooking. If baking the lasagne straight from the freezer, add about 20 minutes to cooking time. Once out of the oven, let lasagne set up for approximately 15 to 20 minutes before cutting (this is critical for ease of serving).

Serves 6 to 8

No-Oil-No-Salt-Added
Marinara Sauce

As much as most of us like our tomato sauce perfumed with extra virgin olive oil, we have all come to appreciate how good and how useful a tomato sauce made with no oil can be. For instance, we use this sauce to make both of our Yellow Line frozen entrées—Skinnystrada (page 143) and Black Bean Lasagne (page 175). And, of course, we recommend it simply for tossing with hot cooked pasta.

This is definitely a recipe where the quality of your canned tomatoes shows. The best-quality ones we have found are the San Marzano brand (see this page). Especially when this sauce is served alone on cooked pasta, the superior flavor of the San Marzano tomatoes helps to make up for the lack of olive oil in the recipe.

PREPARE-AHEAD NOTES:

Like nearly all tomato sauces, this one keeps well for days in the refrigerator and freezes without a flaw for months. Since this recipe makes enough to coat 1½ pounds of pasta (six average adult servings), you may want to tuck some of it away in the freezer. Or, since the sauce doubles without any problems, you may want to make an even bigger batch and really stock your freezer.

SERVING SUGGESTIONS:

Allow a generous cup of this sauce for every ½ pound of fresh pasta or ⅓ pound (5 ounces) of dried pasta—that's an average main course serving for two.

Product Spotlight: San Marzano Tomatoes

Given the poor quality of commercially available fresh tomatoes, good-quality canned ones are often superior for cooking. The best we have found are the San Marzano tomatoes. They are a premium-priced, domestically grown clone of an Italian tomato, available in 28-ounce cans at Pasta & Co. stores and some supermarkets.

When to use the higher-priced, sweet, fresh-tasting San Marzano tomatoes? When their superior flavor is going to show: sliced on a pizza, served (in place of fresh tomatoes) with fresh mozzarella, or for making light-textured soups and sauces where your first choice would be a garden-ripe tomato. Use less-expensive canned tomatoes when tomato solids are important and strong-flavored accompanying ingredients mask the acidic tomato taste, as with robust pasta sauces. We especially like Paradiso and DiNola brand tomatoes when not using San Marzano.

> 2 ¼ cups dry white wine
> 1 teaspoon dried basil
> 1 teaspoon dried oregano
> ¼ teaspoon dried red pepper flakes
> 5 cloves garlic, peeled and put through a press
> 1 can (28 ounces) tomatoes (we suggest San Marzano
>   brand, finely chopped with all juices, or Paradiso
>   or DiNola brand, crushed in purée)

◆ Place the wine, basil, oregano, pepper flakes, and garlic in a heavy 2-quart saucepan. Simmer for 10 to 12 minutes, or until all the alcohol from the wine has evaporated. Add tomatoes. Simmer, partially covered, over low heat for about 20 minutes, stirring occasionally.

Makes 3 ½ cups (enough for 1 ½ pounds fresh pasta or 1 pound dried pasta, 6 average main course servings)

Basic Marinara Sauce

When you want the olive oil, this is our classic marinara sauce—the same that we sell both fresh and in jars.

PREPARE-AHEAD NOTES
AND SERVING SUGGESTIONS:

The same as for the No-Oil-No-Salt-Added Marinara Sauce, page 178.

INGREDIENTS:

3 tablespoons best-quality extra virgin olive oil
¾ teaspoon dried basil
¾ teaspoon dried oregano
¼ teaspoon dried red pepper flakes
2 cloves garlic, peeled and finely minced or put through a press
2 cups dry white wine
1 can (28 ounces) tomatoes (we suggest San Marzano brand, finely chopped with all juices, or Paradiso or DiNola brand, crushed in purée)
½ teaspoon salt, or to taste
Optional: ½ teaspoon sugar

♦ In a heavy 2-quart saucepan over medium heat, sauté basil, oregano, red pepper flakes, and garlic in olive oil for 1 to 2 minutes. Be careful not to brown the garlic. Add wine and simmer for 10 to 12 minutes, or until all the alcohol has evaporated.

♦ Add tomatoes. Simmer, partially covered, over low heat for about 20 minutes, stirring occasionally.

♦ Taste the sauce, and add salt to taste.

♦ Stir sauce and taste again. Now you must make a decision about the sugar. The amount needed will depend upon the residual sugars in the wine you have used. With a very dry California chablis, we use ½ teaspoon sugar to mellow the acidity of the tomatoes and round out the flavor of the sauce. Stir and simmer 1 to 2 minutes longer.

Makes 4 cups (enough for 1 ½ pounds fresh pasta or 1 pound dried pasta, 6 main course servings)

Lentil Sauce

For a big-flavored, vegetarian, low-fat pasta sauce, this one can't be beat. Lentils lend texture and nonfat yogurt cheese fools the palate into thinking that there is something rich and creamy in this sauce, which contains only 4 grams of fat per 1-cup serving.

PREPARE-AHEAD NOTES:

The sauce can be prepared several days ahead of serving and reheated. It also freezes well. Be sure to allow a day for making the yogurt cheese.

SERVING SUGGESTION:

If you're not watching fat, serve the pasta topped with grated Parmesan or crumbled goat cheese.

INGREDIENTS:

2 ¾ cups vegetable or defatted chicken stock, more if needed
1 cup diced yellow onion (½-inch dice)
1 ½ tablespoons finely chopped garlic
⅓ cup uncooked brown lentils (do not use French green lentils), washed and picked over for foreign matter
1 cup canned tomatoes, cut into ¼-inch pieces, with their juice (Paradiso or DiNola brand is a good choice)
1 jalapeño pepper, cored, seeded, and finely chopped
1 ½ teaspoons Pasta & Co. House Herbs (page 166)
1 teaspoon ground cumin
¾ teaspoon salt
¼ teaspoon sweet paprika
Pinch dried red pepper flakes
½ cup peeled, grated carrot
½ cup diced green bell pepper (¼-inch dice)

for more about
**PASTA & CO.
YELLOW LINE
DISHES**
turn to page xv.

2 teaspoons balsamic vinegar
½ cup Nonfat Yogurt Cheese (page 6)
2 tablespoons finely chopped fresh mint
2 tablespoons finely chopped fresh parsley

♦ In a large saucepan, bring 2 cups of the stock, onion, garlic, and lentils to a boil. Cook over medium heat for about 10 minutes. Add tomatoes, jalapeño pepper, herbs, cumin, salt, paprika, and red pepper flakes. Cook over medium heat for another 20 minutes or until lentils are tender. If the lentils become dry, add extra stock.
♦ When the lentils have cooked, stir in the carrots, bell pepper, and balsamic vinegar. Remove from heat. Add Nonfat Yogurt Cheese and the remaining ¾ cup stock and stir until smooth. Add mint and parsley. Taste for seasoning.

Makes 3 cups (enough for 1 pound of fresh pasta or ⅔ pound (11 ounces) dried pasta)

Oven-Roasted Eggplant Sauce

I**f fat watching is not a priority, toss this sauce with rigatoni and cubes of fresh mozzarella cheese. And note that this is more than just a sauce for pasta. It's splendid to serve with beef, chicken, or fish and also makes a great topping for a baked potato.**

PREPARE-AHEAD NOTES:

This sauce keeps well in the refrigerator for a week and rewarms beautifully. Surprisingly for eggplant, it even freezes fine.

SERVING SUGGESTION:

Allow 2 cups sauce to adequately coat ½ pound of fresh pasta or ⅓ pound (5 ounces) of dried pasta—two average main course servings.

Oven-Roasted Wonders

We have found that oven-roasted vegetables develop splendidly intense flavors (see Oven-Roasted Vegetables on page 165 and Oven-Roasted Eggplant Salad on page 120). We hoped that these kinds of flavors would produce pasta sauces with minimum fat. So far, we have had mixed results. The Oven-Roasted Eggplant Sauce (this page) uses only a small amount of fat to yield a marvelous-tasting, great-selling pasta sauce. On the other hand, when the primary ingredient is something as "plain" as the common onion (Oven-Roasted Onion Sauce, page 184), we resort to using generous amounts of high-fat ingredients to meet taste criteria. Introducing more complex flavors in the Oven-Roasted Onion and Fennel Sauce, page 185, permits high-fat and low-fat versions that both make for fine eating. So it goes with our efforts to limit use of fat in our recipes. Sometimes we are successful; sometimes, we are not. Good taste remains the first criteria.

Recommendations for Oven-Roasting:

◆ The sauces mentioned above cook relatively unattended and wait patiently to be rewarmed and tossed with pasta. This is fine winter cooking when the smell of foods roasting in the oven can warm an entire house.

◆ If you double these oven-roasted recipes for great large-group food, be careful not to crowd the vegetables or they will not brown sufficiently. You can use two 9-inch by 13-inch pans, either side by side on the upper shelf or each in its own oven (if you have two ovens) on the upper shelf. Or, use a shallow pan large enough to hold a double recipe.

INGREDIENTS:

¼ cup extra virgin olive oil

2 cans (28 ounces each) whole pear tomatoes (such as San Marzano, Paradiso, or DiNola brand)

1 large eggplant (about 1 ½ pounds), stem end cut off and eggplant cut into cubes no larger than 1 inch

1 large yellow onion, peeled and cut into ½-inch dice (about 2 cups)

1 tablespoon finely minced garlic

2 teaspoons Pasta & Co. House Herbs (page 166), or your choice of dried or fresh herbs

2 bay leaves

1 teaspoon salt

1 teaspoon dark brown sugar, preferably Billington's Premium Dark Brown (page 185)

¼ cup vegetable stock or chicken stock

¼ cup capers, rinsed and well drained

Freshly cracked black pepper to taste

¼ cup finely chopped parsley

◆ Preheat oven to 450° F. Pour the olive oil and one of the cans of tomatoes (broken into coarse chunks and including all juices) into a large, shallow baking pan, such as a 9-inch by 13-inch pan. Stir in the eggplant, onion, garlic, dried herbs (if using fresh herbs, they'll lend more flavor if added immediately before serving), bay leaves, and salt. Top with the brown sugar. Place on upper rack of preheated oven. Roast, stirring at least once midway through cooking time, until eggplant and onions are browned, about 30 minutes. Stir in the second can of tomatoes (breaking them up as before), the stock, and the capers. Lower oven temperature to 300° F and cook another 30 minutes, stirring now and then to keep the vegetables moist. When eggplant is very tender (not rubbery), remove sauce from oven. Taste for seasoning, adding freshly ground pepper to taste. Stir in parsley.

Makes 8 heaping cups (enough to generously coat 2 pounds of fresh pasta or 1 ⅓ pounds of dried pasta— 8 main course servings)

Oven-Roasted Onion Sauce

*T*his sauce tossed with pasta makes a delicious side dish, especially alongside grilled meat. For a contrast to its onion-soup brown, serve it with a bright-colored vegetable— sliced vine-ripened red or yellow tomatoes or blanched sugar snap peas or green beans. Combine the sauce with a short, curly pasta, such as rotini or Pasta & Co. pescine or ripples.

PREPARE-AHEAD NOTES:

The sauce can be stored refrigerated for several days or frozen for weeks.

INGREDIENTS:

> 1 tablespoon extra virgin olive oil
> 3 ounces pancetta, cut into ¼-inch dice (see this page)
> 4 medium yellow onions, peeled and cut into ¼-inch crescents (page 22)
> 4 cloves garlic, peeled and finely minced or put through a press
> 1 teaspoon salt
> ½ teaspoon dried thyme
> 1 heaping tablespoon dark brown sugar, preferably Billington's Premium Dark Brown (page 185)
> 2 cups beef stock
> 2 teaspoons balsamic vinegar
> ½ cup heavy cream

♦ Preheat oven to 425° F. Place olive oil and pancetta in a shallow roasting pan (a 9-inch by 13-inch size works fine). Roast on top rack of oven until pancetta is just golden (not brown, about 5 minutes). Add onions, garlic, salt, and thyme. Top with sugar. (Your pan will appear very full. Do not be concerned; the onions cook down quickly.) Roast for 5 minutes. Lower heat to 325° F and continue roasting for 30 minutes, stirring every 10 minutes. At the end of this time, the onions should be very

Pancetta

*P*ancetta is a rolled and dry-cured Italian-style bacon. It comes in a cylinder about 4 inches in diameter. The fat should be very white and the meat rosy pink to deep red. We recommend purchasing it thinly sliced and storing it in an air-tight bag in your freezer. When you want to use it, remove from freezer and slice or mince while still partially frozen (once thawed, it is difficult to cut because it is so slippery). Any extra amount can be refrozen without discernible harm.

Today's health concerns somewhat limit our use of pancetta. However, its value as a flavoring agent should not be overlooked. In some dishes, it is simply irreplaceable. The closest substitute is bacon that has been simmered in water for 10 minutes, rinsed, and dried before being used in a recipe.

dark golden brown. Add the beef stock and the balsamic vinegar. Roast for another 45 minutes.

♦ While the sauce is finishing roasting, bring the cream to a boil, and boil until reduced to ¼ cup. When the sauce is done, remove from oven and stir in the hot cream. Taste for seasonings.

Makes 5 cups (enough to generously coat 2 pounds of fresh pasta or 1 ⅓ pounds of dried pasta—8 main course servings)

Oven-Roasted Onion and Fennel Sauce

I n this sauce, which is similar to the Oven-Roasted Onion Sauce on page 184, we introduce the more complex taste and texture of fresh fennel plus the flavor of demi-glace and yellow raisins. Voila! We eliminate the need for some of the fat (there is none of the cream that is in the Oven-Roasted Onion Sauce). If you must have an even lower-fat sauce, eliminate the pancetta (see the lower-fat version at end of the recipe).

Pasta & Co. stores sell a shelf-stable demi-glace called Demi-Glace Gold. If you cannot locate demi-glace, you can substitute 2 ½ cups chicken or beef stock that you have boiled until reduced to 1 ¼ cups. If you use this substitute, it could be very salty, so you may want to reduce or eliminate the salt called for in the recipe.

PREPARE-AHEAD NOTES:

The sauce can be stored, refrigerated, for several days or frozen for weeks.

While pasta with Oven-Roasted Onion and Fennel Sauce can be served as an entrée accompanied by nothing more than a blanched vegetable, it is best as a side dish to roasted or grilled meats and a vegetable. Choose a short pasta with lots of ridges, such as Pasta & Co. ripples. Serve topped with either grated Parmesan or toasted bread crumbs (see this page).

INGREDIENTS:

> 1 tablespoon extra virgin olive oil
> 3 ounces pancetta, cut into ¼-inch dice (page 184)
> 1 large onion (about ¾ pound trimmed), peeled and
>   cut into ¼-inch-thick crescents (page 22)
> 1 small bulb fennel, trimmed of all stalks and leaves,
>   bulb cut in half lengthwise and then cut crosswise
>   into ¼-inch-thick slices
> 3 cloves garlic, peeled and finely minced
> 1 teaspoon salt
> ½ teaspoon dried thyme
> 1 tablespoon dark brown sugar, preferably Billington's
>   Premium Dark Brown (page 185)
> 1 tablespoon demi-glace, such as Demi-Glace Gold
>   (see page 41)
> 1 ¼ cups boiling water
> 2 teaspoons balsamic vinegar
> ¼ cup yellow raisins, plumped in boiling water

♦ Preheat oven to 425° F. Place olive oil and pancetta in a shallow baking dish (a 9-inch by 13-inch size works fine). Roast on top rack of oven until pancetta is just golden (not brown), about 5 minutes. Add the onion, fennel, garlic, salt (unless you will be substituting reduced stock for the demi-glace), and thyme. Top with the sugar. Roast for 10 minutes, stirring a couple of times to prevent burning. Lower temperature to 325° F and roast for 30 minutes more, stirring occasionally.

A Low-Fat Pasta Topping: Dry-Toasted Bread Crumbs

Try using homemade bread crumbs instead of cheese to top pasta dishes. Not only do you save fat (1 tablespoon of grated Parmesan contains 1.88 grams of fat, while 1 tablespoon of dry bread crumbs contains .28 grams), but the taste and texture can actually be superior to the much more fat-dense cheese. What is more, the crumbs are a great way to use up stale bread.

To make bread crumbs:

♦ Lightly toast several slices of leftover good-quality, coarse-textured bread, with or without crusts. Break toasted bread into small pieces and place in work bowl of a food processor equipped with a steel blade. Process just until coarsely ground and fluffy. Store any extra crumbs in the freezer. To use, simply warm in a nonstick sauté pan over medium heat until crumbs are crisp.

Even better, make garlic bread crumbs:

◆ For every 2 cups of bread pieces above, add 1 to 2 peeled garlic cloves to the food processor. Process until garlic is chopped very fine and incorporated into the bread crumbs. In rewarming, be careful not to burn the garlic.

◆ Dissolve the demi-glace in the boiling water. Add balsamic vinegar to the demi-glace and pour mixture over the onions. Drain the raisins and add to the sauce. Roast another 40 minutes, or until vegetables are very soft and mixture is thick and syrupy. Taste for seasoning. If sauce is too thick, thin with a bit of water.

Makes about 3 cups (enough to generously coat 1 ¼ pounds of fresh pasta or 1 pound of dried pasta—5 main course servings, or 8 side dish servings)

LOWER-FAT VERSION OF OVEN-ROASTED ONION AND FENNEL SAUCE

◆ Totally eliminate the pancetta. Preheat the oven to 375° F.
◆ Place the tablespoon of olive oil in the shallow baking dish and toss with the onions, fennel, salt, and thyme. Top with the sugar. Roast for 40 minutes, stirring every 15 minutes until the vegetables are well browned. Add the garlic, the demi-glace dissolved in water, and the balsamic vinegar. Lower heat to 325° F and roast for another 40 minutes, or until vegetables are very soft and mixture is thick and syrupy.

Tortellini Sauce

This is one of our most popular pasta sauces. We have recently cut back on the fat, though the sauce still remains deliciously rich. The recipe originally was made only with heavy cream. Now we make it with equal parts cream and half-and-half. It used to call for ⅓ cup olive oil to ¼ cup chicken stock; now we use 2 tablespoons oil and ⅓ cup chicken stock. At this point, we stopped because we did not want to tamper further with a very successful product. In short, we reached our "fat point" (see this page) on this recipe. Fat point, however, is a matter of personal preference. You might well want to cut the fat even more, perhaps replacing another tablespoon of olive oil with a tablespoon of stock, or replacing the cream completely with half-and-half. To compensate, thicken the sauce with a bit more tomato paste. You still will not have a truly low-fat sauce, but you will be eating less fat than if you had used the original recipe.

PREPARE-AHEAD NOTES:

The sauce can be doubled and stored refrigerated for several days or frozen. Just gently reheat.

SERVING SUGGESTIONS:

As its name suggests, this sauce was originally meant to be used with tortellini. It is also excellent over fresh fettuccine noodles, topped with capers, chopped parsley, and a dusting of freshly grated Parmesan cheese. Want it with shellfish? Use clam juice or fish stock in place of the chicken stock.

INGREDIENTS:

> ¼ cup plus 2 tablespoons dry white wine
> ⅓ cup defatted chicken or vegetable stock
> 1 tablespoon tomato paste
> 2 tablespoons extra virgin olive oil

The Fat Point

In our experience at Pasta & Co., almost every recipe can tolerate some fat-trimming without compromising taste. Think in terms of every recipe having a "fat point"—the point where there is just enough fat for your personal taste. Some dishes taste good lean; others need to be deliciously full of fat. You are the best judge.

A Splendid Pasta Accompaniment: Blanched Kale

K ale is more than the leafy green garnish you see overused in delis. In fact, it's a marvelous green to accompany pasta dishes or grilled meats. It cooks up sturdier than spinach and other bitter greens, and its ruffly edges promise a good-looking presentation. Cut in a chiffonade and prepare according to the directions on page 114. Once the kale has had its color set with ice water and is well drained, it can be rewarmed with a little olive oil, salt, pepper, and a tiny dash of vinegar (too much and you lose the good color) and served as a vegetable side dish.

3 medium cloves garlic, peeled and put through
    a press
¼ to ½ teaspoon salt (depending upon saltiness of
    stock)
2 grinds black pepper
¾ cup half-and-half
¾ cup heavy cream
1 tablespoon finely chopped parsley

◆ Whisk together wine, stock, and tomato paste until well blended. Set aside. Place olive oil and garlic in a large sauté pan over medium heat. When oil begins to bubble and garlic barely begins to brown (be careful not to burn the garlic), pour in wine mixture all at once. (If you drizzle it in, you may be spattered with hot oil.) Add salt and pepper. Bring to a steady simmer and cook until mixture has reduced by almost half, about 5 minutes.
◆ In a measuring cup, combine half-and-half and heavy cream. Gradually whisk this mixture into the sauce. Continuing to stir, simmer the sauce until it thickens, about 5 minutes. Stir in 1 tablespoon parsley.

Makes about 1 ⅔ cups sauce, enough to generously coat 1 pound of fresh pasta or ⅔ pound dried pasta (4 main course servings), or to generously coat 2 pounds of fresh tortellini (6 to 8 main course servings)

Pasta with Caprisi Sauce

T his quick-and-easy dish abounds wih the classic Italian taste of vine-ripened tomatoes, garlic, and olive oil, except this sauce uses canned tomatoes. Surprisingly, generous jolts of anchovy (though optional), vinegar, and garlic, combined with the fact that you do not further cook the tomatoes, create an amazingly close facsimile to a fresh tomato sauce. And, of course, with canned tomatoes, you can have *this "fresh" tomato sauce all year long.*

For the best taste, prepare this sauce with the best-quality ingredients you have. Use your best extra virgin olive oil. San Marzano tomatoes (page 178) are the best, but most good-quality Italian-style canned tomatoes work well. Adding the optional fresh mozzarella gives the sauce pleasing substance as the cheese melts against the hot pasta. Substituting fresh herbs, such as basil, for the dried also enhances the sauce. If you do so, triple the quantity of herbs.

PREPARE-AHEAD NOTES:

The sauce can be made several days ahead of serving. Bring to room temperature before tossing with hot pasta.

INGREDIENTS:

1 can (28 ounces) San Marzano or other Italian-style canned tomatoes
3 tablespoons best-quality extra virgin olive oil
Optional, but strongly recommended: 4 good-quality anchovy fillets, rinsed and finely minced (we prefer either Bel Aria or Rusticella brand)
½ tablespoon finely minced garlic
¼ cup finely chopped parsley
1 ½ teaspoons red wine vinegar
½ teaspoon salt
½ teaspoon dried basil
¼ teaspoon Pasta & Co. House Herbs (page 166) other dried herbs of your choice
⅛ teaspoon dried red pepper flakes
Optional, but strongly recommended: 6 to 8 ounces mozzarella (fresh if available), cut coarsely into ¼-inch dice
1 tablespoon salt for pasta water
½ pound dried pasta or ⅔ pound fresh pasta

◆ Place tomatoes and juices into a large bowl. With a paring knife, roughly cut each tomato into ¼-inch slices (hold the tomato down in the bowl so juices don't squirt out).

For more pasta dishes that can be served either hot or at room temperature, see Room-Temperature Pastas (pages 61–80), especially White Truffle Oil on Cappellini (page 78), and other recipes in Room-Temperature Foods (pages 59–140), such as Pasta and Poquitos (page 83).

Exotic Oils

In addition to a bevy of premium extra virgin olive oils, there are also some specialty oils (we call them "exotic oils") that make for extravagant good cooking. Three that we have found especially worthy of attention are the Agribosca White Truffle Oil (page 78); V&R Porcini Oil from Murcia, Spain (see recipe this page); and unrefined, fresh walnut oil from Huilerie J. Leblanc in France's Loire Valley (page 192). Like "condiment" olive oils (page 75), these oils should not be heated, but simply added to hot foods after cooking. All three make delicious pasta dishes that can be eaten hot as soon as they are made or served later at room temperature. Note that there are many other brands of truffle, porcini, and walnut oil, but we have achieved the most stunning results using the three products just specified.

Like olive oil, these specialty oils need to be stored in a cool, dark place. In the case of truffle, porcini, and walnut oils, the refrigerator probably provides the best storage. Bring them back to room temperature before using.

♦ Stir in olive oil, optional anchovy fillets, garlic, parsley, vinegar, the ½ teaspoon salt, basil, herbs, red pepper flakes, and the optional mozzarella.

♦ Bring 6 quarts of water to a boil. Add the 1 tablespoon salt. When water returns to a boil, add pasta and cook until tender.

♦ Drain pasta thoroughly and toss with the tomato mixture, letting the heat of the pasta warm the sauce and partially melt the cheese. Serve immediately or let cool to room temperature.

Serves 4 as a main course

Orzo with Wild Mushrooms and Porcini Oil

This is a gorgeous pasta to serve as a side dish to any meat, from steak to sausage. It is especially good fall and winter eating. The V&R Porcini Oil is made by a special process that extracts the resins from porcini mushrooms and infuses the aroma into a mild-flavored olive oil. The flavor of this oil is so much more intense than other porcini-flavored oils that we think of it more as a flavoring than as an oil.

PREPARE-AHEAD NOTES:

The pasta can be left for an hour or two at room temperature in the sauce (any longer and you begin to lose the aromatic qualities of the porcini oil). Right before serving, re-toss with the sauce and top with the bread crumbs and chives.

1 tablespoon salt for pasta water

½ cup extra virgin olive oil (light-bodied)

1 cup shallots (about 5 shallots), peeled and finely chopped

8 ounces fresh chanterelles or other wild mushrooms, cleaned and thinly sliced

OR: *substitute 4 ounces dried wild mushrooms that have been reconstituted, then sliced or diced*

2 teaspoons finely chopped garlic

1 ½ teaspoons freshly squeezed lemon juice

⅔ pound dried orzo

¼ cup V&R Porcini Oil (one 2-ounce bottle)

½ teaspoon salt or to taste

Freshly ground black pepper to taste (preferably Pasta & Co. No. 4 Pepper Blend with Whole Allspice, page 53)

⅓ cup minced chives

TO TOP:

1 cup garlic bread crumbs (page 186)

♦ Bring 6 quarts of water and the tablespoon of salt to a boil. Meanwhile, heat olive oil in a large skillet (preferably nonstick), add shallots, and sauté over medium heat, stirring occasionally, until golden (about 5 minutes). Add mushrooms and garlic and sauté a couple of minutes until mushrooms are lightly browned. Toss with lemon juice and remove from heat. Cook orzo in the boiling salted water until tender—8 to 10 minutes. Drain and toss with the mushroom mixture over low heat. Remove from heat and toss with the porcini oil, salt, pepper, and chives. Top with bread crumbs and serve immediately or let cool to room temperature.

Serves 4 to 6 as a side dish

Pasta with Walnut Oil Sauce

For a variation on Orzo with Wild Mushrooms and Porcini Oil that has a distinctly different flavor but also makes a superb side dish pasta, omit the chanterelles and substitute ¼ cup walnut oil for the porcini oil; use either ⅔ pound dried orzo or 1 pound fresh fettuccine. Top with freshly grated Parmesan and a sprinkle of chopped, toasted walnuts.

For best results, use the best-quality walnut oil you can find. One possibility is the unrefined walnut oil from Huilerie J. Leblanc. Pasta & Co. has for years sold another very respectable French walnut oil (l'Olivier). It is about a third less costly than the Leblanc oil and it is good walnut oil. However, tasted next to the Leblanc oil, which is pressed only when an order arrives from the U.S. importer and is produced in much smaller quantities with a greater concentration of fresh nuts, the less expensive oil has only a fraction of the flavor and aroma. If you can obtain fresh walnut oil of the quality of Leblanc's, it truly does make for a superior dish.

READY-MADES

Like dressing in ready-to-wear clothing, successful cooking with ready-made foods involves clever touches to create a personal style with minimum time.

The next six recipes are examples of just that: top-notch cases of integrating off-the-shelf products into personal cooking to make stunning dishes in 30 minutes or less.

We include the recipes for our ready-made products (see pages 203–205) in case you are not able to purchase them. However, making these dishes from scratch does not make for quick cooking. The only redeeming feature is that all of them can be made at least a week ahead so that you have your own "ready-mades" waiting in your refrigerator for a spur-of-the-moment meal.

For other recipes featuring ready-made foods, see Easy Easy Risotto with Marinara Sauce (page 162), Endive Leaves Stuffed with Red Bread (page 17), Shrimp and Feta Bake (page 139), South American Soup (page 56), and Eggplant Wraps (page 157).

Hasty Tasty Fettuccine

WITH CHICKEN, SHIITAKE MUSHROOMS, SPINACH, AND ANCHO CHILE BUTTER

This dish comes from a highly successful series of classes called "Hasty Tasty" that we did in 1995. The garlic bread crumbs are a low-fat topping to a high-fat dish that piques both interest and flavor.

PREPARE-AHEAD NOTES:

The sauce can be prepared several hours ahead of serving. Just reheat and toss with the cooked pasta.

INGREDIENTS:

> 1 tablespoon salt for pasta water
>
> 6 tablespoons Pasta & Co. Ancho Chile Butter, pur-
> chased or made according to recipe on page 203
>
> 2 whole boneless, skinless chicken breasts, cut crosswise
> into bite-size pieces—about ¼ inch by 1 ¼ inch
>
> 6 ounces fresh shiitake mushrooms, wiped clean and
> cut into ¼-inch slices
>
> 1 pint Pasta & Co. Slim Alfredo Sauce, purchased or
> made according to recipe on page 204
>
> 1 pound fresh fettuccine
>
> 2 to 3 cups raw spinach leaves, cut into a ¼-inch
> chiffonade (page 132)
>
> Salt and freshly ground pepper to taste

TO TOP:

> 1 cup garlic bread crumbs (page 186)

♦ Bring 4 to 6 quarts of water and the salt to a boil. Meanwhile, in a large sauté pan, heat Ancho Chile Butter over medium-high heat. When butter sizzles, add chicken meat and cook quickly. Do not overcook chicken; it takes only a couple of minutes. As soon as chicken is browned, add mushrooms and cook another 2 minutes. Lower heat and fold in Alfredo sauce, stirring to incorporate any browned bits in the pan. Remove from heat.

♦ Cook the fettuccine in the boiling salted water until tender. Drain well and immediately toss with the sauce. Fold in spinach. Season to taste with salt and pepper. Spoon onto serving plates and top generously with the garlic bread crumbs.

Serves 4 as a main course

Great Pasta Dishes Are a Matter of Great Pairing

A basic truth about great pasta dishes is that they are perfect marriages of tastes, shapes, textures, and colors. The most obvious example is pairing pasta shape with sauce texture. However, there are other considerations. For instance:

◆ Chicken and other mild-flavored meats and fish, to be successful with pasta, need bold flavoring. Otherwise you're dealing with not one but two very neutral ingredients, and the results can be disappointingly bland. In the Hasty Tasty Fettuccine recipe (page 193), for instance, cooking the chicken breast meat in the Ancho Chile Butter (page 203) turns the chicken into a very complementary partner to the neutral pasta.

◆ The perfect mushroom for pasta dishes is the shiitake. It keeps its shape and texture better than the more common brown button mushroom, which easily becomes as soft and flavorless as the pasta itself.

◆ A chiffonade (page 132) of fresh spinach (or other green such as arugula or

Hasty Tasty Pasta Carbonara

Pasta & Co. is peopled with passionate cooks—not just in its kitchens but all through its ranks. This recipe comes from our corporate services manager, David Shuler, who taught the dish at our Hasty Tasty classes. David claims that he and his wife, Kelly (also a Pasta & Co. staffer), use this very quick means of getting dinner on the table at least twice a month. Taking advantage of prepared Alfredo sauce, the dish imitates the taste of the classic carbonara recipe, which traditionally calls for bacon and raw egg. Substituting pancetta for the bacon lends a more sophisticated taste, and adding the chiffonade of raw spinach produces a one-dish meal and is a good way of offsetting the intrinsic richness of the dish.

PREPARE AHEAD NOTES:

The sauce can be prepared a day or two ahead of serving. Cool and refrigerate. Gently reheat while you cook the pasta, assemble the dish, and serve.

INGREDIENTS:

1 tablespoon salt for pasta water
⅓ pound (5 ounces) thinly sliced and frozen pancetta (page 184)
¼ cup dry white wine
1 pint Pasta & Co. Slim Alfredo Sauce, purchased or made according to recipe on page 204
1 pound fresh rigatoni
4 cups raw spinach, cut into ¼-inch chiffonade (page 132)
¼ cup freshly grated Romano or Parmesan cheese

TO TOP:

2 tablespoons finely chopped parsley

♦ Bring 4 to 6 quarts of water and the tablespoon of salt to a boil. Meanwhile, remove pancetta from freezer and let soften for a few minutes. Cut it into ½-inch strips and place them in a skillet, spreading the strips out to separate them. (A nonstick skillet makes cleanup a snap, but a heavy skillet without a nonstick surface will provide more browning for the pancetta and thus more flavor for the sauce.) Place pan over medium heat and, stirring often, cook until pancetta is golden. Some smoking may occur, but do not let the pancetta burn. As the pieces become golden, remove them to a double layer of paper towels to drain.

♦ Remove all but 3 tablespoons of the pancetta drippings from the skillet. Return skillet to medium-low heat and add the wine. Simmer wine for 2 minutes, scraping loose any caramelized bits of pancetta. Add Alfredo sauce and stir to blend. Remove from heat.

♦ Cook the rigatoni in the boiling salted water until tender. Drain well and fold into the Alfredo mixture along with the spinach. Return mixture to low heat and simmer briefly. Fold in the cheese. Spoon pasta and sauce onto serving dishes and top with the parsley.

Serves 4 as a main course

napa cabbage) is one of the niftiest ways we know for composing dazzling pasta dishes. The spinach adds color, texture, and nutrition.

♦ A light sprinkling of a tiny mince of something brightly colored, such as parsley or chives or red or yellow bell pepper, is a dependable finishing touch to almost any plate of pasta. The visual improvement can be striking.

Mary's White Fish with Giardiniera Sauce and Pasta

Mary Neuschwanger has been a Pasta & Co. customer since the company began. This absolutely splendid dish is her quick and easy Friday night standby.

PREPARE AHEAD NOTES:

If time is at a premium, you can prepare the sauce and the fish early in the day up to the point of placing it in the oven. Cover and refrigerate. Go straight from the refrigerator into the oven and allow a little extra baking time. While the dish bakes, proceed with the pasta cooking.

INGREDIENTS:

1 tablespoon salt for pasta water
2 tablespoons capers, drained
Optional: ¼ cup pitted imported olives, quartered
1 pint Pasta & Co. Giardiniera Sauce, purchased or made according to recipe on page 205
1 tablespoon extra virgin olive oil
2 pieces halibut fillet or other firm white fish (about 1 pound)
½ teaspoon salt
Freshly ground black pepper to taste
½ pound fresh pasta (Pasta & Co. pescine is our choice), or ⅓ pound (5 ounces) dried pasta
2 tablespoons extra virgin olive oil

TO TOP:

2 tablespoons finely chopped parsley

◆ Preheat oven to 375° F. Bring 4 to 6 quarts of water and the tablespoon of salt to a boil. Meanwhile, stir capers and optional olives into Giardiniera Sauce and reserve. In a heavy ovenproof skillet (preferably nonstick), heat 1 tablespoon olive oil over high heat until almost smoking. Add halibut and reduce heat to medium high. Brown fish quickly on both sides. Sprinkle with salt and pepper. Pour Giardiniera Sauce mixture over fish and bake, uncovered, on middle rack of preheated oven for approximately 10 minutes, or until fish is barely cooked through.

◆ While fish bakes, cook pasta in boiling salted water until tender. Drain and toss with 1 tablespoon extra virgin olive oil. Distribute pasta between two serving plates. When fish is done, divide fish and sauce between the two plates of pasta. Drizzle remaining 1 tablespoon extra virgin olive oil over both servings and top with the parsley. Serve immediately.

Serves 2 as a main course

Pasta with Oven-Roasted Bell Pepper Cream Sauce

Combine Pasta & Co. Oven-Roasted Bell Peppers and all their delicious juices with pancetta, chicken stock, and cream for a brilliantly flavored pasta dish. Here again, you save time by using a ready-made ingredient.

PREPARE-AHEAD NOTES:

The sauce can be made several days before serving. Refrigerate, then gently reheat while you cook the pasta.

INGREDIENTS:

1 tablespoon salt for pasta water
8 ounces pancetta (page 184), thinly sliced and frozen
1 small yellow onion, peeled and coarsely chopped
1 tablespoon minced or pressed garlic
2 cups chicken stock
1 cup heavy cream
1 pound Pasta & Co. Oven-Roasted Bell Peppers, purchased or made according to the recipe on page 164 (you will need one batch)
1 ¼ pounds fresh fettuccine

TO TOP:

Freshly grated Parmesan cheese
¼ cup finely chopped parsley

♦ Bring 4 to 6 quarts of water and the tablespoon of salt to a boil. Meanwhile, remove pancetta from freezer and let soften for a few minutes. Cut it into ½-inch strips and place them in a skillet, spreading the strips out to separate them. (A nonstick skillet makes cleanup a snap, but a heavy skillet without a nonstick surface will provide more browning for the pancetta and thus more flavor for the sauce.) Place pan over medium heat and, stirring often,

Sporkits

Sporkits are long-handled utensils that are a cross between a spoon and a fork. No avid pasta cook should be without a pair; they are indispensable for tossing long pastas with sauce. Do not use them for filled pastas, however. Rather, use the largest rubber spatula you can obtain.

cook until pancetta is golden. Some smoking may occur, but do not let the pancetta burn. As the pieces become golden, remove them to a double layer of paper towels to drain.

♦ Drain off all but about a tablespoon of the drippings from the skillet. Add the onion and cook over medium heat until softened. Add the garlic and cook 1 minute more. Add stock and cream, raise heat, and bring to a boil, scraping loose any browned bits stuck to the pan. Let mixture boil about 5 minutes. Lower heat to a simmer and add reserved pancetta and roasted peppers, along with all their juices. Let cook over low heat while you cook the fettuccine in the boiling salted water. When fettuccine is tender, drain well and fold into the sauce. Serve immediately, topped with Parmesan and parsley.

Serves 6 as a main course

Pasta with Smoked Chicken and Shiitake Mushrooms

T*his is a hearty, one-dish-meal pasta that takes advantage of ready-made marinara sauce. You'll need nothing more than an appetizer, good wine, and a dessert to get top billing.*

PREPARE-AHEAD NOTES:

The sauce can be prepared a full day ahead, then reheated before tossing with the hot pasta and topping with the cheeses and arugula.

INGREDIENTS:

1 tablespoon salt for pasta water
¼ cup extra virgin olive oil
¼ cup finely minced shallots (about 2 large shallots)

⅓ pound smoked chicken or turkey breast, cut into
    thin strips about 2 inches long and ½ inch wide
¼ pound fresh shiitake mushrooms, trimmed and
    sliced
2 teaspoons finely minced garlic
1 teaspoon Pasta & Co. House Herbs (page 166)
    or your choice of dried herbs
1 jar (16 ounces) Pasta & Co. Marinara Sauce or 2
    cups homemade Basic Marinara Sauce (page 180)
¾ cup defatted chicken stock
¼ teaspoon salt
10 grinds black pepper
⅔ pound (11 ounces) dried penne or pappardelle
    noodles or 1 pound fresh pasta (fettuccine is a
    good choice)

TO TOP:

⅓ cup freshly grated Parmesan cheese
3 tablespoons goat cheese, such as Montrachet
1 heaping cup arugula, cut into a thin chiffonade
    (page 132) (if you do not like or cannot get
    arugula, use fresh spinach or skip the greens and
    just top each serving with minced parsley or chives)

◆ Bring 4 quarts water and the 1 tablespoon salt to a boil.
Meanwhile, heat olive oil in a large sauté pan over medium
heat. Add shallots and cook until softened. Raise heat to
medium high, add smoked chicken, and cook until it
begins to turn golden. Stir in mushrooms, garlic, and
herbs and cook just until mushrooms take on a little color,
stirring occasionally. Add marinara sauce, stock, ¼ teaspoon salt, and pepper. Heat to blend flavors. Remove
from heat and reserve.
◆ Cook pasta in the boiling salted water until tender.
Drain well and add to sauce in sauté pan, tossing to
mix. Reheat briefly, if necessary. Divide among four to six
plates, and top each portion with Parmesan, goat cheese,
and arugula.

Serves 4 to 6 as a main course

Salt-Packed Capers

For truest flavor and best texture, look for capers packed in salt as opposed to brine. Ironically, the packing salt affects the flavor of the caper less than the more common brine. Just rinse very well and use.

Salami Puttanesca

Using prepared marinara sauce makes this dish quick to prepare. Paper-thin slivers of good salami put a tasty spin on puttanesca sauce, the zesty pasta sauce named for Italian harlots, known as putane. You decide how much red pepper or anchovy to use—if any (we like lots). Note that because of the saltiness of the ingredients, we do not salt the pasta cooking water for this dish.

PREPARE-AHEAD NOTES:

The sauce can be prepared several days before serving. Refrigerate, then gently reheat while you cook the pasta.

INGREDIENTS:

⅓ cup extra virgin olive oil

¼ pound salami, very thinly sliced and cut into fine julienne (or if you like the sauce very spicy, use copa)

4 large cloves garlic, peeled and finely chopped

1 teaspoon dried oregano

⅛ teaspoon dried red pepper flakes, or to taste

1 jar (16 ounces) Pasta & Co. Marinara Sauce or 2 cups homemade Basic Marinara Sauce (page 180)

¼ cup niçoise olives, rinsed and well drained

¼ cup capers (see this page), rinsed and well drained

4 firm-textured anchovy fillets, well rinsed and coarsely chopped

⅓ cup finely chopped fresh parsley

1 ¼ pounds fresh fettuccine, or ¾ pound dried spaghetti

TO TOP:

Additional finely chopped parsley
Freshly grated Parmesan cheese

◆ Bring 4 to 6 quarts of water to a boil. Meanwhile, in a large sauté pan, heat the olive oil over medium-high heat, add the salami, and sauté about 3 minutes. Lower the heat to medium, add the garlic, oregano, and red pepper flakes, and cook until salami is slightly golden, being careful not to burn the garlic. Stir in marinara sauce, olives, capers, anchovies, and parsley. Simmer for a few minutes to blend flavors. Remove from heat.

◆ Cook pasta in the boiling salted water until tender. Drain well and toss with the heated sauce. Top with the additional parsley and Parmesan. Serve immediately.

Serves 4 to 5 as a main course

Ancho Chile Butter

The great thing about composed butters is that they keep so well and have so many uses. Let this butter, for example, hang around your refrigerator for a couple of months. Toss pasta with it. Make your next omelet with it. Sauté boneless chicken in it. Dollop some on a piece of grilled fish. Cook shrimp in it. Spread it on slices of a baguette, run them under the broiler, and serve as an appetizer that will bring guests back for more. And do not forget to melt some of the butter over a baked potato.

This particular butter—a staple for years at Pasta & Co. stores—uses the mild dried ancho chile pepper to give it a Southwest flavor and rich, rusty color.

PREPARE-AHEAD NOTES:

The butter will keep, refrigerated, for at least three months.

INGREDIENTS:

2 teaspoons vegetable oil

1 dried ancho chile

5 cloves garlic, unpeeled

1 teaspoon ground coriander

Heaping ¼ teaspoon salt

⅓ teaspoon chili powder

Zest of ½ lemon

1 pound salted butter, at room temperature

2 tablespoons finely chopped parsley

◆ Fill a small bowl with very hot tap water. Place oil in small skillet and set over medium-high heat. When oil barely begins to smoke, add chile and roast, turning until skin is soft and slightly puffed. Remove chile to the hot water and let soak for 30 minutes.

◆ In the same skillet, again over medium-high heat, roast garlic cloves, shaking the pan until skins are golden brown and shriveling. Remove from heat. When cloves are cool to the touch, squeeze garlic from skin and reserve.

◆ When the chile has finished soaking, drain, seed, and stem it. Place the chile and the garlic in the bowl of a food processor equipped with a steel blade. Add coriander, salt, chili powder, lemon zest, and one-fourth of the butter. Process until all ingredients are well puréed. Gradually add the rest of the butter and process until it is incorporated. Add parsley and process a second more just to fold in.

♦ Remove to a storage container and refrigerate or freeze to store. To use, melt the butter over low heat.

Makes 2 ½ cups

Slim Alfredo Sauce

Years ago, we substituted defatted chicken stock for 25 percent of the cream, butter, and cheese in our Alfredo Sauce and called it Slim Alfredo Sauce. The sauce is neither low fat nor Yellow Line, but it is a flavorful, lighter-textured alternative to the traditional Alfredo Sauce. This recipe makes enough to sauce up to 1 ½ pounds of filled pasta or 1 pound of unfilled pasta.

PREPARE-AHEAD NOTES:

This sauce reheats well. It also freezes well.

INGREDIENTS:

> 1 cup heavy cream
> ¾ cup chicken stock
> 3 tablespoons butter
> 3 grinds black pepper (preferably Pasta & Co. No. 4 Pepper Blend
>   with Whole Allspice, page 53)
> Pinch ground nutmeg
> ¾ cup freshly grated Parmesan cheese

♦ Place cream, stock, butter, black pepper, and nutmeg in a heavy 12-inch skillet (preferably nonstick). Bring mixture to a simmer. Let simmer 8 minutes, stirring occasionally. Remove pan from heat and whisk in Parmesan cheese.

Makes 2 cups

Giardiniera Sauce

This is the vegetarian red sauce that has been a daily favorite in our stores since shortly after Pasta & Co. opened for business. It is zesty. The vegetables are cut tiny and cooked crunchy.

PREPARE-AHEAD NOTES:

The recipe makes four times the amount you need for Mary's White Fish with Giardiniera Sauce (page 196), but if you make less you will have a lot of leftover vegetables. So use what you need and freeze the rest in pint containers.

INGREDIENTS:

⅓ cup extra virgin olive oil

6 cloves garlic, peeled and finely minced or put through a press

1 cup diced onion (¼-inch dice)

1 teaspoon dried basil

1 teaspoon dried oregano

½ bay leaf

½ to ¾ teaspoon dried red pepper flakes

1 ½ cups dry white wine

1 can (28 ounces) crushed tomatoes in purée (we use Paradiso or DiNola brand)

¼ cup tomato paste

1 ¼ cups diced cauliflower (¼-inch dice)

1 ¼ cups diced zucchini (¼-inch dice)

1 cup diced celery (¼-inch dice)

1 diced green bell pepper, cored (¼-inch dice)

1 cup diced carrots (¼-inch dice)

½ teaspoon salt

½ teaspoon sugar, or to taste

◆ In a 4-quart saucepan, combine olive oil, garlic, onion, basil, oregano, bay leaf, and red pepper flakes. Cook mixture over medium heat until onion is translucent. It should not brown. Stir to prevent garlic from burning. Add wine. Bring to a simmer. Simmer 10 to 12 minutes, uncovered, until alcohol evaporates. Add tomatoes, tomato paste, cauliflower, zucchini, celery, bell pepper, carrots, salt, and sugar. Simmer, partially covered, about 5 minutes. The vegetables should be crunchy.

Makes 8 cups

sweets

SIMPLY PUT, WE'VE NOT DARED ATTACK THE SUBJECT OF FAT IN OUR SWEETS. DESSERT RECIPES ARE A HOUSE OF CARDS WHEN IT COMES TO CUTTING FAT. GOOD RECIPES FOR CAKES, COOKIES, AND THE LIKE ARE SUCH A FINE BALANCE OF CHEMISTRIES THAT TO START SUBSTITUTING THIS FOR THAT IN THE INTEREST OF FAT GRAMS IS A MOST IMPOSING TASK. SOME GOOD WORK HAS BEEN DONE ON LOWER-FAT DESSERTS BY OTHERS. BOTH ALICE MEDRICH IN HER CHOCOLATE AND THE ART OF LOW-FAT DESSERTS AND NANCY BAGGETT IN HER DREAM DESSERTS HAVE PRODUCED INSPIRED DESSERTS WITH LESS FAT. OUR DESSERT RECIPES, ON THE OTHER HAND, ARE JUST DEPENDABLY GOOD SWEETS.

Santori: The Apple Cake Recipe Customers Beg For

L ura Throssel volunteered this family recipe years ago. Judy Birkland (who has been a part of Pasta & Co. since we opened our first store) claims it is the best thing we bake. Certainly, Santori is a hugely popular Pasta & Co. staple, as appropriate for a summer picnic as a winter feast. If you want to dress it up, serve it in a pool of caramel sauce with the proverbial dollop of whipped cream on top.

PREPARE-AHEAD NOTES:

The cake is very moist and stores well for at least a week, refrigerated.

INGREDIENTS:

> 3 cups sugar
> 1 tablespoon baking soda
> 1 ½ teaspoons ground cinnamon
> 1 ¼ teaspoons salt
> ¾ cup vegetable oil
> 3 eggs
> 1 ½ teaspoons vanilla extract
> 6 cups (approximately 4 apples) peeled, cored, and sliced tart cooking apples such as Granny Smith
> 1 ½ cups very coarsely chopped walnuts
> 3 cups flour

♦ Preheat oven to 325° F if using a metal pan; 300° F if using a glass one. Lightly butter a 9-inch by 13-inch shallow baking pan. (At the stores, we use a large commercial metal loaf pan, but when baking at home, we prefer the shallow pan, since it gives more surface for the delicious crust to form.)

♦ In a large bowl, combine sugar, baking soda, cinnamon, salt, oil, eggs, and vanilla. Mix well and stir in apples and walnuts until they are coated with batter. Stir in flour. Batter will be quite firm. Spoon into prepared pan.

♦ Bake in preheated oven for 1 hour and 20 minutes if using a metal pan, 1 hour and 30 minutes if using a glass pan. Check for doneness by inserting a toothpick. If batter clings to the toothpick, bake for up to another 20 minutes, checking every 10 minutes. When done, remove from oven and let cool on a rack before cutting into squares.

Makes one 9-inch by 13-inch cake

Fresh Ginger Gingerbread
WITH APRICOT SAUCE

There are some secrets in this recipe that turn typically plain-fare gingerbread into a striking dessert: the use of both fresh and candied ginger (adds piquancy), the touch of cocoa powder (deepens the flavor), and most of all, the crowning of the gingerbread with a warm apricot sauce (contributes an exquisitely unexpected taste).

Use the following tip for working with fresh ginger: freeze the whole knob of ginger. Peel the frozen ginger with a vegetable peeler. As the ginger begins to thaw and soften slightly, slice and then coarsely chop.

PREPARE-AHEAD NOTES:

The gingerbread keeps well for several days and can be rewarmed.

INGREDIENTS:

2-ounce knob fresh ginger, peeled and chopped (about 5 tablespoons)
2 tablespoons vegetable oil
1 egg

½ cup packed dark brown sugar, preferably
  Billington's Premium Dark Brown (page 185)
½ cup vegetable oil
¼ cup molasses
¼ cup dark Karo corn syrup
1 ounce candied ginger, finely minced
1 ½ cups flour
1 teaspoon baking soda
½ teaspoon ground cinnamon
2 teaspoons unsweetened cocoa powder
¼ teaspoon salt
½ cup buttermilk, at room temperature
Apricot Sauce (page 212)
Optional: barely sweetened, whipped cream

♦ Butter an 8-inch-square Pyrex pan. Set aside. Preheat oven to 350° F. Place fresh ginger and the 2 tablespoons of vegetable oil in food processor bowl equipped with a steel blade. Process until ginger is very finely minced. Reserve.

♦ In a 2-quart bowl, beat egg. Add sugar, the ½ cup vegetable oil, molasses, corn syrup, reserved ginger and oil mixture, and candied ginger. Mix with whisk until smooth. In another bowl, mix together flour, baking soda, cinnamon, cocoa powder, and salt. Mix half the dry mixture into the batter, add half the buttermilk, and repeat. When ingredients are well blended, pour into prepared pan. Bake in upper third of preheated oven for 35 to 40 minutes. Remove from oven and cool on a wire rack.

♦ Serve warm or at room temperature with the warm Apricot Sauce (page 212) and dollops of whipped cream if you wish.

Makes one 8-inch-square gingerbread

Apricot Sauce

Pasta & Co. Apricot Preserves are incomparable for spreading over hot toast. They also make an unbeatable sauce with the luxurious taste of fresh summer apricots all year long. You'll want this sauce for glazing fruit tarts (great for apple or cranberry holiday concoctions), for topping cheesecakes and pound cakes, for drizzling hot over bread pudding or fresh gingerbread, and for spooning over ice cream.

PREPARE-AHEAD NOTES:

Once made, the sauce will keep for a couple of months in the refrigerator—of course, it will never last that long (it's way too tempting late at night by the spoonful).

INGREDIENTS:

> 1 jar (10 ounces) Pasta & Co. Apricot Preserves (or 1 scant cup of the best quality apricot preserves you have)
>
> 2 tablespoons dry white wine (or even better, a late-harvest Riesling, Sauternes, or other sweet dessert wine)
>
> 1 teaspoon vanilla extract, preferably Tahitian
>
> 2 tablespoons freshly squeezed lemon juice, more if needed

♦ Combine all ingredients in a small saucepan over low heat. Stir occasionally, mashing the apricot pieces against the side of the pan while heating. After about 15 minutes, when flavors are blended, remove from heat. At this point, the sauce will be thick with apricot pieces. If you desire a finer-textured sauce, briefly purée mixture in food processor equipped with steel blade. Do not over-process.

A Sweet Idea

Do beautiful desserts sometimes seem too daunting? With a little advance preparation, the final course is still replete with fun and easy possiblities. Days before company is scheduled to arrive, make Apricot Sauce (this page) and Two-Cherries Jubilee Sauce (page 222). The day of the gathering, pre-scoop and refreeze an assortment of your favorite ice cream flavors. Your lavish dessert is simply make-your-own ice cream sundaes, with intriguing jewel-toned sauces from your own kitchen. Anyone lucky enough to be invited is sure to be charmed.

♦ Taste for flavor. Sauce should be pleasantly tart; add more lemon juice if necessary. Store covered and refrigerated.

Makes about 1 ½ cups

The Chocolate Cupcake

We bake dozens of these cupcakes every day in our stores. They are a classic "black bottom" cream cheese concoction. The frosting we use is on page 214.

PREPARE-AHEAD NOTES:

The cream cheese filling makes these cakes nice and moist so that they keep well for two or three days. On warm days, you will want to keep the frosted cakes cool—even refrigerated—since the frosting softens readily.

CUPCAKES:

1 ½ cups flour
1 cup plus 2 tablespoons sugar
¼ cup unsweetened cocoa powder
1 teaspoon baking soda
½ teaspoon salt
1 cup lukewarm water
⅓ cup vegetable oil
2 ¼ teaspoons distilled vinegar
2 teaspoons vanilla extract

CREAM CHEESE FILLING:

1 package (8 ounces) cream cheese, softened
½ cup sugar
1 egg
1 teaspoon vanilla extract

♦ Preheat oven to 350° F.

♦ For the cupcakes, sift flour, sugar, cocoa, baking soda, and salt together into a large mixing bowl. In a separate bowl whisk together water, oil, vinegar, and the 2 teaspoons vanilla. Add liquid mixture to dry mixture, whisking to combine thoroughly without overmixing.

♦ For the filling, with an electric mixer, combine cream cheese and sugar until very smooth. Beat in the egg, scrape down sides of bowl, and add the 1 teaspoon vanilla. Continue to mix until very smooth.

♦ Place paper liners in cupcake pans. Fill each liner a little more than half full with the chocolate batter. Spoon a heaping tablespoon of filling onto each cup of chocolate batter.

♦ Bake in preheated oven for 25 to 30 minutes, or until puffed and resilient to the touch. Let cool completely in pans before removing. Frost with Chocolate Frosting (below).

Makes 12 cupcakes

Chocolate Frosting

Y*ou will prize this Chocolate Frosting recipe, which makes a satiny ganache to enhance almost any cake or torte.*

PREPARE AHEAD NOTES:

The frosting can be made and stored in the refrigerator for at least a couple of weeks, or it can be frozen. The recipe makes about 4 cups—well more than you will need for frosting the 12 cupcakes in the previous recipe. If you do not want a stash of frosting, cut the recipe in half. Allow refrigerated frosting to return to room temperature before using.

½ pound bittersweet chocolate

¾ cup plus 1 tablespoon salted butter

1 teaspoon espresso powder dissolved in 1 tablespoon hot water

2 teaspoons vanilla extract

2 teaspoons rum

1 ½ cups sifted powdered sugar (measure after sifting)

3 tablespoons unsweetened cocoa powder

½ cup plus 2 tablespoons salted butter

1 cup heavy cream

♦ Chop chocolate into small chunks on a clean cutting board. Place the chocolate and the ¾ cup plus 1 tablespoon butter in a medium-size stainless steel bowl. Place the bowl over a saucepan with about 3 inches of hot water in it. (Or use a double boiler.) Place saucepan over medium heat.

♦ Watch closely, whisking chocolate and butter together as they soften. As soon as they are melted and combined, remove from heat and stir in espresso, vanilla, and rum. Let cool to room temperature.

♦ Sift together the sifted powdered sugar and the cocoa.

♦ Place the ½ cup plus 2 tablespoons butter and half the cocoa/powdered sugar mixture in work bowl of food processor equipped with steel blade. Process, scraping down sides of work bowl with a rubber spatula. Add the rest of the cocoa/powdered sugar mixture and gradually add the cream, processing for about 10 seconds.

♦ Making sure the melted chocolate/espresso mixture is at room temperature, combine with the butter/cocoa mixture, whisking all together in a large bowl until thoroughly combined. Use immediately or refrigerate.

♦ To frost cupcakes, the frosting needs to be at room temperature. If it has been refrigerated or frozen, you may need to stir it until it returns to its original shiny, smooth consistency. Place a large dollop (2 heaping tablespoons) of frosting on each cupcake and spread over the top.

Makes about 4 cups frosting

White on White Cakes

Made into either a couple dozen cupcakes or two single-layer cakes, this is one of the most versatile, dependable cake recipes we know. We use it for the white cupcakes we sell daily, frosting them with the Cream Cheese Frosting that follows. The preceding Chocolate Frosting is another good choice. You can also leave the cakes unfrosted—they make a perfect foil for seasonal fruits and are great picnic fare.

You can buy almond paste, which is made of finely ground almonds and sugar, at most grocery stores. You will probably have an odd amount left. Almond paste freezes well, so just tuck it away for your next batch of cakes.

PREPARE-AHEAD NOTES:

The cakes keep very well for several days and also can be frozen.

INGREDIENTS:

> 1 ⅓ cups sugar
> 1 cup packed (about 10 ounces) almond paste, at room temperature
> 1 ⅓ cups salted butter, at room temperature
> 6 eggs, at room temperature
> ½ teaspoon vanilla extract
> 1 ⅓ cups unsifted all-purpose flour
> 1 teaspoon baking powder

♦ Preheat oven to 350° F.
♦ Place sugar in the work bowl of a food processor equipped with a steel blade. Break almond paste into rough chunks and add to work bowl. Process until almond paste and sugar are thoroughly combined (a couple of minutes). Add butter 2 tablespoons or so at a time, processing until mixture is smooth, scraping sides of work bowl with a spatula several times. Then add eggs, one at a

The Dessert Buffet: Entertaining Made Easy

When there is little time to cook, a dazzling way to fete guests is the dessert buffet. Assemble a bounty of desserts—homemade or purchased—and present them with your best serving pieces (your own, borrowed, or even rented). Confections of all sorts, from cakes to cookies, pies to puddings, make stunning still-life presentations, especially when surrounded by fresh fruit, flowers, and, if suitable, candlelight (the warm glow flatters food and minimizes the need for dusting). The idea works well for groups large and small, implying great indulgence, when, in fact, assembling the buffet may have been less work (and perhaps more fun) than doing a simple dinner for four. Remember that many desserts lend themselves to prepare-ahead cooking—avoid those that do not.

time, processing until each is incorporated. Add vanilla and process very briefly to combine.

♦ In a separate bowl, mix together flour and baking powder. Add to the batter in the food processor and process until well blended, being careful not to overprocess. You will need to scrape the sides of the work bowl once or twice.

♦ Place paper liners in cupcake pans, or line two 8- or 9-inch cake pans with foil. Fill each liner two-thirds full with the batter (about ⅓ cup per liner—do not overfill), or distribute the batter evenly between the two cake pans. Bake in upper third of the preheated oven for approximately 25 minutes for cupcakes; 50 to 60 minutes for layer cakes. Test for doneness by touching the middle of a cake. If the cake is firm to the touch and springs back with no indentation, the cakes are done. If not, bake a few minutes more and test again. When done, remove the cakes from the oven. Lift the cupcakes out of their tins and let cool on a rack. Remove the layer cakes from their pans by lifting the foil. Place them on racks and let them cool in the foil.

♦ When cakes are cool, remove foil (if making the layer cake) and frost with Cream Cheese Frosting (page 218) or with another frosting of your choice, or serve the cakes unfrosted with fresh fruit, if desired.

♦ If the cakes are to be saved for later use, wrap well and refrigerate or freeze. The layer cakes can be wrapped in the foil they were baked in, with a second piece of foil to cover the top.

Makes 24 cupcakes or two 8- or 9-inch cake layers

Cream Cheese Frosting

This is our version of cream cheese frosting—rich but not too sweet. We recommend the optional touches of fresh lemon juice and nutmeg, though we do not use them on the cakes we sell in our stores.

PREPARE-AHEAD NOTES:

Any extra frosting keeps well for a week if refrigerated and can also be frozen. Allow frosting to return to room temperature before using.

INGREDIENTS:

¾ cup salted butter, at room temperature
1 ¾ cups plus 2 tablespoons sifted powdered sugar
   (measure after sifting)
1 teaspoon vanilla extract, or 1 to 2 tablespoons
   freshly squeezed lemon juice
2 packages (8 ounces each) cream cheese, at room
   temperature
Optional: whole nutmeg for grating over frosted cakes

♦ Place butter in the work bowl of a food processor equipped with a steel blade. Process until it is creamy. Add half the powdered sugar and the vanilla. Mix well. Remove to a mixing bowl. Into the same processor work bowl place the cream cheese and remaining powdered sugar. Process until smooth but not liquid. Fold cream cheese mixture into the butter mixture until thoroughly combined.
♦ To frost cupcakes, place a dollop (about 2 tablespoons) of frosting in the middle of each cake and spread over the top. To frost layer cakes, spoon 1 ½ cups of frosting onto each cake. Spread over top and sides of cake to cover.
♦ A lovely flavor fillip comes from dusting the frosted cakes with the optional freshly grated nutmeg.

Makes 3 cups (enough to frost 1 batch of White on White cupcakes or 2 White on White single layer cakes—page 216)

What's Topping Sugar?

We discovered years ago that using a coarse sugar such as Whitworth's Cane Demerara Sugar produces a desirable crunchy top to cookies, cakes, and bread puddings. Whitworth's is difficult to find, so several years ago we began to package a similar sugar under our own label—Pasta & Co. Topping Sugar. If you have access to neither Whitworth's sugar nor ours, check the sugar section of your grocery store for anything that has large, light brown crystals (C&H Raw Sugar will do). Whatever that product may be, it will probably give you comparable results.

Hasty Tasty Gingerbread Men

If you don't have access to Pasta & Co.'s frozen Ginger Crinkle Cookie Dough, read no further. This recipe will be of no use to you. But if you do and you want to use a shortcut for some of your holiday baking, definitely try it. You'll be pleased with the results.

INGREDIENTS:

> 1 package (28 ounces) frozen Pasta & Co. Ginger Crinkle Cookie Dough
> ½ cup flour
> 5 teaspoons ground ginger
> 5 teaspoons cocoa powder
> Pasta & Co. Topping Sugar (see this page) or your choice of frostings and other decorations

◆ Thaw dough. In a small bowl mix together flour, ginger, and cocoa. Knead mixture into thawed dough until it is completely incorporated and dough is firm enough to roll.

◆ Preheat oven to 350° F. On a very lightly floured board, roll dough out ¼-inch thick and cut into desired shapes. Place on parchment-lined baking sheets. Top with Topping Sugar (unless you plan to frost cookies after baking). Chill in refrigerator for about 5 minutes, then bake in upper third of preheated oven until edges are lightly browned—8 to 10 minutes. Remove from baking sheets and cool on rack.

Makes about 4 dozen average-size gingerbread men

Gratinée of Garden Berries

This gratinée is an unassuming and easy way to use up summer's bumper crop of raspberries, boysenberries, and strawberries—fresh at the top of the season or frozen all year long. The fruit is topped with whipped cream flavored with lemon juice and brandy and a layer of brown sugar that, when the dish is run under the broiler, forms a burnt sugar crust like the top of a crème brûlée.

Serve in bowls with big spoons so that you can enjoy every ounce of the good juices. Frozen fruits will yield more juice than fresh—either way, the dish could not be better.

You will need a shallow broilerproof au gratin dish large enough to hold the fruit in a layer 1 to 2 inches deep, leaving 1 inch for the topping. A 10-inch by 14-inch oval dish works perfectly. (If you do not allow ample room, the dessert bubbles out of the dish when it is broiled, making a nasty oven mess.)

PREPARE-AHEAD NOTES:

You can assemble the dish a couple of hours ahead, then top with the sugar and broil it right before serving.

INGREDIENTS:

> 5 cups fresh or frozen raspberries or boysenberries
>   OR 5 cups fresh strawberries, cut in half or
>   quartered (do not use frozen strawberries)
> 1 cup heavy cream
> ¼ cup sugar
> 1 ½ tablespoons freshly squeezed lemon juice
> 1 tablespoon brandy
> Brown sugar (¾ to 1 cup) to cover the fruit and
>   cream

◆ Spoon fruit and any juices evenly into a shallow, broilerproof dish. Fruit should be no more than 2 inches deep.

◆ In a medium-sized bowl, whip cream until slightly thickened. Continue whipping while gradually adding sugar, lemon juice, and brandy. Spoon cream mixture over fruit, completely covering it. At this point, the dish can sit for a couple of hours.

◆ Immediately before serving, crumble brown sugar over the top to make a ¼-inch-thick layer. Place dish under broiler and broil just until sugar caramelizes and forms a crust (2 to 4 minutes). Watch closely. It is done when the cream is bubbling and the sugar has turned dark brown. Remove immediately. Let the dish set for 5 minutes for the brown sugar to form its crackling crust.

◆ Spoon the warm mixture into small bowls, being sure that everyone gets a share of the sugar crust and lots of sauce.

Serves 4 to 6

The Berry Sauce

T*his dessert sauce recipe is so outstanding that after years of making it fresh and selling it in our stores each summer, we turned it into a shelf-stable jarred product, called The Berry Sauce. If you are lucky enough to have a bumper crop of summer berries, you may want to make your own. Use it on ice creams and sorbets, or to make a pool for serving individual crèmes brûlée or slices of dense chocolate cake.*

PREPARE-AHEAD NOTES:

The sauce will keep for several weeks refrigerated.

INGREDIENTS:

1 quart frozen or fresh boysenberries OR mixed raspberries and boysenberries, thawed if frozen (use all the juices given off as berries thaw)

½ cup water

Juice of 1 lemon

1 cup plus 2 tablespoons sugar (more or less depending
    upon the tartness of your fruit)

2 sprigs (1 inch each) fresh mint

1 teaspoon arrowroot

2 tablespoons kirsch (cherry brandy)

♦ Combine berries, including any juices, water, and lemon juice in a food processor bowl equipped with a steel blade. Purée berries until smooth and strain through a fine sieve to remove all seeds.

♦ Pour strained berry mixture into a saucepan and add the sugar and mint. Bring to a boil over medium-high heat. Simmer for 15 minutes, tasting every 5 minutes; if mint flavor is becoming too intense, remove the sprigs. (The mint flavor in the finished sauce is intended to be very subtle.)

♦ Dissolve the arrowroot in the kirsch and stir into the berry mixture. Remove from heat and cool. If you have not already removed the mint springs, do so now. Cover and refrigerate.

Makes about 3 cups

Two-Cherries Jubilee Sauce

C herries jubilee was a wildly popular dessert in the early 1970s. Cooks would mix together canned big dark cherries with brandy, flame the concoction, and pour it over vanilla ice cream. It seemed ravishingly "gourmet" and in fact was quite yummy.

We've adapted this household classic to use the popular Fabri cherries from Italy. You can buy these cherries in their distinctive blue and white crocks at all Pasta & Co. stores and other specialty food stores. To the very sweet Fabri

Product Spotlight: Dried Sour Cherries

Since we first discovered these exquisitely sour morsels in 1986, we have used them in everything from pasta dishes to granola to cranberry sauce. They pair astonishingly well with dried or glacéed apricots, and in our second book, *Pasta & Co. By Request,* we even combined them with fresh kumquats and Cognac for a dessert sauce. Consider using them to replace other dried fruits such as raisins in almost any baking recipe. And don't miss them as a delicious, healthy snack. You can purchase dried sour cherries under numerous labels, including our own.

cherries, we add dried sour cherries, which give a tart and chewy character, and then a whopping dose of good Scotch, bourbon, or Cognac. The result is an astonishingly good dessert sauce for serving over unfrosted cakes. For instance, make the White on White Cakes (page 216), but instead of frosting them, serve them with a generous topping of this sauce. Of course, over ice cream, the sauce will invoke not only memories of cherries jubilee, but also a conviction that some things do get better.

PREPARE-AHEAD NOTES:

The sauce can be prepared ahead and served either cold or reheated. It keeps well for months in the refrigerator and is a welcome staple to have on hand for quick desserts. One 21-ounce jar of Fabri cherries is exactly the amount you need for a double recipe, which makes 6 cups. Since the sauce keeps so well, we recommend making the double batch. If you can't use it all yourself, give some away. It makes a splendid hostess or holiday gift.

INGREDIENTS:

> 1 cup dried sour cherries
> ¾ cup warm water
> 1 cup Fabri cherries, with their syrup
> Zest of 1 orange, finely chopped
> Juice of 1 orange, strained (about ⅓ cup)
> ½ cup single-malt Scotch, premium bourbon,
>   or Cognac

◆ Soak dried cherries in the water for 1 hour. Drain and reserve the cherries.

◆ In a small sauté pan, warm the Fabri cherries over low heat. Add orange zest, orange juice, and reserved dried cherries, and simmer over low heat for about 5 minutes. Remove from heat. Stir in liquor. The sauce can be served immediately or allowed to cool for later use.

Makes about 3 cups

INDEX